PowerPoint® 2013

FOR DUMMIES®

A Wiley Brand

PowerPoint® 2013

A Wiley Brand

by Doug Lowe

COVENTRY UNIVERSITY LONDON CAMPUS
East India House,
109-117 Middlesex Street, London, E1 7JF
Tel: 020 7247 3666 | Fax: 020 7375 3048
www.coventry.ac.uk/londoncampus

A Wiley Brand

PowerPoint® 2013 For Dummies®

Published by
John Wiley & Sons, Inc.
111 River Street
Hoboken, NJ 07030-5774

www.wiley.com

For general information on our other products and services, please contact our Customer Care Department within the U.S. at 877-762-2974, outside the U.S. at 317-572-3993, or fax 317-572-4002.

For technical support, please visit www.wiley.com/techsupport.

Wiley publishes in a variety of print and electronic formats and by print-on-demand. Some material included with standard print versions of this book may not be included in e-books or in print-on-demand. If this book refers to media such as a CD or DVD that is not included in the version you purchased, you may download this material at http://booksupport.wiley.com. For more information about Wiley products, visit www.wiley.com.

Library of Congress Control Number: 2012956420

ISBN 978-1-118-50253-2 (pbk); ISBN 978-1-118-50260-0 (ebk); ISBN 978-1-118-50259-4 (ebk); ISBN 978-1-118-50261-7 (ebk)

Manufactured in the United States of America

10 9 8 7 6 5 4 3 2

About the Author

Doug Lowe has written enough computer books to line all the birdcages in California. His other books include *Word 2010 All-in-One For Dummies*, *Java All-in-One For Dummies*, and *Networking For Dummies*, 9th Edition.

Although Doug has yet to win a Pulitzer Prize, he remains cautiously optimistic. He is hopeful that James Cameron will pick up the film rights to this book and suggests Avatar II: The Phantom Presentation as a working title.

Doug lives in sunny Fresno, California, which is kind of boring but fortunately close to non-boring places like Disneyland, Yosemite, and San Francisco.

Dedication

To Rebecca, Sarah, and Bethany.

Author's Acknowledgments

I'd like to thank the whole crew at Wiley who helped with this edition, especially Blair Pottenger who did a great job keeping the entire project moving along when deadlines came and chapters didn't. Copy editor Beth Taylor dotted all the t's and crossed all the i's, or something like that, and managed to get my crude prose readable. Ryan Williams gave the entire manuscript a thorough technical review and made many excellent suggestions. And, of course, many other people pitched in.

I'd also like to thank everyone who helped out with previous editions of this book: Kim Darosett, Virginia Sanders, Mark Enochs, Kala Schrager, Jennifer Riggs, Rebecca Mancilla, Doug Sahlin, Andrea Boucher, Garret Pease, Steve Hayes, Kel Oliver, Nancy DelFavero, Grace Jasmine, Rev Mengle, Tina Sims, Pam Mourouzis, Leah Cameron, Jim McCarter, Kezia Endsley, Becky Whitney, and Michael Partington.

Publisher's Acknowledgments

We're proud of this book; please send us your comments at http://dummies.custhelp.com. For other comments, please contact our Customer Care Department within the U.S. at 877-762-2974, outside the U.S. at 317-572-3993, or fax 317-572-4002.

Some of the people who helped bring this book to market include the following:

Acquisitions and Editorial

Project Editor: Blair J. Pottenger

Acquisitions Editor: Amy Fandrei

Copy Editor: Beth Taylor

Technical Editor: Ryan Williams

Editorial Manager: Kevin Kirschner

Editorial Assistant: Annie Sullivan

Sr. Editorial Assistant: Cherie Case

Cover Photo: © Goldmund Lukic / iStockphoto

Composition Services

Project Coordinator: Katie Crocker

Layout and Graphics: Jennifer Creasey, Joyce Haughey

Proofreaders: Lindsay Amones, Debbye Butler

Indexer: BIM Indexing & Proofreading Services

Publishing and Editorial for Technology Dummies

Richard Swadley, Vice President and Executive Group Publisher

Andy Cummings, Vice President and Publisher

Mary Bednarek, Executive Acquisitions Director

Mary C. Corder, Editorial Director

Publishing for Consumer Dummies

Kathleen Nebenhaus, Vice President and Executive Publisher

Composition Services

Debbie Stailey, Director of Composition Services

Contents at a Glance

Table of Contents

Part II: Creating Great-Looking Slides............................ 87

Part IV: Working with Others 261

Chapter 17: Collaborating in the Cloud.................263

Chapter 18: Using a Slide Library and Other Ways to Reuse Slides....275

Chapter 19: Exporting Your Presentation to Other Formats 281

Part V: The Part of Tens 293

Chapter 20: Ten PowerPoint Commandments...................295

Introduction

Welcome to *PowerPoint 2013 For Dummies,* the book written especially for people who are lucky enough to use this latest and greatest version of PowerPoint and want to find out just enough to finish that presentation that was due yesterday.

Do you ever find yourself in front of an audience, no matter how small, flipping through flip charts or shuffling through a stack of handwritten transparencies? You need PowerPoint! Have you always wanted to take your notebook computer with you to impress a client at lunch, but you haven't known what to do with it between trips to the salad bar? You *really* need PowerPoint!

Or maybe you're one of those unfortunate folks who bought Microsoft Office because it was such a bargain and you needed a Windows word processor and spreadsheet anyway, and hey, you're not even sure what PowerPoint is, but it was free. Who can resist a bargain like that?

Whichever circumstance you find yourself in, you're holding the perfect book right here in your formerly magic-marker-stained hands. Help is here, within these humble pages.

This book talks about PowerPoint in everyday — and often irreverent — terms. No lofty prose here; the whole thing checks in at about the fifth-grade reading level. I have no Pulitzer expectations for this book. My goal is to make an otherwise dull and lifeless subject at least tolerable, and maybe even kind of fun.

About This Book

This isn't the kind of book that you pick up and read from start to finish as though it were a cheap novel. If I ever see you reading it at the beach, I'll kick sand in your face. This book is more like a reference — the kind of book you can pick up, turn to just about any page, and start reading. It has 22 chapters, each one covering a specific aspect of using PowerPoint — such as printing, animating your slides, or using clip art.

Each chapter is divided into self-contained chunks, all related to the major theme of the chapter.

For example, the chapter on using charts contains nuggets like these:

- Understanding charts
- Adding a chart to your presentation
- Pasting a chart from Excel
- Changing the chart type
- Working with chart data

You don't have to memorize anything in this book. It's a need-to-know book: You pick it up when you need to know something. Need to know how to create an organization chart? Pick up the book. Need to know how to override the Slide Master? Pick up the book. After you find what you're looking for, put it down and get on with your life.

How to Use This Book

This book works like a reference. Start with the topic that you want to find out about: To get going, look for it in the table of contents or in the index. The table of contents is detailed enough that you should be able to find most of the topics that you look for. If not, turn to the index, where you find even more detail.

When you find your topic in the table of contents or the index, turn to the area of interest and read as much or as little as you need or want. Then close the book and get on with it.

This book is loaded with information, of course, so if you want to take a brief excursion into your topic, you're more than welcome. If you want to know all about Slide Masters, read the chapter on templates and Masters. If you want to know all about animation, read the chapter on animation. Read whatever you want. This is *your* book — not mine.

On occasion, this book directs you to use specific keyboard shortcuts to get things done. When you see something like Ctrl+Z, this instruction means to hold down the Ctrl key while pressing the Z key and then release both together. Don't type the plus sign.

Sometimes I tell you to use a command that resides on the new Ribbon interface like this: Choose Home⇨Editing⇨Find. That means to click the Find button, which you can find in the Editing group on the Home tab.

Whenever I describe a message or information that you see onscreen, it looks like this:

```
Are we having fun yet?
```

Anything you're instructed to type appears in bold like so: Type **a:setup** in the Run dialog box. Type exactly what you see, with or without spaces.

Another nice feature of this book is that whenever I discuss a certain button that you need to click in order to accomplish the task at hand, the button appears either in the margin or in a helpful table that summarizes the buttons that apply to a particular task. This way, you can easily locate it on your screen.

What You Don't Need to Read

Some parts of this book are skippable. I carefully place extra-technical information in self-contained sidebars and clearly mark them so that you can give them a wide berth. Don't read this stuff unless you just gots to know. Don't worry; I won't be offended if you don't read every word.

Foolish Assumptions

I make only three assumptions about you:

- You use a computer.
- It's a Windows computer — not a Macintosh. This book works just as well whether you're using Windows 8 or Windows 7. (PowerPoint 2013 requires at least Windows 7.)
- You use or are thinking about using PowerPoint 2013.

Nothing else. I don't assume that you're a computer guru who knows how to change a controller card or configure memory for optimal use. These types of computer chores are best handled by people who like computers. My hope is that you're on speaking terms with such a person. Do your best to stay there.

How This Book Is Organized

Inside this book are chapters arranged in six parts. Each chapter is broken down into sections that cover various aspects of the chapter's main subject. The chapters have a logical sequence, so it makes sense to read them in order if you want. But you don't have to read the book that way; you can flip it open to any page and start reading.

Here's the lowdown on what's in each of the five parts:

Part I: Getting Started with PowerPoint 2013

In this part, you review the basics of using PowerPoint. This is a good place to start if you're clueless about what PowerPoint is, let alone how to use it.

Part II: Creating Great-Looking Slides

The chapters in this part show you how to make presentations that look good. Most important are the chapters about themes (Chapter 8), and Masters and templates (Chapter 10). Get the theme, template, and Masters right, and everything else falls into place.

Part III: Embellishing Your Slides

One of the nifty new features of PowerPoint 2013 is the Insert tab on the Ribbon. It's loaded with things you can insert into your presentations. The chapters in this part explore the various goodies to be found here, such as pictures, clip art, charts, SmartArt objects, sounds, movies, tables, Ginsu knives, and more!

Part IV: Working with Others

The chapters in this part show you how to use PowerPoint's many collaboration features, such as sharing files in the Cloud via Microsoft's new SkyDrive feature, creating slide libraries, and exporting slide shows to other formats.

Part V: The Part of Tens

This wouldn't be a *For Dummies* book without lists of interesting snippets: ten PowerPoint commandments, ten tips for creating readable slides, and ten ways to keep your audience awake.

Icons Used in This Book

As you're reading all this wonderful prose, you occasionally see the following icons. They appear in the margins to draw your attention to important information. They're defined as follows:

Watch out! Some technical drivel is just around the corner. Read it only if you have your pocket protector firmly attached.

Pay special attention to this icon — it tells you that some particularly useful tidbit is at hand, perhaps a shortcut or a way of using a command that you might not have considered.

Danger! Danger! Danger! Stand back, Will Robinson!

Did I tell you about the memory course I took? Paragraphs marked with this icon simply point out details that are worth committing to memory.

Where to Go from Here

Yes, you can get there from here. With this book in hand, you're ready to charge full speed ahead into the strange and wonderful world of desktop presentations. Browse through the table of contents and decide where you want to start. Be bold! Be courageous! Be adventurous! Above all else, have fun!

Part I

getting started
with
PowerPoint
2013

 Visit www.dummies.com for great Dummies content online.

In this part . . .

✔ Get a bird's-eye view of PowerPoint 2013 and what you can do with it.

✔ Find out how to edit the content on PowerPoint slides, from the text itself to text objects to other types of objects, such as clip art pictures or drawn shapes.

✔ Understand how to work in Outline View so you can focus on your presentation's main points and subpoints without worrying about appearance.

✔ Learn to proof your presentation with PowerPoint and avoid embarrassing mistakes.

✔ Discover how to create speaker notes to help you get through your presentation.

✔ Know how to finish the final preparations by printing copies of your slides, notes, and handouts, as well as how to set up a projector and actually deliver your presentation.

✔ Visit www.dummies.com for great Dummies content online.

Welcome to PowerPoint 2013

In This Chapter

▶ Discovering PowerPoint

▶ Firing up PowerPoint

▶ Making sense of the PowerPoint screen and the Ribbon

▶ Visiting backstage

▶ Creating a presentation

▶ Viewing presentation outlines

▶ Saving and closing your work

▶ Retrieving a presentation from the hard drive

▶ Getting help

▶ Getting out of PowerPoint

*T*his chapter is a grand and gala welcoming ceremony for PowerPoint 2013, Microsoft's popular slide-presentation program.

This chapter is sort of like the opening ceremony of the Olympics, in which all the athletes parade around the stadium and people make speeches in French. In much the same way, this chapter marches PowerPoint 2013 around the stadium so you can get a bird's-eye view of what the program is and what you can do with it. I might make a few speeches, but not in French (unless, of course, you're reading the French edition of this book).

Banded   Basis   Cel

Facet   Frame   Inte

Mesh

What in Sam Hill Is PowerPoint?

PowerPoint is a program that comes with Microsoft Office (although you can buy it separately, as well). Most people buy Microsoft Office because it's a great bargain: You get Word, Excel, and Outlook all together in one inexpensive package. And PowerPoint is thrown in for good measure. Of course, depending on which edition of Office you buy, you might get other goodies as well, such as Access, Publisher, a complete set of Ginsu knives, and a Binford VegaPneumatic Power Slicer and Dicer. (Always wear eye protection.)

You know what Word is — it's the world's most loved and most hated word processor, and it's perfect for concocting letters, term papers, and great American novels. I'm thinking of writing one as soon as I finish this book. Excel is a spreadsheet program used by bean counters the world over. Outlook is that program you use to read your e-mail. But what the heck is PowerPoint? Does anybody know or care? (And as long as I'm asking questions, who in Sam Hill was Sam Hill?)

PowerPoint is a *presentation* program, and it's one of the coolest programs I know. It's designed to work with a projector to display presentations that will bedazzle your audience members and instantly sway them to your point of view, even if you're selling real estate on Mars, season tickets for the Oakland Raiders, or a new increase to a congressman in an election year. If you've ever flipped a flip chart, you're going to love PowerPoint.

Here are some of the many uses of PowerPoint:

- **Business presentations:** PowerPoint is a great timesaver for anyone who makes business presentations, whether you've been asked to speak in front of hundreds of people at a shareholders' convention, a group of sales reps at a sales conference, or your own staff or co-workers at a business meeting.

- **Sales presentations:** If you're an insurance salesperson, you can use PowerPoint to create a presentation about the perils of not owning life insurance and then use your laptop or tablet computer to show it to hapless clients.

- **Lectures:** PowerPoint is useful for teachers or conference speakers who want to reinforce the key points in their lectures with slides.

- **Homework:** PowerPoint is a great program to use for certain types of homework projects, such as those big history reports that count for half your grade.

- **Church:** People use PowerPoint at churches to display song lyrics on big screens so everyone can sing or to display sermon outlines so everyone can take notes. If your church still uses hymnals or prints the outline in the bulletin, tell the minister to join the 21st century.

- **Information stations:** You can use PowerPoint to set up a computerized information kiosk that people can walk up to and use. For example, you can create a museum exhibit about the history of your town or set up a tradeshow presentation to provide information about your company and products.

- **Internet presentations:** PowerPoint can even help you to set up a presentation that you can broadcast over the Internet so people can join in on the fun without having to leave the comfort of their own homes or offices.

Introducing PowerPoint Presentations

PowerPoint is similar to a word processor such as Word, except that it's geared toward creating *presentations* rather than *documents.* A presentation is kind of like those Kodak Carousel slide trays that your grandpa filled up with 35mm slides of the time he took the family to the Grand Canyon in 1965. The main difference is that with PowerPoint, you don't have to worry about dumping all the slides out of the tray and figuring out how to get them back into the right order.

Word documents consist of one or more pages, and PowerPoint presentations consist of one or more *slides.* Each slide can contain text, graphics, animations, videos, and other information. You can easily rearrange the slides in a presentation, delete slides that you don't need, add new slides, or modify the contents of existing slides.

You can use PowerPoint both to create your presentations and to actually present them.

You can use several different types of media to actually show your presentations:

- ✔ **Computer screen:** Your computer screen is a suitable way to display your presentation when you're showing it to just one or two other people.

- ✔ **Big-screen TV:** If you have a big-screen TV that can accommodate computer input, it's ideal for showing presentations to medium-sized audiences — say 10 to 12 people in a small conference room.

- ✔ **Computer projector:** A computer projector projects an image of your computer monitor onto a screen so large audiences can view it.

- ✔ **Webcast:** You can show your presentation over the Internet. That way, your audience doesn't all have to be in the same place at the same time. Anyone with a web browser can sit in on your presentation.

- ✔ **Printed pages:** Printed pages enable you to distribute a printed copy of your entire presentation to each member of your audience. (When you print your presentation, you can print one slide per page, or you can print several slides on each page to save paper.)

- ✔ **Overhead transparencies:** Overhead transparencies can be used to show your presentation using an overhead projector. It's a little old-school to be sure, but some people still do it this way.

- ✔ **35mm slides:** For a fee, you can have your presentation printed onto 35mm slides either by a local company or over the Internet. Then, your presentation really is just like your grandpa's old Kodak Carousel slide tray!

Your presentations will be much more interesting if you show them using one of the first four methods (computer monitor, TV, projector, or webcast) because you can incorporate animations, videos, sounds, and other whiz-bang features in your presentation. Printed pages, overheads, and 35mm slides can show only static content.

Presentation files

A *presentation* is to PowerPoint what a document is to Word or a worksheet is to Excel. In other words, a presentation is a file that you create with PowerPoint. Each presentation that you create is saved on your computer's hard drive as a separate file.

PowerPoint 2013 presentations have the special extension `.pptx` added to the end of their filenames. For example, `Sales Conference.pptx` and `History Day.pptx` are both valid PowerPoint filenames. When you type the filename for a new PowerPoint file, you don't have to type the `.pptx` extension, because PowerPoint automatically adds the extension for you. Windows may hide the `.pptx` extension, in which case a presentation file named `Conference.pptx` often appears as just `Conference`.

I recommend you avoid the use of spaces and special characters, especially percent signs (%), in your filenames. If you want the effect of a space in a filename, use an underscore character instead. Spaces and percent signs in filenames can cause all kinds of problems if you post your presentation files to the Internet, either on a web page or even as a File Transfer Protocol (FTP) upload.

Versions of PowerPoint prior to 2007 save presentations with the extension `.ppt` instead of `.pptx`. The *x* at the end of the newer file extension denotes that the new file format is based on an open XML standard data format that makes it easier to exchange files among different programs. PowerPoint 2013 can still save files in the old `.ppt` format, but I recommend you do so only if you need to share presentations with people who haven't yet upgraded to PowerPoint 2007 or later. (You can download a program called the Microsoft Office Compatibility Pack from `http://www.microsoft.com/en-us/download/details.aspx?id=3` that enables PowerPoint 2002 or 2003 to read and write files in `.pptx` format. This program enables you to share your `.pptx` files with people who haven't yet upgraded.)

PowerPoint is set up initially to save your presentation files in the Documents folder, but you can store PowerPoint files in any folder of your choice on your hard drive or on any other drive. You can also save your presentation to online file storage, such as Microsoft's SkyDrive. And, if you wish, you can write a presentation to a USB flash drive or a writable CD or DVD disc.

What's in a slide?

PowerPoint presentations comprise one or more slides. Each slide can contain text, graphics, and other elements. A number of PowerPoint features work together to help you easily format attractive slides:

✔ **Slide layouts:** Every slide has a slide layout that controls how information is arranged on the slide. A slide layout is simply a collection of one or more placeholders, which set aside an area of the slide to hold information. Depending on the layout that you choose for a slide, the placeholders can hold text, graphics, clip art, sound or video files, tables, charts, graphs, diagrams, or other types of content.

✔ **Background:** Every slide has a background, which provides a backdrop for the slide's content. The background can be a solid color; a blend of two colors; a subtle texture, such as marble or parchment; a pattern, such as diagonal lines, bricks, or tiles; or an image file. Each slide can have a different background, but you usually want to use the same background for every slide in your presentation to provide a consistent look.

✔ **Themes:** Themes are combinations of design elements such as color schemes and fonts that make it easy to create attractive slides that don't look ridiculous. You can stray from the themes if you want, but you should do so only if you have a better eye than the design gurus who work for Microsoft.

✔ **Slide Masters:** Slide Masters are special slides that control the basic design and formatting options for slides in your presentation. Slide Masters are closely related to layouts — in fact, each layout has its own Slide Master that determines the position and size of basic title and text placeholders; the background and color scheme used for the presentation; and font settings, such as typefaces, colors, and sizes. In addition, Slide Masters can contain graphic and text objects that you want to appear on every slide.

You can edit the Slide Masters to change the appearance of all the slides in your presentation at once. This helps to ensure that the slides have a consistent appearance.

All the features described in the preceding list work together to control the appearance of your slides in much the same way that style sheets and templates control the appearance of Word documents. You can customize the appearance of individual slides by adding any of the following elements:

✔ **Title and body text:** Most slide layouts include placeholders for title and body text. You can type any text that you want into these placeholders. By default, PowerPoint formats the text according to the Slide Master, but you can easily override this formatting to use any font, size, styles like bold or italic, or text color that you want.

✔ **Text boxes:** You can add text anywhere on a slide by drawing a text box and then typing text. Text boxes enable you to add text that doesn't fit conveniently in the title or body text placeholders.

✔ **Shapes:** You can use PowerPoint's drawing tools to add a variety of shapes to your slides. You can use predefined AutoShapes, such as rectangles, circles, stars, arrows, and flowchart symbols. Alternatively, you can create your own shapes by using basic line, polygon, and freehand drawing tools.

✔ **Illustrations:** You can illustrate your slides by inserting clip art, photographs, and other graphic elements. PowerPoint comes with a large collection of clip art pictures you can use, and Microsoft provides an even larger collection of clip art images online. And, of course, you can insert photographs from your own picture library.

✔ **Charts and diagrams:** PowerPoint includes a slick diagramming feature called *SmartArt* that enables you to create several common types of diagrams, including organization charts, cycle diagrams, and others. In addition, you can insert pie charts, line or bar charts, and many other chart types.

✔ **Video and Sound:** You can add sound clips or video files to your slides. You can also add background music or a custom narration.

Starting PowerPoint

Here's the procedure for starting PowerPoint in Windows 8:

1. **Get ready.**

   Light some votive candles. Take two Tylenol. Put on a pot of coffee. If you're allergic to banana slugs, take an allergy pill. Sit in the lotus position facing Redmond, Washington, and recite the Windows creed three times:

   Bill Gates is my friend. Resistance is futile. No beer and no TV make Homer something something . . . .

2. **Press the Windows key on your keyboard.**

   The Windows key is the one that has the fancy Windows flag printed on it. On most keyboards, it's located between the Alt and Tab keys. When you press this button, Windows brings up the Windows 8 Start screen, which lists your commonly used applications in large tiles.

3. **Click the PowerPoint 2013 tile.**

   That's all there is to it — PowerPoint starts up in a flash. (Note that you might have to scroll the Start screen to the right to find the PowerPoint 2013 tile.)

If you're using Windows 7, the procedure is a little different:

1. **Click the Start button.**

   The Start button is ordinarily found in the lower-left corner of the Windows display. When you click it, the Start menu appears. The Start menu works pretty much the same, no matter which version of Windows you're using.

If you can't find the Start button, try moving the cursor all the way to the bottom edge of the screen and holding it there a moment. With luck on your side, you see the Start button appear. If not, try moving the cursor to the other three edges of the screen: top, left, and right. Sometimes the Start button hides behind these edges.

2. **Point to All Programs on the Start menu.**

After you click the Start button to reveal the Start menu, move the cursor up to the words *All Programs* and hold it there a moment. Yet another menu appears, revealing a bevy of commands.

3. **Choose Microsoft Office⇨Microsoft Office PowerPoint 2013.**

Your computer whirs and clicks and possibly makes other unmentionable noises while PowerPoint comes to life.

If you use PowerPoint frequently, it might appear in the *Frequently Used Programs* list directly on the Start menu so you don't have to choose All Programs⇨Microsoft Office to get to it. If you want PowerPoint to always appear at the top of the Start menu, choose Start⇨All Programs⇨Microsoft Office. Then, right-click Microsoft Office PowerPoint 2013 and choose the Pin to Start Menu command.

If you hate clicking through menus but don't mind typing, another way to start PowerPoint is to press your keyboard's Windows key (usually found between the Ctrl and Alt keys), type the word **powerpoint**, and press the Enter key. (Note that this trick works only in Windows 7.)

Navigating the PowerPoint Interface

When you start PowerPoint, it greets you with the screen shown in Figure 1-1. This screen lets you create a blank presentation, open a recently used presentation, or create a new presentation based on a template. You can also take a video tour of PowerPoint.

For the purposes of this chapter, click Blank Presentation to get started with a new presentation. You will next be greeted with a screen that's so cluttered with stuff that you're soon ready to consider newsprint and markers as a viable alternative for your presentations. The center of the screen is mercifully blank, but the top part of the screen is chock-full of little icons and buttons and doohickeys. What is all that stuff?

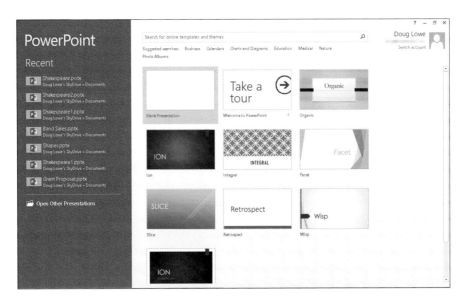

Figure 1-1: PowerPoint's opening screen.

Figure 1-2 shows the basic PowerPoint screen in all its cluttered glory. The following list points out the more important parts of the PowerPoint screen:

✔ **The Ribbon:** Across the top of the screen, just below the Microsoft PowerPoint title, is PowerPoint's main user-interface gadget, called the *Ribbon.* If you've worked with earlier versions of PowerPoint, you were probably expecting to see a menu followed by one or more toolbars in this general vicinity. After meticulous research, Microsoft gurus decided that menus and toolbars are hard to use. So they replaced the menus and toolbars with the Ribbon, which combines the functions of both. The Ribbon takes some getting used to, but after you figure it out, it actually does become easier to use than the old menus and toolbars. The deepest and darkest secrets of PowerPoint are hidden on the Ribbon. Wear a helmet when exploring it.

Note that the exact appearance of the Ribbon varies a bit depending on the size of your monitor. On smaller monitors, PowerPoint may compress the Ribbon a bit by using smaller buttons and arranging them differently (for example, stacking them on top of one another instead of placing them side by side).

For more information about working with the Ribbon, see the section "Unraveling the Ribbon," later in this chapter.

File tab

Quick Access toolbar

Slides pane

Ribbon

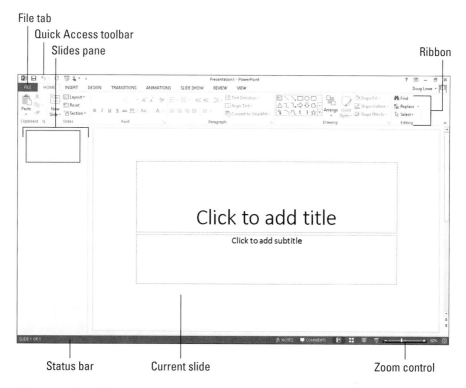

Status bar   Current slide   Zoom control

Figure 1-2: PowerPoint's cluttered screen.

- **The File tab:** The first tab on the Ribbon is called the File tab. You can click it to switch the program into a special mode called *Backstage View,* which provides access to various functions such as opening and saving files, creating new presentations, printing, and other similar chores. For more information, see the section "Taking the Backstage Tour," later in this chapter.

- **Quick Access toolbar:** Just above the Ribbon is the *Quick Access toolbar,* also called the QAT for short. Its sole purpose in life is to provide a convenient resting place for the PowerPoint commands you use the most often.

  Initially, this toolbar contains just three: Save, Undo, and Redo. However, you can add more buttons if you want. To add any button to the QAT, right-click the button and choose Add to Quick Access Toolbar. You can also find a pull-down menu at the end of the QAT that lists several frequently used commands. You can use this menu to add these common commands to the QAT.

- **Current slide:** Right smack in the middle of the screen is where your current slide appears.

✔ **Slides pane:** To the left of the slide is an area that shows thumbnail icons of your slides. You can use this area to easily navigate to other slides in your presentation.

✔ **Task pane:** To the right of the slide is an area called the *task pane.* The task pane is designed to help you complete common tasks quickly. When you first start PowerPoint, the task pane isn't visible, so you can't see it in Figure 1-1. However, it appears whenever it's needed, and you can see plenty of examples of it throughout this book.

✔ **Status bar:** At the very bottom of the screen is the *status bar,* which tells you the slide that is currently displayed (for example, Slide 1 of 1).

You can configure the status bar by right-clicking anywhere on it. This right-click reveals a list of options that you can select or deselect to determine which elements appear on the status bar.

✔ **Zoom control:** PowerPoint automatically adjusts its zoom factor so that Slide View displays each slide in its entirety. You can change the size of your slide by using the zoom control slider that appears at the bottom right of the window.

You'll never get anything done if you feel that you have to understand every pixel of the PowerPoint screen before you can do anything. Don't worry about the stuff that you don't understand; just concentrate on what you need to know to get the job done and worry about the bells and whistles later.

Unraveling the Ribbon

The Ribbon is Microsoft's primary user interface gadget. Across the top of the Ribbon is a series of tabs. You can click one of these tabs to reveal a set of controls specific to that tab. For example, the Ribbon in Figure 1-2 (earlier in the chapter) shows the Home tab. Figure 1-3 shows the Ribbon with the Insert tab selected.

Figure 1-3: The Ribbon with the Insert tab selected.

Initially, the Ribbon displays the tabs described in Table 1-1.

Table 1-1	Basic Tabs on the Ribbon
Tab	**Actions You Can Perform**
File	Open, close, print, and share presentations
Home	Create and format slides
Insert	Insert various types of objects on slides
Design	Tweak the layout of a slide
Transitions	Change the transition effects that are applied when you switch from one slide to the next
Animations	Add animation effects to your slides
Slide Show	Present your slide show
Review	Proof and add comments to your presentations
View	Change the view

Besides these basic tabs, additional tabs appear from time to time. For example, if you select a picture, a Picture Tools tab appears with commands that let you manipulate the picture.

The commands on a Ribbon tab are organized into groups. Within each group, most of the commands are simple buttons that are similar to toolbar buttons in previous versions of PowerPoint.

The View from Here Is Great

Near the right edge of the status bar is a series of four View buttons. These buttons enable you to switch among the various *views,* or ways of looking at your presentation. Table 1-2 summarizes what each View button does.

Table 1-2	View Buttons
Button	**What It Does**
🔲	Switches to Normal View, which shows your slide, outline, and notes all at once. This is the default view for PowerPoint.
▦	Switches to Slide Sorter View, which enables you to easily rearrange slides and add slide transitions and other special effects.
📖	Switches to Reading View, which displays your slide show within a window.
📺	Switches to Slide Show View, which displays your slides in full-screen mode. This is the view you use when you're actually giving your presentation.

Taking the Backstage Tour

Every summer, I attend plays at the Oregon Shakespeare Festival in Ashland, Oregon. A few years ago, I took the special backstage tour, which revealed all kinds of nifty secrets worthy of a Dan Brown novel.

This section takes a brief look at PowerPoint's Backstage View feature, which provides access to document management features previously found on the File menu. When you click the File tab in the top-left corner of the PowerPoint window, PowerPoint switches to Backstage View, as shown in Figure 1-4.

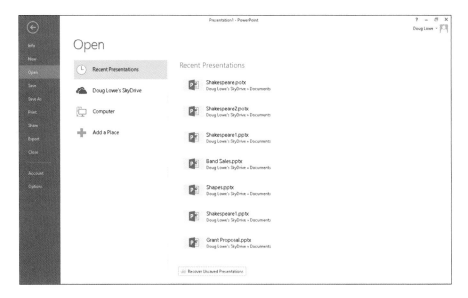

Figure 1-4: Backstage View.

Initially, Backstage View displays information about the current presentation. However, the menu on the left — which bears a striking resemblance to what used to be called the File menu back in the day when programs had plain menus instead of fancy ribbons — provides access to the hidden features of PowerPoint available only to those who venture backstage.

You find out how to use the most important of these commands later in this chapter, and several of the more advanced commands on this menu are presented in later chapters.

Okay, the only secret I learned on the backstage tour at Ashland that was really worthy of a Dan Brown novel is the one about Psalm 46 in the King James translation of the Bible, which was published in 1611 — when William Shakespeare turned 46. If you count 46 words from the start of the Psalm, you get the word

Shake. And if you count 46 words backwards from the end of the Psalm, you get the word *Spear.* Which clearly means that there's a treasure buried directly beneath the stage in Ashland's outdoor theater. Next year I'm taking a shovel.

Creating a New Presentation

The simplest way to create a new presentation is to start PowerPoint, click Blank Presentation on the opening screen (see Figure 1-1), and then edit the blank presentation to your liking.

After PowerPoint is started, you can also create a new presentation by clicking the File tab to switch to Backstage View and then clicking the New command. This action brings up the screen shown in Figure 1-5, which offers several ways to create a new presentation:

- **Choose Blank Presentation:** Double-click Blank Presentation to start a new presentation from scratch.

- **Choose a template:** You can select one of the displayed templates to create a new presentation based on the template's design. Several templates are displayed on the New screen.

- **Search for a template:** You can type a search phrase into the Search text box and then click the magnifying glass icon. Doing this opens a list of templates that match your search criteria. Double-click one of these templates to create a presentation based on it.

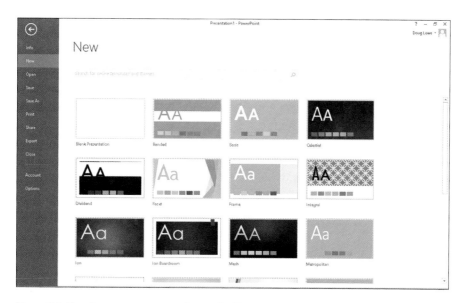

Figure 1-5: Creating a new presentation on the New screen in Backstage View.

Editing text

In PowerPoint, slides are blank areas that you can adorn with various objects. The most common type of object is a *text placeholder,* a rectangular area that's specially designated for holding text. (Other types of objects include shapes, such as circles or triangles; pictures imported from clip art files; and graphs.)

Most slides contain two text objects: one for the slide's title and the other for its body text. However, you can add more text objects if you want, and you can remove the body text or title text object. You can even remove both to create a slide that contains no text.

 Whenever you move the cursor over a text object, the cursor changes from an arrow to the *I-beam,* which you can use to support bridges or build aircraft carriers. Seriously, when the cursor changes to an I-beam, you can click the mouse button and start typing text.

When you click a text object, a box appears around the text, and an insertion pointer appears at the spot where you clicked. PowerPoint then becomes like a word processor. Any characters that you type are inserted into the text at the insertion pointer location. You can press Delete or Backspace to demolish text, and you can use the arrow keys to move the insertion pointer around in the text object. If you press Enter, a new line of text begins within the text object.

When a text object contains no text, a placeholder message appears in the object. For example, a title text object displays the message `Click to add title`. Other placeholders display similar messages. The placeholder message magically vanishes when you click the object and begin typing text.

 If you start typing without clicking anywhere, the text that you type is entered into the title text object — assuming that the title text object doesn't already have text of its own. If the title object is not empty, any text that you type (with no text object selected) is simply ignored.

After you finish typing text, press Esc or click anywhere outside the text object.

In Chapter 2, you find many details about playing with text objects, but hold your horses. You have more important things to attend to first.

Adding a new slide

When you first create a presentation, it has just one slide, which is useful only for the shortest presentations. Fortunately, PowerPoint gives you about 50 ways to add new slides to your presentation. You see only three of them here:

  ✓ On the Home tab, click the New Slide button in the Slides group, as
    shown in Figure 1-6.

  ✓ Press Ctrl+M.

  ✓ Right-click in the Slides pane on the left and then choose New Slide.

In all three cases, PowerPoint adds a blank slide with a standard layout
that includes a title and content area, as shown in Figure 1-5. If you want to
choose a different layout, click the Layout button in the Home tab to display
the gallery of slide layouts. This pane enables you to pick from several types
of slide layouts. Just click the one that you want to use, and PowerPoint sets
the new slide to the layout of your choosing.

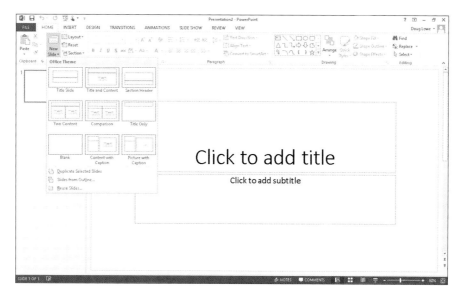

Figure 1-6: Choosing a slide layout.

Each slide layout has a name. For example, the *Title and Content* layout
includes a text object in addition to the title area. This is probably the layout
you'll use most. It's the best format for presenting a topic along with several
supporting points. For example, Figure 1-7 shows a typical bulleted list slide.

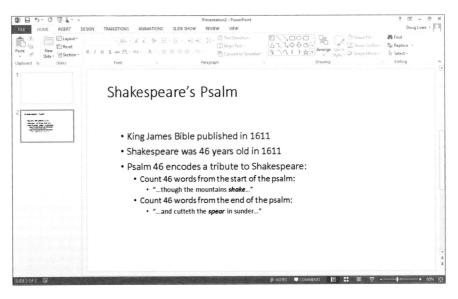

Figure 1-7: A typical text slide.

Moving from slide to slide

You have several ways to move forward and backward through your presentation, from slide to slide:

- ✔ **Click one of the double-headed arrows at the bottom of the vertical scroll bar.** Doing so moves you through the presentation one slide at a time.

- ✔ **Press the Page Up and Page Down keys.** Using these keys also moves one slide at a time.

- ✔ **Use the scroll bar.** When you drag the box in the scroll bar, a tooltip appears to display the number and title of the current slide. Dragging the scroll bar is the quickest way to move directly to any slide in your presentation.

- ✔ **In the list of slides on the left side of the window, click the thumbnail for the slide that you want to display.** If the thumbnails are not visible, click the Slides tab above the outline.

Choosing a design

In Parts II and III of this book, you discover many different ways to create great-looking slides. However, you don't have to wait until then to apply some basic style to your presentation. I've already mentioned that Office 2013 comes preloaded with a handful of professionally designed themes that enable you to create polished presentations with just the click of a mouse. To apply one of these themes, just select the Design tab on the Ribbon and then click the theme you want to apply in the Themes group. Figure 1-8 shows a presentation after a theme has been applied.

Because of space constraints, PowerPoint doesn't display all the available themes on the Ribbon at the same time. But just to the right of the themes is a scroll bar that you can use to scroll through the themes. And the button at the bottom of the scroll bar brings up a gallery that displays all the themes that come with Office 2013.

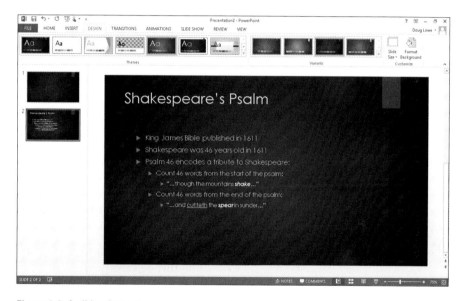

Figure 1-8: A slide after a theme has been applied.

Displaying Your Presentation

When your masterpiece is ready, you can show it on the screen. Just follow these steps:

From Beginning

1. **Choose the Slide Show tab on the Ribbon and then click the From Beginning button in the Start Slide Show group (shown in the margin).**

   There are several shortcuts to this command. You can also start the show by pressing F5 or by clicking the Slide Show button, located with the other view buttons in the lower-right corner of the screen.

2. **Behold the first slide.**

   The slide fills the screen.

3. **Press Enter to advance to the next slide.**

   You can keep pressing Enter to call up each slide in the presentation. If you don't like the Enter key, you can use the spacebar instead.

   If you want to go back a slide, press Page Up.

4. **Press Esc when you're done.**

   You don't have to wait until the last slide is shown. If you find a glaring mistake in a slide or if you just get bored, you can press Esc at any time to return to PowerPoint.

For the complete lowdown on showing your presentation, kindly turn to Chapter 6.

Saving Your Work

Now that you've spent hours creating the best presentation since God gave Moses the Ten Commandments, it's time to save your work to a file. If you make the rookie mistake of turning off your computer before you've saved your presentation, *poof!* Your work vanishes as if David Copperfield were in town.

Like everything else in PowerPoint, you have at least four ways to save a document:

- ✔ Click the Save button on the Quick Access toolbar.
- ✔ Click the File tab to switch to Backstage View and then choose Save.
- ✔ Press Ctrl+S.
- ✔ Press Shift+F12.

If you haven't yet saved the file to your hard drive, the magical Save As dialog box appears. Type the name that you want to use for the file in the Save As dialog box and click OK to save the file. After you save the file once, subsequent saves update the hard drive file with any changes that you made to the presentation since the last time you saved it.

Also note that after you save a file for the first time, the name in the presentation window's title area changes from *Presentation* to the name of your file. This is simply proof that the file has been saved.

Keep the following tips in mind when saving files:

✔ Put on your Thinking Cap when assigning a name to a new file. The filename is how you can recognize the file later on, so pick a meaningful
name that suggests the file's contents.

✔ Don't work on your file for hours at a time without saving it. I've learned
the hard way to save my work every few minutes. After all, I live in
California, so I never know when a rolling blackout will hit my neighbor-
hood. Get into the habit of saving every few minutes, especially after
making a significant change to a presentation, such as adding a covey of
new slides or making a gaggle of complicated formatting changes.

✔ If you want to save a copy of the presentation you're working on using
a different filename, choose File➪Save As. Type a new name for the file
and then click Save.

✔ The File➪Save As command includes a Save As Type option that lets you
change the file format your presentation file is saved in. The most important use of this option is to save your file as a PDF or XPS file. A *PDF* file
is a widely used file format that lets any user display the contents of the
file whether or not he or she owns a copy of the software used to create
the file. PDF was developed and marketed by Adobe. *XPS* has a similar
purpose, but was developed and marketed by Microsoft.

✔ One of the best new features of Office 2013 is *SkyDrive,* which provides
an online location for you to save your files. When you save a file to your
SkyDrive account, you can later retrieve it from any other computer that
has an Internet connection. To save to SkyDrive, just click on SkyDrive in
the Save As dialog box, type a name for your file, and click Save.

Opening a Presentation

After you save your presentation to your hard drive, you can retrieve it later
when you want to make additional changes or to print it. As you might guess,
PowerPoint gives you about 2,037 ways to accomplish the retrieval. Here are
the two of the most common:

✔ Click the File tab to switch to Backstage View and then choose the Open
command.

✔ Press Ctrl+O.

Both options take you to the Open screen in Backstage View, as shown in
Figure 1-9. From here, you can select a file from a list of recently opened
presentations.

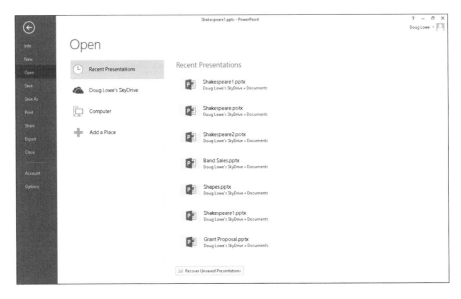

Figure 1-9: Opening a file in Backstage View.

To browse your computer for a file, double-click Computer. This brings up a standard Open dialog box, as shown in Figure 1-10. The Open dialog box has controls that enable you to rummage through the various folders on your hard drive in search of your files. If you know how to open a file in any Windows application, you know how to do it in PowerPoint (because the Open dialog box is pretty much the same in any Windows program).

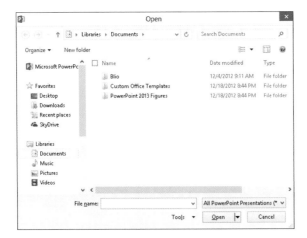

Figure 1-10: The Open dialog box.

If you seem to have lost a file, rummage around in different folders to see whether you can find it. Perhaps you saved a file in the wrong folder by accident. Also, check the spelling of the filename. Maybe your fingers weren't on the home row when you typed the filename, so instead of Shakespeare1.pptx, you saved the file as Djslrd[rstr2.pptx. I hate it when that happens.

The fastest way to open a file from the Open dialog box is to double-click the file. This spares you from having to click the file once and then click OK. Double-clicking also exercises the fast-twitch muscles in your index finger.

PowerPoint keeps track of the files you've recently opened and displays them on the File menu. To open a file that you recently opened, click the File tab, select Recent in Backstage View, and then inspect the list of files on the right side of the menu. If the file that you want is in the list, click it to open it.

Closing a Presentation

Having finished and saved your presentation, you have come to the time to close it. Closing a presentation is kind of like gathering your papers, putting them neatly in a file folder, and returning the folder to its proper file drawer. The presentation disappears from your computer screen. Don't worry: It's tucked safely away on your hard drive where you can get to it later if you need to.

To close a file, click the Close button that appears at the top right of the PowerPoint window. Alternatively, you can click the File tab and then choose Close, or use the keyboard shortcut Ctrl+W. But clicking the Close button is the easiest way to close a file.

You don't have to close a file before exiting PowerPoint. If you exit PowerPoint without closing a file, PowerPoint graciously closes the file for you. The only reason that you might want to close a file is that you want to work on a different file and you don't want to keep both files open at the same time.

If you've made changes since the last time you saved the file, PowerPoint offers to save the changes for you. Click Save to save the file before closing or click Don't Save to abandon any changes that you've made to the file.

If you close all the open PowerPoint presentations, you might discover that most of the PowerPoint commands have been rendered useless. (They are grayed on the menu.) Fear not. If you open a presentation or create a new one, the commands return to life.

Getting Help

The ideal way to use PowerPoint would be to have a PowerPoint expert sitting patiently at your side, answering your every question with a straightforward answer, gently correcting you when you make silly mistakes, and otherwise minding his or her own business. All you'd have to do is occasionally toss the expert a Twinkie and let him or her outside once a day.

Short of that, the next best thing is to find out how to coax PowerPoint itself into giving you the answers you need. Fortunately, PowerPoint includes a nice built-in Help feature that can answer your questions. No matter how deeply you're lost in the PowerPoint jungle, help is never more than a few mouse clicks or keystrokes away.

As with everything else in Office, more than one method is available for calling up help when you need it. The easiest thing to do would be to yell, "Skipper!!!" in your best Gilligan voice. Otherwise, you have the following options:

- Press F1 or click the Help button, located just above the right edge of the Ribbon. This activates PowerPoint's main Help system, shown in Figure 1-11.

- Whenever a dialog box is displayed, you can click the question mark button in the top-right corner of the dialog box to summon help.

- When you hover the mouse over an item in the Ribbon, a tooltip appears explaining what the item does. Many of these tooltips include the phrase "Press F1 for more help." In that case, you can press F1 to get help specific to that item.

The Help dialog box in Figure 1-11 offers several ways to access the help you need. The following paragraphs describe the various ways you can work your way through PowerPoint's Help feature:

- **Help window links:** You can click any of the links that appear in the Help window to display help on a particular topic. For example, if you click the Working with Charts link, you'll find a page of useful information about creating charts.

- **Search:** If you can't find what you're looking for, try entering a word or phrase in the Search text box and clicking the Search button. This displays a list of topics that pertain to the word or phrase you entered.

 Pushpin icon: Normally, the Help window always displays on top. In many cases, this obscures your access to the PowerPoint window. If you don't want the Help window to always stay on top, you can click the button with the pushpin icon. Then the Help window will minimize like any other window.

✔ **Back button:** You can retrace your steps by clicking the Help window's Back button. You can use the Back button over and over again, retracing all your steps if necessary.

✔ **Home button:** Takes you back to the Help home page.

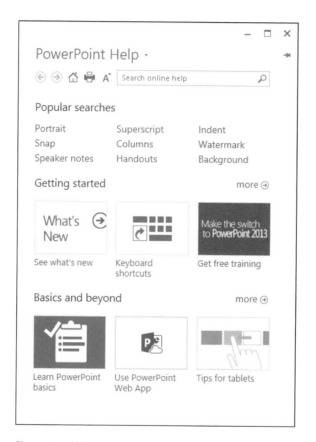

Figure 1-11: Help!

Exiting PowerPoint

Had enough excitement for one day? Use either of these techniques to shut down PowerPoint:

✔ Click the X box at the top-right corner of the PowerPoint window.

✔ Press Alt+F4.

Bam! PowerPoint is history.

You should know a couple things about exiting PowerPoint (or any application):

- PowerPoint doesn't let you abandon ship without first considering whether you want to save your work. If you've made changes to any presentation files and haven't saved them, PowerPoint offers to save the files for you. Lean over and plant a fat kiss right in the middle of your monitor — PowerPoint just saved you your job.

- Never, never, never, ever, never turn off your computer while PowerPoint or any other program is running. Bad! Always exit PowerPoint and all other programs that are running before you turn off your computer.

Editing Slides

In This Chapter

▷ Moving around in a presentation

▷ Working with objects and editing text

▷ Undoing a mistake and deleting slides

▷ Finding and replacing text

▷ Rearranging slides

*1*f you're like Mary Poppins ("Practically Perfect in Every Way"), you can skip this chapter. Perfect people never make mistakes, so everything that they type in PowerPoint comes out right the first time. They never have to press Backspace to erase something they typed incorrectly, or go back and insert a line to make a point they left out, or rearrange their slides because they didn't add them in the right order to begin with.

If you're more like Jane ("Rather Inclined to Giggle; Doesn't Put Things Away") or Michael ("Extremely Stubborn and Suspicious"), you probably make mistakes along the way. This chapter shows you how to go back and correct those mistakes.

Reviewing your work and correcting it if necessary is called *editing*. It's not a fun job, but it has to be done. A spoonful of sugar usually helps.

This chapter focuses mostly on editing text objects. Many of the techniques also apply to editing other types of objects, such as clip art pictures or drawn shapes. For more information about editing other types of objects, see Part III.

akespeare's Psalm

► King James Bible published in 1611

► Shakespeare was 46 years old in 1611

► Psalm 46 encodes a tribute to Shakespear

  ► Count 46 words from the start of the psalm:

    ► "...though the mountains *shake*..."

  ► Count 46 words from the end of the psalm:

    ► "...and cutteth the *spear* in sunder..."

Moving from Slide to Slide

The most common way to move in a PowerPoint presentation is to press the Page Down and Page Up keys:

- **Page Down:** Press Page Down to move forward to the next slide in your presentation.

- **Page Up:** Press Page Up to move backward to the preceding slide in your presentation.

You can also use the vertical scroll bar on the right side of the window to navigate through your presentation:

- **Double-headed arrows:** You can move forward or backward through your presentation one slide at a time by clicking the double-headed arrows at the bottom of the vertical scroll bar.

- **Single-headed arrows:** You can also scroll forward or backward through your presentation by clicking and holding the single-headed arrow at the top or bottom of the vertical scroll bar. (Note that if the zoom factor is set so that a single slide is visible in the presentation window, clicking the single-headed arrows moves to the next or preceding slide.)

- **Scroll box:** Another way to move quickly from slide to slide is by dragging the scroll bar up or down. When you drag the scroll bar, a little tooltip pops up next to it to tell you which slide will be displayed if you stop dragging at that point.

Working with Objects

In the beginning, the User created a slide. And the slide was formless and void, without meaning or content. And the User said, "Let there be a Text Object." And there was a Text Object. And there was evening and there was morning, one day. Then the User said, "Let there be a Picture Object." And there was a Picture Object. And there was evening and there was morning, a second day. This continued for forty days and forty nights, until there were forty objects on the slide, each after its own kind. And the User was laughed out of the auditorium by the audience who could not read the slide.

I present this charming little parable solely to make the point that PowerPoint slides are nothing without objects. *Objects* are items — such as text, pictures, and charts — that give meaning and content to otherwise formless and empty slides. When it comes to objects, however, sometimes less is more. Don't overdo it by cluttering your slides with so many objects that the main point of the slide is obscured.

Most of the objects on your slides are text objects, which let you type text on your slides. For more information about working with text objects, see Chapter 7.

Every slide has a slide layout that consists of one or more placeholders. A *placeholder* is simply an area on a slide that's reserved for text, clip art, a graph, or some other type of object. For example, a slide that uses the Title layout has two placeholders for text objects: one for the title and the other for the subtitle. You use the Slide Layout task pane to select the layout when you create new slides. You can change the layout later, as well as add more objects to the slide. You can also delete, move, or resize objects if you want. For more information about slide layouts, see Chapter 1.

You can add many different types of objects, such as clip art, charts, graphs, shapes, and so on. You can add more objects to your slide with one of the tools that appears on the Drawing toolbar at the bottom of the screen or by using the icons that appear in the center of slides created using the Content layouts. For more information about adding objects to your slides, see Chapters 11 through 16.

Each object occupies a rectangular region on the slide. The contents of the object may or may not visually fill the rectangular region, but you can see the outline of the object when you select it. (See the next section "Selecting objects.")

Objects can overlap. Usually, you don't want them to, but sometimes doing so creates a jazzy effect. You may lay some text on top of some clip art, for example.

Selecting objects

Before you can edit anything on a slide, you have to select the object that contains whatever it is that you want to edit. For example, you can't start typing away to edit text onscreen. Instead, you must first select the text object that contains the text you want to edit. Likewise, you must select other types of objects before you can edit their contents.

Note that you must be in Normal view to select individual objects on the slide. In Slide Sorter view, you can select whole slides but not the individual elements on them.

Here are some guidelines to keep in mind when selecting objects:

  ✔ **Text objects:** To select a text object so that you can edit its text, move the insertion point over the text that you want to edit and then click. A rectangular box appears around the object, and a text insertion point appears so that you can start typing away.

✔ **Non-text objects:** Other types of objects work a little differently. Click an object, and the object is selected. The rectangular box appears around the object to let you know that you've hooked it. After you've hooked the object, you can drag it around the screen or change its size, but you can't edit its contents.

✔ **The Ctrl key:** You can select more than one object by selecting the first object and then holding down the Ctrl key while clicking to select additional objects.

✔ **Click and drag:** Another way to select an object — or more than one object — is to use the insertion point to drag a rectangle around the objects that you want to select. Point to a location above and to the left of the object(s) that you want to select, and then click and drag the mouse down and to the right until the rectangle surrounds the objects. When you release the button, all the objects within the rectangle are selected.

✔ **The Tab key:** Also, you can press the Tab key to select objects. Press Tab once to select the first object on the slide. Press Tab again to select the next object. Keep pressing Tab until the object that you want is selected.

Pressing Tab to select objects is handy when you can't easily point to the object that you want to select. This problem can happen if the object that you want is buried underneath another object or if the object is empty or otherwise invisible and you're not sure of its location.

Resizing or moving an object

When you select an object, an outline box appears around it, as shown in Figure 2-1. If you look closely at the box, you can see that it has love handles, one on each corner and one in the middle of each edge. You can use these love handles to adjust the size of an object. You can also grab the box edge between the love handles to move the object on the slide. (Technically, the love handles are called *sizing handles.*)

In addition, for many types of objects, a circular arrow called the *rotate handle* appears, floating above the object. You can rotate the object by grabbing this handle and dragging it around in a circle. (Not all types of objects can be rotated, however. For example, you can't rotate charts.)

To change the size of an object, click the object to select it and then grab one of the love handles by clicking. Hold down the mouse button and then move the mouse to change the object's size.

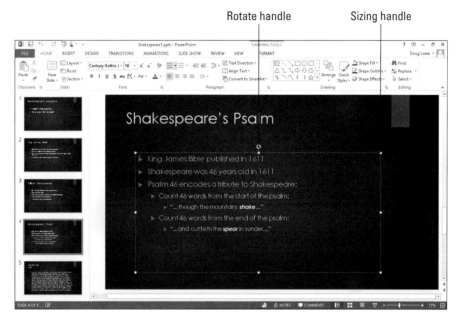

Figure 2-1: You can resize this object by taking hold of its love handles.

The various handles on an object give you different ways to change the object's size:

- ✏ The handles at the corners enable you to change both the height and the width of the object.

- ✏ The handles on the top and bottom edges enable you to change just the object's height.

- ✏ The handles on the right and left edges change just the width of the object.

If you hold down the Ctrl key while you drag one of the love handles, the object stays centered at its current position on the slide as its size adjusts. Try it to see what I mean. Also, try holding down the Shift key while you drag an object by using one of the corner love handles. This combination maintains the object's proportions when you resize it.

Changing a text object's size doesn't change the size of the text in the object; it changes only the size of the *frame* that contains the text. Changing the width of a text object is equivalent to changing margins in a word processor: It makes the text lines wider or narrower. To change the size of the text within a text object, you must change the font size. For more information, see Chapter 7.

To move an object, click anywhere on the outline box — except on a love handle — and then drag the object to its new locale. Note that for shapes and other graphic objects, you don't have to click precisely on the outline box — you can click and drag anywhere within the object to move it. But for objects that contain text, you must click the outline box itself to drag the object to a new location.

The outline box can be hard to see if you have a fancy background on your slides. If you select an object and have trouble seeing the outline box, try squinting or cleaning your monitor screen. Or, in severe weather, try selecting the View tab on the Ribbon and then choosing one of the Color/Grayscale options:

- **Color:** Displays slides in full color
- **Grayscale:** Displays colors as shades of gray
- **Pure Black and White:** Shows the slides in black and white

Viewing the slide in Grayscale or Pure Black and White might make the love handles easier to spot. To switch back to full-color view, click Back to Color View.

Editing a Text Object

When you select a text object for editing, PowerPoint transforms into a baby word processor so you can edit the text. Note that PowerPoint automatically wraps text so that you don't have to press Enter at the end of every line. Press Enter only when you want to begin a new paragraph.

Text in a PowerPoint presentation is usually formatted with a *bullet character* at the beginning of each paragraph. The default bullet character depends on the theme you've applied to the slide. But if you don't like the bullet provided by the theme, you can change it to just about any shape that you can imagine. The point to remember here is that the bullet character is a part of the paragraph format, and not a character that you have to type in your text.

Some word-processing software enables you to switch between *Insert mode* and *Typeover mode* by pressing the Insert key on the right side of your keyboard. In Insert mode, any characters that you type are inserted at the insertion point (the blinking vertical line that appears within the text). In Typeover mode, each character that you type replaces the character at the insertion point. However, PowerPoint always works in Insert mode, so any text that you type is inserted at the insertion point. Pressing Insert has no effect on the way text is typed.

You can move around within a text object by pressing the arrow keys or by using the mouse. You can also use the End and Home keys to take the insertion point to the start or end of the line that you're on. Additionally, you can use the arrow keys in combination with the Ctrl key to move around even faster. For example, press the Ctrl key and the left- or right-arrow key to move left or right an entire word at a time.

You delete text by pressing the Delete or Backspace key. To delete from the insertion point to the start or end of a word, use the Ctrl key along with the Delete or Backspace key. If you first select a block of text, the Delete and Backspace keys delete the entire selection. (The next section, "Selecting Text," has some tips for selecting text.)

Selecting Text

Some text-editing operations — such as amputations and transplants — require that you first select the text on which you want to operate. The following list shows you the methods for selecting blocks of text:

- ✓ **When you use the keyboard,** hold down the Shift key while you press any of the arrow keys to move the insertion point.
- ✓ **When you use the mouse,** point to the beginning of the text that you want to mark and then click and drag over the text. Release the mouse button when you reach the end of the text that you want to select.

PowerPoint has an automatic word-selection option that tries to guess when you intend to select an entire word. If you use the mouse to select a block of text that spans the space between two words, you notice that the selected text jumps to include entire words while you move the mouse. If you don't like this feature, you can disable it by clicking the File tab and Options button in Backstage View. Then deselect the When Selecting, Automatically Select Entire Word check box.

You can use the following tricks to select different amounts of text:

- ✓ **A single word:** To select a single word, point the insertion point anywhere in the word and double-click.
- ✓ **An entire paragraph:** To select an entire paragraph, point the insertion point anywhere in the paragraph and triple-click.

After you have selected text, you can edit it in the following ways:

- ✓ **Delete text:** To delete the entire block of text that you've selected, press Delete or Backspace.
- ✓ **Replace text:** To replace an entire block of text, select it and then begin typing. The selected block vanishes and is replaced by the text that you're typing.

✔ **Cut, Copy, and Paste:** You can use the Cut, Copy, and Paste commands from the Clipboard group with selected text blocks. The following section describes these commands.

Using Cut, Copy, and Paste

Like any good Windows program, PowerPoint uses the standard Cut, Copy, and Paste commands. These commands work on text that you've selected, or if you've selected an entire object, the commands work on the object itself. In other words, you can use the Cut, Copy, and Paste commands with bits of text or with entire objects.

Cut, Copy, and Paste all work with one of the greatest mysteries of Windows — the *Clipboard.* The Clipboard is where Windows stashes stuff so that you can get to it later. The Cut and Copy commands add stuff to the Clipboard, and the Paste command copies stuff from the Clipboard to your presentation.

For basic cutting, copying, and pasting, you can use the standard Windows keyboard shortcuts: Ctrl+X for Cut, Ctrl+C for Copy, and Ctrl+V for Paste. Because these three keyboard shortcuts work in virtually all Windows programs, memorizing them pays off.

The Ribbon buttons for working with the Clipboard are found in the Clipboard group of the Home tab. Three of the four buttons in this section are for working with the Clipboard:

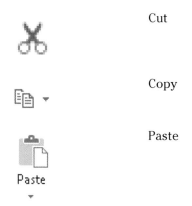

Cut

Copy

Paste

Notice that the Copy button includes a drop-down arrow. If you click the Copy icon itself, the selected object is copied to the Clipboard. But if you click the drop-down arrow instead, a small menu with two icons is displayed. The first copies the selection; the second makes a duplicate. For more information about creating duplicates, see the next section, "Duplicating an Object."

Here's a cool feature: PowerPoint 2013 lets you preview how the contents of the Clipboard will appear before you actually paste it into your slide. To use this feature, copy or cut something to the Clipboard. Then, click the down arrow beneath the Paste button. This reveals a menu with several buttons representing different ways to paste the selection. Hover the mouse over each icon to see a preview of how the item will appear when pasted. When you find a button whose paste preview you approve of, click the button to paste the item.

If you want to blow away an entire object permanently, select it and then press Delete or Backspace. This step removes the object from the slide but doesn't copy it to the Clipboard. It's gone forever. Well, sort of — you can still get it back by using the Undo command, but only if you act fast. See the section, "Oops! I Didn't Mean It (The Marvelous Undo Command)" for more information.

To include the same object on each of your slides, you can use a better method than copying and pasting: Add the object to the *Slide Master,* which governs the format of all the slides in a presentation. (See Chapter 10.)

Duplicating an Object

PowerPoint has a Duplicate command you can use to quickly create copies of objects. First, select the object you want to duplicate. Then, press Ctrl+D to create a duplicate of the object. You probably need to move the duplicate object to its correct location.

An even easier way to duplicate an object is to select the object, hold down the Ctrl key, then press and hold the left mouse button and drag the object to a new location on the slide. After you release the mouse button, a duplicate copy of the object is created.

Using the Clipboard Task Pane

The Clipboard task pane lets you gather up to 24 items of text or graphics from any Office program and then selectively paste them into your presentation. To summon the Clipboard task pane, click the dialog box launcher in the Home tab on the Ribbon at the bottom right of the Clipboard group. Then, the Clipboard task pane appears, as shown in Figure 2-2. Here you can see the Clipboard task pane at the left side of the PowerPoint window, with several objects held in the Clipboard.

To paste an item from the Clipboard task pane, simply click the item you want to insert.

Dialog box launcher
Clipboard task pane

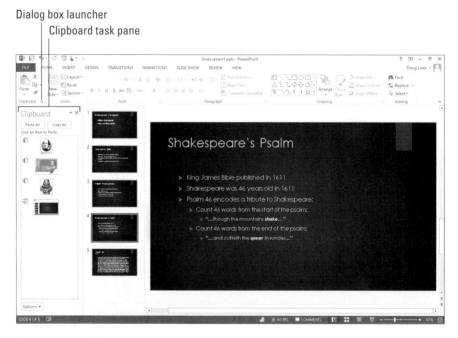

Figure 2-2: The Clipboard task pane.

Oops! 1 Didn't Mean 1t (The Marvelous Undo Command)

Made a mistake? Don't panic. Use the Undo command. Undo is your safety net. If you mess up, Undo can save the day.

You have two ways to undo a mistake:

- ✔ Click the Undo button in the Quick Access toolbar.
- ✔ Press Ctrl+Z.

Undo reverses whatever you did last. If you deleted text, Undo adds it back. If you typed text, Undo deletes it. If you moved an object, Undo puts it back where it was. You get the idea.

Undo is such a useful command that committing the Ctrl+Z keyboard short-cut to memory is a good idea. If you want, think of the word *Zip!* to help you remember how to zip away your mistakes.

Undo remembers up to 20 of your most recent actions. You can undo each action one at a time by repeatedly using the Undo command. Or you can click the down arrow next to the Undo button (shown in the margin) on the Quick Access toolbar and then choose the actions you want to undo from the list that appears. However, as a general rule, you should correct your mistakes as soon as possible. If you make a mistake, feel free to curse, kick something, or fall on the floor in a screaming tantrum if you must, *but don't do anything else on your computer!* If you use the Undo command immediately, you can reverse your mistake and get on with your life.

 PowerPoint also offers a Redo command (shown in the margin), which is sort of like an Undo for Undo. In other words, if you undo what you thought was a mistake by using the Undo command and then decide that it wasn't a mistake after all, you can use the Redo command. Here are two ways to use the Redo command:

✔ Click the Redo button on the Quick Access toolbar.

✔ Press Ctrl+Y.

Note that if the last action you performed wasn't an Undo command, the Redo button is replaced by a Repeat button. You can click the Repeat button to repeat the last command.

Deleting a Slide

Want to delete an entire slide? No problem. Simply move to the slide that you want to delete and click the Delete button in the Slides group of the Home tab on the Ribbon. Zowie! The slide is history.

Another way to delete a slide is to click the miniature of the slide in the Slide Preview pane (on the left side of the screen) and then press the Delete key or the Backspace key.

Deleted the wrong slide, eh? No problem. Just press Ctrl+Z or click the Undo button to restore the slide.

Duplicating a Slide

PowerPoint sports a Duplicate Slide command that lets you duplicate an entire slide — text, formatting, and everything else included. That way, after you toil over a slide for hours to get its formatting just right, you can create a duplicate to use as the basis for another slide.

To duplicate a slide — or slides — select the slide(s) you want to duplicate. Then open the Home tab on the Ribbon, click the arrow at the bottom of the Add Slide button in the Slides group, and click the Duplicate Selected Slides button. A duplicate of the slide is inserted into your presentation.

If you're a keyboard shortcut fanatic, all you have to do is select the slide that you want to duplicate in the Slides pane (located on the left side of the screen) and then press Ctrl+D.

Finding Text

You know that buried somewhere in that 60-slide presentation about Configurable Snarfblats is a slide that lists the options available on the Vertical Snarfblat, but where is it? This sounds like a job for the PowerPoint Find command!

The Find command can find text buried in any text object on any slide. These steps show you the procedure for using the Find command:

1. **Think of what you want to find.**

   Snarfblat will suffice for this example.

 2. **Click the Find button in the Editing group of the Home tab (as shown in the margin) or use the keyboard shortcut Ctrl+F.**

   The Find dialog box appears, as shown in Figure 2-3, which contains the secrets of the Find command.

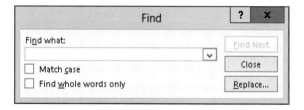

Figure 2-3: The Find dialog box.

3. **Type the text that you want to find.**

   It displays in the Find What box.

4. **Press Enter.**

   Or click the Find Next button. Either way, the search begins.

If the text that you type is located anywhere in the presentation, the Find command zips you to the slide that contains the text and highlights the text.

You can then edit the text object or search for the next occurrence of the text within your presentation. If you edit the text, the Find dialog box stays onscreen to make it easy to continue your quest.

Here are some facts to keep in mind when using the Find command:

- **Find the next occurrence:** To find the next occurrence of the same text, press Enter or click the Find Next button again.

- **Edit the text:** To edit the text you found, click the text object. The Find dialog box remains onscreen. To continue searching, click the Find Next button again.

- **Start anywhere:** You don't have to be at the beginning of your presentation to search the entire presentation. When PowerPoint reaches the end of the presentation, it automatically picks up the search at the beginning and continues to the point at which you started the search.

- **Give up:** You might receive the following message:

  ```
  PowerPoint has finished searching the presentation. The
          search item wasn't found.
  ```

  This message means that PowerPoint has given up. The text that you're looking for just isn't anywhere in the presentation. Maybe you spelled it wrong, or maybe you didn't have a slide about Snarfblats after all.

- **Match case:** If the right mix of uppercase and lowercase letters is important to you, select the Match Case check box before beginning the search. This option is handy when you have, for example, a presentation about Mr. Smith the Blacksmith.

- **Find whole words:** Use the Find Whole Words Only check box to find your text only when it appears as a whole word. If you want to find the slide on which you discuss Smitty the Blacksmith's mitt, for example, type **mitt** for the Find What text and select the Find Whole Words Only check box. That way, the Find command looks for *mitt* as a separate word. It doesn't stop to show you the *mitt* in *Smitty*.

- **Replace text:** If you find the text that you're looking for and decide that you want to replace it with something else, click the Replace button. This step changes the Find dialog box to the Replace dialog box, which is explained in the following section.

- **Close the Find dialog box:** To make the Find dialog box go away, click the Close button or press Esc.

Replacing Text

Suppose that the Rent-a-Nerd company decides to switch to athletic consulting, so it wants to change the name of its company to Rent-a-Jock. Easy. Just use the handy Replace command to change all occurrences of the word *Nerd* to *Jock.* The following steps show you how:

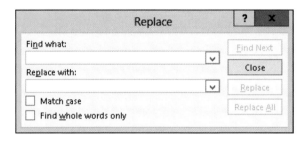

1. **Click the Replace button (found in the Editing group on the Home tab on the Ribbon) or use the keyboard shortcut Ctrl+H.**

   The Replace dialog box, shown in Figure 2-4, appears.

Figure 2-4: The Replace dialog box.

2. **In the Find What box, type the text that you want to find.**

   Enter the text that you want to replace with something else (**Nerd**, in this example).

3. **Type the replacement text in the Replace With box.**

   Enter the text you want to use to replace the text that you typed in the Find What box (**Jock**, in this example).

4. **Click the Find Next button.**

   PowerPoint finds the first occurrence of the text.

5. **Click the Replace button to replace the text.**

   Read the text first to make sure that it found what you're looking for.

6. **Repeat the Find Next and Replace sequence until you're finished.**

   Click Find Next to find the next occurrence, click Replace to replace it, and so on. Keep going until you finish.

If you're absolutely positive that you want to replace all occurrences of your Find What text with the Replace With text, click the Replace All button. This step dispenses with the Find Next and Replace cycle. The only problem is that you're bound to find at least one spot where you didn't want the replacement to occur. Replacing the word *mitt* with *glove,* for example, results in *Sglovey* rather than *Smitty.* Don't forget that you can also use the Find Whole Words Only option to find and replace text only if it appears as an entire word.

If you totally mess up your presentation by clicking Replace All, you can use the Undo command to restore sanity to your presentation.

Rearranging Your Slides in Slide Sorter View

Normal View is the view that you normally work in to edit your slides, move things around, add text or graphics, and so on. However, Normal View has one serious limitation: It doesn't give you a big picture of your presentation. You can see the details of only one slide at a time, and the Slide Preview pane lets you see snapshots of only a few slides. To see an overall view of your presentation, you need to work in Slide Sorter View.

You can switch to Slide Sorter View in two easy ways:

✔ Click the Slide Sorter button at the right side of the status bar (as shown in Figure 2-5).

✔ Select the View tab on the Ribbon and then click the Slide Sorter button in the Presentation Views group.

The PowerPoint Slide Sorter View is shown in Figure 2-5.

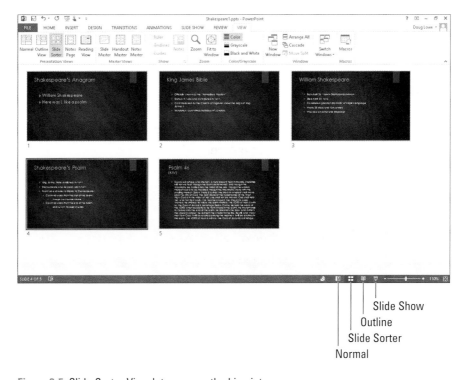

Figure 2-5: Slide Sorter View lets you see the big picture.

The following list tells you how to rearrange, add, or delete slides from Slide Sorter View:

- **Move a slide:** To move a slide, click and drag it to a new location. Point to the slide and then hold down the mouse button. Drag the slide to its new location and release the button. PowerPoint adjusts the display to show the new arrangement of slides.

- **Delete a slide:** To delete a slide, click the slide to select it and then press Delete or Backspace. This works only in Slide Sorter View.

- **Add a new slide:** To add a new slide, click the slide that you want the new slide to follow and then click the New Slide button. The Slide Layout task pane appears so that you can select the layout for the new slide. To edit the contents of the slide, return to Normal View via the view buttons (shown in Figure 2-5) or the View tab on the Ribbon or by double-clicking the new slide.

If your presentation contains more slides than can fit onscreen at one time, you can use the scroll bars to scroll through the display. Or you can use the zoom slider at the bottom-right corner of the screen to make the slides smaller.

Slide Sorter View might seem kind of dull and boring, but it's also the place where you can add jazzy transitions, build effects, or add cool animation effects to your slides. For example, you can make your bullets fall from the top of the screen like bombs and switch from slide to slide by using strips, wipes, or blinds. Chapter 9 describes all this cool stuff.

Working in Outline View

*M*any presentations consist of slide after slide of bulleted lists. You might see a chart here or there and an occasional bit of clip art thrown in for comic effect, but the bread and butter of the presentation is the bulleted list. It sounds boring — and it often is. But in some cases, an endless stream of bullet points turns out to be the best way to get you through.

Such presentations lend themselves especially well to out-lining. PowerPoint's Outline View lets you focus on your presentation's main points and subpoints. In other words, it enables you to focus on content without worrying about appearance.

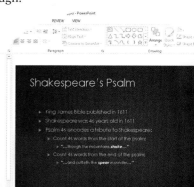

Calling Up the Outline

Outline View

In Normal View, the left side of the PowerPoint window is devoted to showing thumbnail images of your slides. But you can easily switch your presenta-tion into Outline View by clicking the Outline View button in the Ribbon's View tab (shown in the margin). Then, your presentation appears as an outline, with the title of each slide as a separate heading at the highest level of the outline, and the text on each slide appears as lower-level headings subordinate to the slide headings. See Figure 3-1. (Note that if a slide doesn't have a title, the slide still appears in the outline, but the top-level heading for the slide is blank.)

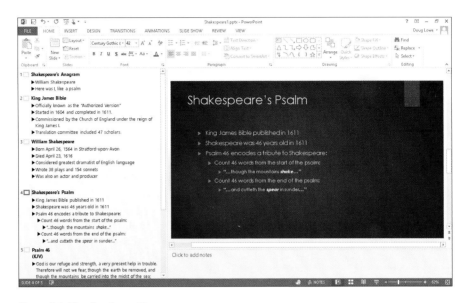

Figure 3-1: Viewing the outline.

You can expand the area devoted to the outline by clicking and dragging the border of the Outline pane.

The following list highlights a few important things to notice about the outline:

- ✔ **The outline is comprised of the titles and body text of each slide.** Any other objects that you add to a slide — such as pictures, charts, and so on — are not included in the outline. Also, if you add any text objects to the slide in addition to the basic title and body text placeholders in the slide layout, the additional text objects are not included in the outline.

- ✔ **Each slide is represented by a high-level heading in the outline.** The text of this heading is taken from the slide's title, and an icon that represents the entire slide appears next to the heading. Also, the slide number appears to the left of the Slide icon.

- ✔ **Each text line from a slide's body text appears as an indented heading.** This heading is subordinate to the slide's main title heading.

- ✔ **An outline can contain subpoints that are subordinate to the main points on each slide.** PowerPoint enables you to create as many as nine heading levels on each slide, but your slides will probably get too complicated if you go beyond two headings. You can find more about working with heading levels in the section "Promoting and Demoting Paragraphs," later in this chapter.

Selecting and Editing an Entire Slide

When you work with the Outline tab, you often have to select an entire slide. You can do that by clicking the icon for the slide. This selects the slide title and all its body text. In addition, any extra objects, such as graphics, that are on the slide are also selected even though those objects don't appear in the outline.

You can delete, cut, copy, or duplicate an entire slide:

- **Delete:** To delete an entire slide, select it and then press Delete.

- **Cut or copy:** To cut or copy an entire slide to the Clipboard, select the slide and then press Ctrl+X (Cut) or Ctrl+C (Copy), or use the Cut or Copy button on the Home tab on the Ribbon. You can then move the cursor to any location in the outline and press Ctrl+V or use the Paste button to paste the slide from the Clipboard. (You can also cut or copy a slide by right-clicking the slide and choosing Cut or Copy from the menu that appears.)

- **Duplicate:** To duplicate a slide, select it and then press Ctrl+D. This step places a copy of the selected slide immediately after it. (Actually, you don't have to select the entire slide to duplicate it. Just click anywhere in the slide's title or body text.)

Selecting and Editing One Paragraph

You can select and edit an entire paragraph along with all its subordinate paragraphs. To do so, just click the bullet next to the paragraph that you want to select. To delete an entire paragraph along with its subordinate paragraphs, select it and then press Delete.

To cut or copy an entire paragraph to the Clipboard along with its subordinates, select it and then press Ctrl+X (Cut) or Ctrl+C (Copy). You can then press Ctrl+V to paste the paragraph anywhere in the presentation.

Promoting and Demoting Paragraphs

To *promote* a paragraph is to move it up one level in the outline. If you promote the "Psalm 46 encodes a tribute to Shakespeare" paragraph in Figure 3-1, for example, that paragraph becomes a separate slide rather than a bullet under "Shakespeare's Psalm."

To promote a paragraph, place the cursor anywhere in the paragraph and then press Shift+Tab or click the Decrease List Level button in the Paragraph group on the Home tab. (Note that you can't promote a paragraph that is already at the highest outline level.)

 To *demote* a paragraph is to do just the opposite: The paragraph moves down one level in the outline. If you demote the "Shakespeare was 46 years old in 1611" paragraph in Figure 3-1, it becomes a subpoint under "King James Bible published in 1611" rather than a separate main point.

To demote a paragraph, place the cursor anywhere in the paragraph and then either press the Tab key or click the Increase List Level button in the Paragraph group on the Home tab.

Note that you can't promote a slide title. Slide title is the highest rank in the outline hierarchy. If you demote a slide title, the entire slide is *subsumed* into the preceding slide. In other words, the slide title becomes a main point in the preceding slide.

You can promote or demote paragraphs by using the mouse, but the technique is a little tricky. When you move the cursor over a bullet (or the Slide button), the pointer changes from a single arrow to a four-cornered arrow. This arrow is your signal that you can click to select the entire paragraph (and any subordinate paragraphs). Then, you can use the mouse to promote or demote a paragraph along with all its subordinates by dragging the selected paragraph left or right.

Be sensitive when you demote paragraphs. Being demoted can be an emotionally devastating experience.

Adding a New Paragraph

To add a new paragraph to a slide with the outline that appears on the Outline tab, move the insertion point to the end of the paragraph that you want the new paragraph to follow and then press Enter. PowerPoint creates a new paragraph at the same outline level as the preceding paragraph.

Note that if you move the insertion point to the end of the title line and press Enter, PowerPoint creates a new slide. However, you can then press the Tab key to change the new slide to a paragraph on the preceding slide.

If you position the insertion point at the beginning of a paragraph and press Enter, the new paragraph is inserted above the cursor position. If you position the cursor in the middle of a paragraph and press Enter, the paragraph is split in two.

After you add a new paragraph, you might want to change its level in the outline. To do that, you must promote or demote the new paragraph (as described in the preceding section). To create a subpoint for a main point, for example, position the cursor at the end of the main point and press Enter. Then, demote the new paragraph by pressing the Tab key.

Adding a New Slide

You can add a new slide in many ways when you're working with the outline. This list shows the most popular methods:

- **Promote existing text:** Promote an existing paragraph to the highest level. This method splits a slide into two slides.

- **Promote new text:** Add a new paragraph and then promote it to the highest level.

- **Press Enter:** Place the cursor in a slide's title text and press Enter. This method creates a new slide before the current slide. Whether the title text stays with the current slide, goes with the new slide, or is split between the slides depends on the location of the cursor within the title when you press Enter.

- **Press Ctrl+Enter:** Place the cursor anywhere in a slide's body text and press Ctrl+Enter. This method creates a new slide immediately following the current slide. The position of the cursor within the existing slide doesn't matter; the new slide is always created after the current slide. (The cursor must be in the slide's body text, however, in order for this method to work. If you put the cursor in a slide title and press Ctrl+Enter, the cursor jumps to the slide's body text without creating a new slide.)

- **Insert a new slide:** Place the cursor anywhere in the slide and use the keyboard shortcut Ctrl+M or click the Add Slide button in the Slides group of the Home Ribbon tab.

- **Duplicate an existing slide:** Select an existing slide by clicking the slide's icon or triple-clicking the title, and then press Ctrl+D to duplicate it.

Because the outline focuses on slide content rather than on layout, new slides receive the basic Title and Content layout, which includes title text and body text formatted with bullets.

Moving Text Up and Down

The outline is a handy way to rearrange your presentation. You can easily change the order of individual points on a slide, or you can rearrange the order of the slides.

You can rearrange your presentation by right-clicking the paragraphs that you want to move and then clicking the Move Up or Move Down button in the menu that appears. Or you can point to the bullet next to the paragraph that you want to move. Then, when the cursor changes to the four-cornered arrow, click and drag the paragraph up or down. A horizontal line appears, showing the horizontal position of the selection. Release the mouse button when the horizontal line is positioned where you want the text.

Be careful when you're moving text in a slide that has more than one level of body text paragraphs. Notice the position of the horizontal line when you drag the selection; the entire selection is inserted at that location, which might split up subpoints. If you don't like the result of a move, you can always undo it by pressing Ctrl+Z or clicking the Undo button.

Collapsing and Expanding the Outline

If your presentation has many slides, you might find that grasping its overall structure is difficult, even when looking at the outline. Fortunately, PowerPoint enables you to *collapse* the outline so that only the slide titles are shown. Collapsing an outline doesn't delete the body text; it merely hides the body text so that you can focus on the order of the slides in your presentation.

Expanding a presentation restores the collapsed body text to the outline so that you can once again focus on details. You can collapse and expand an entire presentation, or you can collapse and expand one slide at a time.

To collapse the entire presentation, right-click anywhere in the outline and then choose Collapse⇨Collapse All or use the keyboard shortcut Alt+Shift+1. To expand the presentation, right-click and choose Expand⇨Expand All or press Alt+Shift+9.

To collapse a single slide, right-click anywhere in the slide and then choose Collapse⇨Collapse from the menu that appears. To expand a single slide, right-click the collapsed slide and choose Expand⇨Expand.

Proofing Your Presentations

In This Chapter

▶ Checking your spelling

▶ Using the Thesaurus

▶ Capitalizing and punctuating the right way

▶ Using the AutoCorrect feature

1 was voted Worst Speller in the sixth grade. Not that being Worst Speller qualifies me to run for president or anything, but it shows how much I appreciate computer spell checkers. Spelling makes no sense to me. I felt a little better after watching *The Story of English* on public television. Now at least I know whom to blame for all the peculiarities of English spelling — the Anglos, the Norms (including the guy from *Cheers*), and the Saxophones.

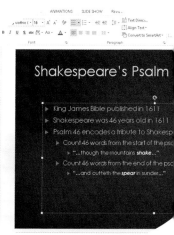

Fortunately, PowerPoint 2013 has a pretty decent spell checker. In fact, the spell checker in PowerPoint is so smart that it knows that you've made a spelling mistake almost before you make it. The spell checker watches over your shoulder as you type and helps you to correct your spelling errors as you work.

Checking Spelling As You Go

Spelling errors in a word-processing document are bad, but at least they're small. In a PowerPoint presentation, spelling errors are small only until you use a projector to throw your presentation onto a 30-foot screen. Then they get all blown out of proportion. Nothing is more embarrassing than a 3-foot-tall spelling error. And if you're like me, you probably try to look for mistakes in other people's presentations just for kicks. Thank goodness for PowerPoint's on-the-fly spell checker.

The PowerPoint spell checker doesn't make you wait until you finish your presentation and run a special command to point out your spelling errors. It boldly points out your mistakes right when you make them by underlining any word it doesn't recognize with a wavy red line, as shown on the word "yars" in the second bullet point in Figure 4-1.

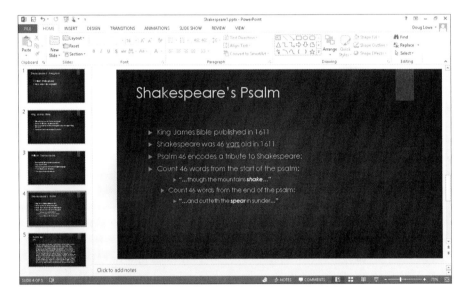

Figure 4-1: PowerPoint usually knows before you do that you've misspelled a word.

When you see the telltale wavy red line, you have several options:

- **Make the correction:** You can retype the word using the correct spelling.

- **Let PowerPoint help:** You can right-click the word to call up a menu that lists suggested spellings for the word. In most cases, PowerPoint can figure out what you meant to type and suggests the correct spelling. To replace the misspelled word with the correct spelling, just click the correctly spelled word in the menu.

- **Ignore the misspelling:** Sometimes, you want to misspell a word on purpose (for example, if you run a restaurant named "The Koffee Kup"). More likely, the word is correctly spelled, but PowerPoint just doesn't know about the word. The right-click menu will help in either case: You can right-click the word in question and then choose either Ignore All to ignore the misspelling or Add to Dictionary to add it to PowerPoint's spelling dictionary.

The spell checker can't tell you when you've used the wrong word but spelled it correctly. For example, the second bullet point in Figure 4-1 mentions *dime navels* instead of *dime novels.* Cheap literature might be a bad thing, but cheap citrus certainly is not.

Spell Checking After-the-Fact

If you prefer to ignore the constant nagging by PowerPoint about your spelling, you can always check your spelling the old-fashioned way: by running the spell checker after you finish your document. The spell checker works its way through your entire presentation, looking up every word in its massive list of correctly spelled words and bringing any misspelled words to your attention. It performs this task without giggling or snickering. As an added bonus, the spell checker even gives you the opportunity to tell it that you're right and it's wrong and that it should discern how to spell words the way you do.

The following steps show you how to check the spelling for an entire presentation:

ABC

Spelling

1. **If the presentation that you want to spell check is not already open, open it.**

2. **Open the Review tab on the Ribbon and then click the Spelling button found in the Proofing group (shown in the margin).**

3. **Tap your fingers on your desk.**

    PowerPoint is searching your presentation for embarrassing spelling errors. Be patient.

4. **Don't be startled if PowerPoint finds a spelling error.**

    If PowerPoint finds a spelling error in your presentation, it switches to the slide that contains the error, highlights the offensive word, and displays the misspelled word along with a suggested correction, as shown in Figure 4-2.

5. **Choose the correct spelling and click the Change button. Alternatively, click Ignore and laugh in PowerPoint's face.**

    If you agree that the word is misspelled, scan the list of corrections that PowerPoint offers and select the one that you like. Then click the Change button.

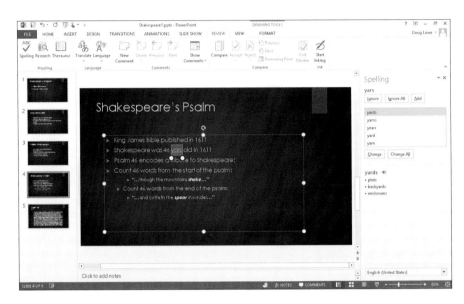

Figure 4-2: The PowerPoint spell checker points out a boo-boo.

If you like the way that you spelled the word in the first place (maybe it's an unusual word that isn't in the PowerPoint spelling dictionary, or maybe you like to spell the way Chaucer did), click the Ignore button. Watch as PowerPoint turns red in the face.

If you want PowerPoint to ignore all occurrences of a particular misspelling within the current presentation, click the Ignore All button. Likewise, if you want PowerPoint to correct all occurrences of a particular misspelling, click the Change All button.

6. **Repeat Steps 4 and 5 until PowerPoint gives up.**

When you see the following message, you're finished:

```
Spell check complete. You're good to go!
```

PowerPoint always checks spelling in the entire presentation, beginning with the first slide — unless you specify a single word or group of words by highlighting them first. PowerPoint checks the spelling of titles, body text, notes, and text objects added to slides. It doesn't check the spelling in embedded objects, however, such as charts or graphs.

If you get tired of PowerPoint always complaining about a word that's not in its standard dictionary, click Add to add the word to the custom dictionary. If you can't sleep at night until you know more about the custom dictionary, read the following sidebar titled "Don't make me tell you about the custom dictionary."

Don't make me tell you about the custom dictionary

The PowerPoint spell checker can use more than one spelling dictionary. Besides the standard dictionary, which contains untold thousands of words that were all reviewed for correctness by Noah Webster himself (just kidding), you can have one or more custom dictionaries, which contain words that you have added by clicking the Add button when the spell checker found a spelling error.

Custom dictionaries are shared by other Microsoft programs that use spell checkers — most notably Microsoft Word. So if you add a word to a custom dictionary in Word, the PowerPoint spell checker knows about the word, too.

What if you accidentally add a word to the dictionary? Then you have a serious problem. You have two alternatives. You can petition Noah Webster to have your variant spelling officially added to the English language, or you can edit the `Custom.dic` file, search through the file until you find the bogus word, and then delete it. The easiest way to edit the `Custom.dic` file is to click the File tab, and then in Backstage View, click Options, click Proofing, and then click the Custom Dictionaries button. You can then select the `Custom.dic` file and click Edit Word List to edit its contents.

The PowerPoint spell checker is good, but it isn't perfect. It does a reasonably good job of catching *your* when you meant *you're* or *its* when you meant *it's*. But it can't catch an error such as "In a few ours we can go home." Thus, spell checking is no substitute for good, old-fashioned proofreading. Print your presentation, sit down with a cup of cappuccino, and *read* it.

Using the Thesaurus

PowerPoint includes a built-in thesaurus that can quickly show you synonyms for a word that you've typed. Using it is easy:

1. **Right-click a word that you've typed and choose Synonyms from the menu that appears.**

   A menu listing synonyms for the word appears. (Sometimes PowerPoint throws an antonym into the list just to be contrary.)

2. **Select the word that you want to use to replace your word.**

   PowerPoint replaces the original word with your selection.

Thesaurus

If you choose Thesaurus from the Synonyms menu or click the Thesaurus button in the Ribbon (shown in the margin), the Thesaurus section of the Research task pane appears with the synonyms listed, as shown in Figure 4-3. The Thesaurus lets you look up words to find even more synonyms. For example, if you select *falloff* from the list of synonyms, you get another set of words. You can keep clicking words to find other synonyms as long as you'd like, until you're ready to get back to real work.

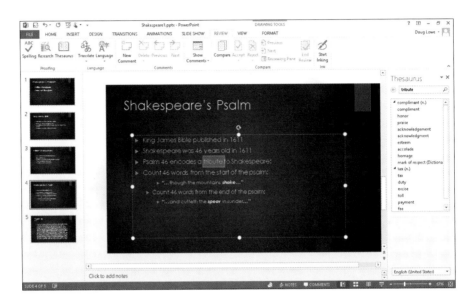

Figure 4-3: The Thesaurus appears in the Research task pane.

Capitalizing Correctly

The PowerPoint Change Case command enables you to capitalize the text in your slides properly. These steps show you how to use it:

1. **Select the text that you want to capitalize.**

2. **Choose the Home tab on the Ribbon and then click the Change Case button in the Font section (shown in the margin).**

   Doing so reveals a menu of Change Case choices.

3. **Study the options for a moment and then click the one that you want.**

   Here are the case options:

   - *Sentence case:* The first letter of the first word in each sentence is capitalized. Everything else is changed to lowercase.

   - *lowercase:* Everything is changed to lowercase.

   - *UPPERCASE:* Everything is changed to capital letters.

- *Capitalize Each Word:* The first letter of each word is capitalized.

- *tOGGLE cASE:* This option turns uppercase into lowercase and turns lowercase into uppercase, for a ransom-note look.

4. Check the results.

Always double-check your text after using the Change Case command to make sure that the result is what you intended. This is especially true when you select Capitalize Each Word. In most cases, you should *not* capitalize articles (like *a* and *the*) and prepositions (like *of* and *from*). The Capitalize Each Word option capitalizes every word in the title, so you'll have to manually change articles and prepositions back to lowercase.

Slide titles should almost always use title case. The first level of bullets on a slide can use title case, where all words except articles like *a* or *the* and prepositions like *for* and *to* are capitalized, or sentence case, where only the first word of each sentence is capitalized. Lower levels usually should use sentence case.

Avoid uppercase if you can. IT'S HARD TO READ AND LOOKS LIKE YOU'RE SHOUTING.

Using the AutoCorrect Feature

PowerPoint includes an AutoCorrect feature that can automatically correct spelling errors and style errors as you type them. For example, if you accidentally type teh, PowerPoint automatically changes your text to the. And if you forget to capitalize the first word of a sentence, PowerPoint automatically capitalizes it for you. AutoCorrect can even catch certain multi-word mistakes. For example, if you type their are, AutoCorrect will substitute there are.

Any time PowerPoint makes a correction that you don't like, just press Ctrl+Z to undo the correction. For example, if you really intended to type teh, press Ctrl+Z immediately after PowerPoint corrects it to the.

If you move the insertion pointer back to a word that has been corrected (or if you click the word), a small blue line appears beneath the first letter of the word. Point the mouse at this blue line, and the button with a lightning bolt in it appears. You can then click this button to bring up a menu that enables you to undo the correction that was made, tell PowerPoint to stop making that type of correction, or summon the AutoCorrect options dialog box to adjust your AutoCorrect settings.

To control PowerPoint's AutoCorrect feature, click the File tab to switch to Backstage View and then click Options. This summons the PowerPoint Options dialog box. Next, choose the Proofing tab on the left side of the PowerPoint Options dialog box, and then click the AutoCorrect Options button to display the dialog box shown in Figure 4-4.

Figure 4-4: The AutoCorrect Options dialog box.

As you can see, the AutoCorrect Options dialog box contains check boxes for a variety of options that govern how AutoCorrect works:

- **Show AutoCorrect Options buttons:** This option displays the AutoCorrect button beneath words that were changed by the AutoCorrect feature, which allows you to undo the change or tell PowerPoint to stop making that particular type of correction.

- **Correct TWo INitial CApitals:** Looks for words with two initial capitals and changes the second one to lowercase. For example, if you type `BOther`, PowerPoint changes it to `Bother`. However, if you type three or more capitals in a row, PowerPoint assumes that you did it on purpose, so no correction is made.

- **Capitalize first letter of sentences:** Automatically capitalizes the first word of a new sentence if you forget.

- **Capitalize first letter of table cells:** Automatically capitalizes the first word in table cells.

✔ **Capitalize names of days:** You know, Monday, Tuesday, Wednesday, and so forth.

✔ **Correct accidental use of cAPS LOCK key:** This is an especially cool feature. If PowerPoint notices that you're capitalizing everything backwards, it assumes that you accidentally pressed the Caps Lock key. So it turns off Caps Lock and corrects the words that you capitalized backwards.

✔ **Replace text as you type:** This option is the heart of the AutoCorrect feature. It consists of a list of words that are frequently typed wrong, along with the replacement word. For example, teh is replaced by the, and adn is replaced by and. The AutoCorrect list also contains some shortcuts for special symbols. For example, (c) is replaced by the copyright symbol (©), and (tm) is replaced by the trademark symbol (™).

You can add your own words to this list. In the Replace text box, type the word that you want PowerPoint to watch for. In the With text box, type the word that you want PowerPoint to substitute for the first word. Then click Add.

The AutoCorrect feature also includes several formatting options that can automatically apply formats as you type. To set these options, click the AutoFormat As You Type tab. The options shown in Figure 4-5 appear. These options let you control formatting features, such as automatically converting straight quotes to curly quotes, changing fractions such as $1/2$ to fraction symbols such as $^1/_2$, and so on.

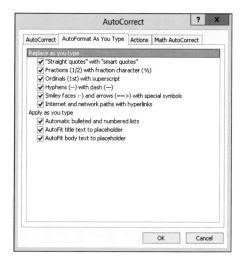

Figure 4-5: The AutoFormat As You Type options.

5

Don't Forget Your Notes!

*E*ver had the fear — or maybe the actual experience — of showing a beautiful slide, complete with snappy text and perhaps an exquisite chart, and suddenly forgetting why you included the slide in the first place? You stumble for words. "Well, as you can see, this is a beautiful chart, and, uh, this slide makes the irrefutable point that, uh, well, I'm not sure — are there any questions?"

Fear not! One of the slickest features in PowerPoint 2013 is its capability to create speaker notes to help you get through your presentation. You can make these notes as complete or as sketchy as you want or need. You can write a complete script for your presentation or just jot down a few key points to refresh your memory.

The best part about speaker notes is that you're the only one who sees them. They don't actually show up on your slides for all the world to see. Instead, notes pages are displayed separately on your computer's monitor but not displayed by the projector. And, you can print your notes pages so that you can have them available as a handy reference during your presentation.

Don't you think that it's about time for a short chapter? Although notes pages are one of the slickest features in PowerPoint, creating notes pages isn't all that complicated — hence the brevity of this chapter.

Understanding Notes

Notes are like an adjunct attachment to your slides. They don't appear on the slides themselves but are displayed separately. Each slide in your presentation has its own page of notes.

Notes are usually hidden at the bottom of the screen in a tiny Notes pane that's just large enough to display a line or two of text. You can recognize the Notes pane because it initially contains the words "Click to add notes." To work with notes, you should first enlarge the Notes pane to give yourself some room to work. For more information, see the section "Adding Notes to a Slide," later in this chapter.

Notes
Page

PowerPoint also has a separate view designed for working with notes pages, called (you guessed it) Notes Page View. To call up Notes Page View, choose the View tab on the Ribbon and then click the Notes Page button found in the Presentation Views group (this button is shown in the margin). Each Notes Page consists of a reduced version of the slide and an area for notes, as shown in Figure 5-1.

Depending on the size of your monitor, these notes are too small to see or work with in Notes Page View unless you increase the zoom setting. But on smaller monitors, you can zoom in to see your work.

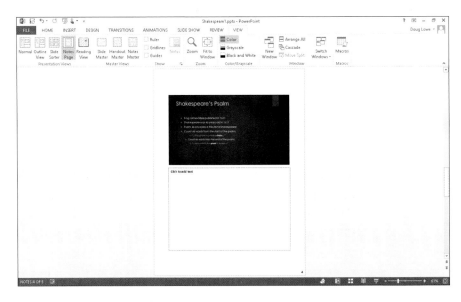

Figure 5-1: Notes Page View lets you see your notes.

Unfortunately, no keyboard shortcut is available to switch directly to Notes Page View. Earlier versions of PowerPoint included a button for this alongside the other view buttons in the lower-right corner of the screen. But for some mysterious reason, Microsoft decided to omit this button in recent versions of PowerPoint. So the only way to get to Notes Page View now is to use the Ribbon's Notes Page button.

Adding Notes to a Slide

To add notes to a slide, as shown in Figure 5-2, follow this procedure:

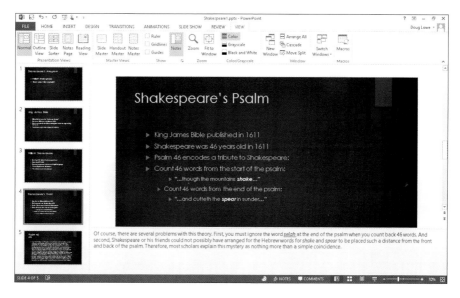

Figure 5-2: A slide with notes.

1. **In Normal View, move to the slide to which you want to add notes.**
2. **Click and drag the Notes pane border, if necessary, to bring the notes text into view.**
3. **Click the notes text object, where it reads `Click to add notes`.**
4. **Type away.**

The text that you type appears in the notes area. As you create your notes, you can use any of the PowerPoint standard word-processing features, such as Cut, Copy, and Paste. Press Enter to create new paragraphs.

Note that there is also a Notes button in the status bar at the bottom of the PowerPoint screen. You can click this button to hide or reveal notes.

Adding an Extra Notes Page for a Slide

PowerPoint doesn't provide a way to add more than one page of notes for each slide. However, these steps show you a trick that accomplishes essentially the same thing:

1. **Create a duplicate slide immediately following the slide that requires two pages of notes.**

   To duplicate the slide, move to the slide that you want to duplicate in Normal View and press Ctrl+D to duplicate the slide.

2. **Click the Notes Page button in the Presentation Views group of the View tab.**

   The Notes Page for the new duplicate slide appears.

3. **Delete the slide object at the top of the duplicate notes page.**

   To do so, click the slide object at the top of the page and press Delete.

4. **Extend the notes area up so that it fills the page.**

   To extend the notes area, just drag the top-center love handle of the notes area up.

5. **Type the additional notes for the preceding slide on this new notes page.**

   Add a heading, such as "Continued from slide 23," at the top of the text to help you remember that this portion is a continuation of notes from the preceding slide.

6. **Return to Normal View.**

   Click the Normal button in the Presentation Views group of the View tab.

7. **Open the Slide Show tab on the Ribbon and then click the Hide Slide button in the Set Up group.**

   The Hide Slide button hides the slide, which means that it isn't included in an onscreen slide show.

The result of this trick is that you now have two pages of notes for a single slide, and the second notes page doesn't have an image of the slide on it and is not included in your slide show.

If you're printing overhead transparencies, you might want to deselect the Print Hidden Slides check box in the Print dialog box. This way, the hidden slide isn't printed. Be sure to select the check box when you print the notes pages, though. Otherwise, the notes page for the hidden slide isn't printed either — and the reason you created the hidden slide in the first place was to print a notes page for it!

 Think twice before creating a second page of notes for a slide. Do you really have that much to say about a single slide? Maybe the slide contains too much to begin with and should be split into two slides.

Adding a New Slide from Notes Page View

If you're working in Notes Page View and realize that you want to create a new slide, you don't have to return to Normal View. Just click the Add Slide button in the Slides group on the Home tab to add the new slide. Or press Ctrl+M.

If you want to work on the slide's appearance or contents, however, you must switch back to Normal View. You can't modify a slide's appearance or contents from Notes Page View.

Printing Notes Pages

If you don't have a computer that can show your slides on a projector and your notes on a separate monitor, you can always print your notes on paper and then use the printed notes while you give your presentation. These steps show you how to print your notes:

1. **Choose the Print command from the Office button menu.**

   The Print dialog box appears.

2. **Use the Print What list box to choose the Notes Pages option.**

3. **Make sure that the Print Hidden Slides check box is selected if you want to print notes pages for hidden slides.**

   The Print Hidden Slides check box is dimmed if the presentation doesn't have any hidden slides.

4. **Click OK or press Enter.**

You can find more information about printing in Chapter 6.

Displaying Notes on a Separate Monitor

As you discover in the next chapter, PowerPoint can display your presentation in a special mode called Presenter View, which displays the slides on a projector and helpful information that includes your notes on your computer's main monitor. As shown in Figure 5-3, Speaker View shows the main slide on the left and a thumbnail of the next slide on the right, with your notes immediately below the next slide preview. To activate this view, simply select the Use Presenter View option in the Monitors group on the Slide Show tab.

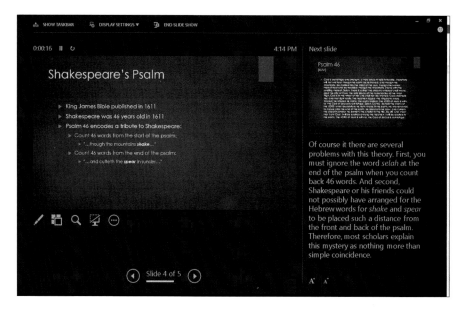

Figure 5-3: Speaker View shows you your notes during a slide show.

6

Show Time!

In This Chapter

▶ Printing slides

▶ Printing handouts, notes, and outlines

▶ Previewing your output

▶ Showing your presentation on your computer screen or the big screen

▶ Wrestling a projector into submission

▶ Working in Presentation View

▶ Showing your presentation online

Overture, curtains, lights. This is it — the night of nights.
No more rehearsing and nursing a part,
We know every part by heart.
Overture, curtains, lights. This is it, you'll hit the heights.
And Oh, what heights we'll hit,
On with the show, this is it.

*T*he old Bugs Bunny theme song (written by Mack David and Jerry Livingston) strikes a chord when your presentation is all finished and all that remains is to present it to your audience.

This chapter shows you how to finish the final preparations by printing copies of your slides, notes, and handouts. Then the chapter delves into the task of setting up a projector and actually presenting your show.

This is it!

The Quick Way to Print

The Print command. The Printmeister. Big presentation comin' up. Printin' some slides. The Printorama. The Mentor of de Printor. Captain Toner of the Good Ship Laseroo.

Don't worry — when you print a PowerPoint presentation, no one's waiting to ambush you with annoying one-liners like that guy who used to be on *Saturday Night Live.* All that awaits you is a handful of boring dialog boxes with boring check boxes. Point-point, click-click, print-print.

The fastest way to print your presentation is to click the Quick Print button, which appears on the Quick Access toolbar. This button does not appear on your Quick Access toolbar by default. To add it, click the down arrow to the right of the Quick Access toolbar and then click the Quick Print button.

Clicking this Quick Print button prints your presentation without further ado, using the current printer settings, which I explain in the remaining sections of this chapter. Usually, this action results in printing a single copy of all the slides in your presentation. But if you have altered the settings on the Print screen in Backstage View during the current PowerPoint session, clicking the Print button uses the altered settings automatically.

You find more information about printing from Backstage View in the next section.

Printing from Backstage View

For precise control over how you want your presentation to be printed, you must switch to Backstage View and conjure up the Print screen, shown in Figure 6-1. To summon this screen, choose Office➪Print or press Ctrl+P.

After you call up the Print screen, click the big Print button (shown in the margin) or press Enter to print all the slides in your presentation. Fiddle around with the settings to print a select group of slides, to print more than one copy, or to print handouts, speaker notes, or an outline. The following sections show you the treasures that lie hidden in this screen.

Printing can be es-el-oh-double-ewe, so don't panic if your presentation doesn't start printing right away. PowerPoint printouts tend to demand a great deal from the printer, so sometimes the printer has to work for a while before it can produce a finished page. Be patient. The Printer Wizard has every intention of granting your request.

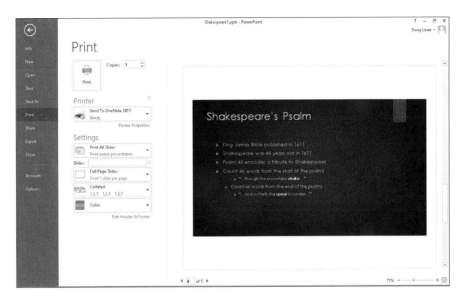

Figure 6-1: Behold the Print screen.

Printing more than one copy

The Copies field lets you print more than one copy of your presentation. You can click one of the arrows next to this field to increase or decrease the number of copies, or you can type directly in the field to set the number of copies.

Changing printers

If you're lucky enough to have two or more printers at your disposal, you can use the Printer list to pick which printer you want to use. Each printer must first be successfully installed in Windows — a topic that's beyond the reach of this humble book. However, you can find plenty of information about installing printers in the appropriate version of Andy Rathbone's *Windows For Dummies.*

Printing part of a document

The Print All Slides drop-down list lets you choose how much (or what part) of your presentation you want to print. When you first access the Print page in Backstage view, the Print All Slides option is selected so that your entire presentation prints. The other options in this drop-down list enable you to tell PowerPoint to print distinct portions of your presentation:

- ✔ **Print Selection:** Prints just the portion of the presentation that you selected before invoking the Print command. First, select the slides that you want to print. Then call up the Print command, click the Selection option, and click OK. (Note that this option is grayed out if nothing is selected when you call up the Print dialog box.)

- ✔ **Print Current Slide:** Prints just the current slide. Before you invoke the Print command, you should move to the slide that you want to print. Then select this option in the Print dialog box and click OK. This option is handy when you make a change to one slide and don't want to reprint the entire presentation.

- ✔ **Custom Range:** Lets you type specific slide numbers you want to print.

- ✔ **Custom Shows:** If you set up one or more custom slide shows, you can use this option to select the show that you want to print. (See "Using Custom Shows" later in this chapter.)

But wait, there's more! Beneath the Print All Slides drop-down list are several other controls:

- ✔ **Full Page Slides:** Lets you indicate how many slides per page you want to print. You can also use this same drop-down list to print Notes Pages or the outline rather than slides.

- ✔ **Collated:** This option tells PowerPoint to print each copy of your presentation one at a time. In other words, if your presentation consists of ten slides and you select three copies and select the Collate check box, PowerPoint first prints all ten slides of the first copy of the presentation, then all ten slides of the second copy, and then all ten slides of the third copy. If you don't select the Collate check box, PowerPoint prints three copies of the first slide, followed by three copies of the second slide, followed by three copies of the third slide, and so on.

- ✔ **Color:** This drop-down list lets you choose whether to print your slides in color, black and white, or with shades of gray.

Using Print Preview

The Print screen of Backstage View includes a Print Preview feature that lets you see how your pages will appear before actually printing them.

From the Print screen, you can zoom in to examine the preview more closely by clicking anywhere in the preview area. You can also scroll through the pages by using the scroll bar or the navigation arrows beneath the preview area.

Setting Up a Slide Show

The PowerPoint printing features are useful, but PowerPoint is really designed to create slides that are presented directly on a screen rather than printed out. The screen can be your computer's own monitor, a projector, or an external monitor, such as a giant-screen television. This section and the sections that follow show you how to set up and show a presentation.

In most cases, the default settings for showing a presentation are adequate. However, in some cases, you may need to change the default settings. To do so, first open the presentation that you want to set up and then open the Slide Show tab on the Ribbon and click Set Up Slide Show (found in the Set Up group). This action summons the Set Up Show dialog box, which is shown in Figure 6-2. With this dialog box, you can twiddle with the various options that are available for presenting slide shows.

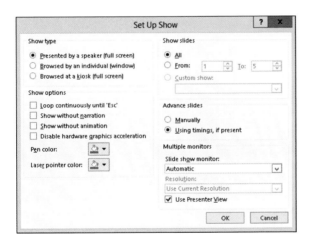

Figure 6-2: The Set Up Show dialog box.

With the options on the Set Up Show dialog box, you can do the following:

- **Configure the presentation:** You can configure the presentation for one of three basic slide show types: Presented by a Speaker (Full Screen), Browsed by an Individual (Window), or Browsed at a Kiosk (Full Screen).

- **Loop through slides:** Select the Loop Continuously until 'Esc' check box if you want the show to run indefinitely. If you enable this setting, the show jumps back to the first slide after the last slide is shown, and the show continues to repeat until you press Esc.

- ✔ **Simplify the presentation:** Deselect the Show Without Narration and Show Without Animation options if you want to simplify the presentation by not playing narrations that you've recorded or animations that you've created.

- ✔ **Select pen and laser pointer color:** Select the color to use for the pen or laser pointer. (See the sections "Scribbling on Your Slides" and "Using the Laser Pointer," later in this chapter, for more information about using the pen and the laser pointer.)

- ✔ **Select slides:** In the Show Slides area, select All to include all slides in the slide show or choose From and supply starting and ending slide numbers if you want to display just some of the slides in the presentation.

- ✔ **Set up custom shows:** Choose Custom Show if you have set up any custom shows within your presentation. (See the section "Using Custom Shows," later in this chapter, for more information.)

- ✔ **Choose to change slides manually:** In the Advance Slides area, choose Manually to advance from slide to slide by pressing Enter, pressing the spacebar, or clicking. Or, if you want the show to proceed automatically, select the Using Timings, If Present option if it's available.

- ✔ **Select a monitor:** If your computer has two monitors, select the monitor to use for the slide show by using the drop-down list in the Multiple Monitors area.

Starting a Slide Show

When you want to do a slide show in a one-on-one or small group setting without a projector, beginning the show is just a click away. To start a slide show immediately, click the Slide Show button located (along with the other View buttons) in the lower-right corner of the screen (shown in the margin). PowerPoint fills the entire screen with the first slide of the slide show. To advance to the next slide, click the mouse button or press Enter, the down arrow, Page Down, or the spacebar.

If you're in a hurry and have a good memory for keyboard shortcuts, just press F5.

You can also start a slide show by opening the Slide Show tab on the Ribbon and clicking one of the following buttons:

From
Beginning

- ✔ **From Beginning:** Starts the slide show from the first slide. Clicking this button is the same as clicking the Slide Show button in the lower-right corner of the screen or pressing F5.

From
Current Slide

- ✔ **From Current Slide:** Starts the show from the currently selected slide.

Working in Presenter View

If you have a projector or second monitor connected to your computer, PowerPoint will show the presentation's slides on the projector or second monitor and switch the primary monitor to Presenter View. Figure 6-3 shows Presenter View in action.

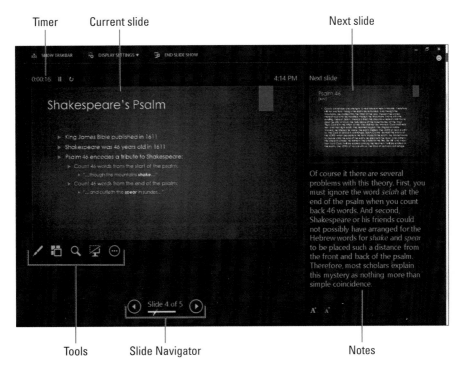

Figure 6-3: Presenter View.

The following paragraphs describe the various features that are available in Presenter View:

- **Current slide:** The current slide is displayed in the center-left portion of the screen.

- **Next slide:** The next slide to be displayed is shown at the top right of the screen.

- **Notes:** Any notes you have created for the current slide are shown at the bottom right of the screen.

- **Timer:** A timer appears above the current slide to help you keep track of how long your presentation has dragged on.

✓ **Tools:** Beneath the current slide are icons representing various tools that let you draw on your slides, magnify the slide to draw the audience's attention to a particular point, hide the current slide so you can draw the audience's attention away from the screen and to you, and perform a few other interesting onscreen tricks. These tools are described in the section "Using Presentation Tools," later in this chapter.

✓ **Slide Navigator:** These controls let you advance forward or backward through your slide show.

Setting Up a Projector

If you're going to present your show by using a computer projector and a laptop, you need to know how to connect the computer to your laptop as well as how to set up the projector, turn it on, focus it, and so on. Most of these details vary from one projector to the next, so you have to consult the manual that came with the projector or bribe someone to set up the projector for you. The following list provides a few general tips that might help:

✓ **Connecting the projector:** Most laptops have an external video port on the back or side, and most projectors have a video input connection. Newer projects and laptops use HDMI connectors, but older projectors or laptops may use other types of connectors, such as DVI or VGA. Note that depending on the type of connector on your laptop and on your projector, you may need a special adapter to match the laptop's connector to the projector's connector. At any rate, make sure you have the correct cable and adapter to connect your projector to your laptop.

✓ **Activating the external video port:** To use the laptop with a projector, you must first activate the external video port. Some laptops automatically detect a projector when it is connected. On others, you must press a key or combination of keys to activate the external port.

✓ **Selecting the projector's video input:** Most projectors can accept input from more than one source. For example, you might be able to connect a computer and a DVD player to the projector. The projector should have some buttons or perhaps a menu setting that lets you select the input that is used to display the projected image. If you connect your computer to the projector and everything else seems okay but you still don't get a picture, make sure that the projector is set to the correct input.

✓ **Using the projector's remote control:** If you want to use the projector's remote control to operate your presentation, you need the appropriate cable to connect the projector to your laptop's mouse port or USB. The correct cable should come with the projector.

✓ **Using sound:** If your presentation has sound, you need to connect your computer's sound outputs to a set of amplified speakers or, if you're showing the presentation in a large auditorium, a PA system. The correct cable to connect to a PA system depends on the PA system, but a cable with a mini-stereo plug on one end and a ¼-inch plug on the other will probably do the trick. Note that if you're using an HDMI connection, the sound output will be supplied to the projector or TV via the HDMI output.

Keyboard and Mouse Tricks for Your Slide Show

During an onscreen slide show, you can use the keyboard and mouse to control your presentation. Tables 6-1 and 6-2 list the keys and clicks that you can use.

If the cursor is hidden, you can summon it by jiggling the mouse. Then, when the cursor is visible, a faint menu appears in the lower-left corner of the slide. You can use this menu to activate various slide show features.

Table 6-1	Keyboard Tricks for Your Slide Show
To Do This	**Press Any of These Keys**
Display next slide	Enter, spacebar, Page Down, or N
Display preceding slide	Backspace, Page Up, or P
Display first slide	1+Enter
Display specific slide	Slide number+Enter
Toggle screen black	B or . (period)
Toggle screen white	W or , (comma)
Show or hide pointer	A or = (equal sign)
Erase screen doodles	E
Stop or restart automatic show	S or + (plus sign)
Display next slide even if hidden	H
Display specific hidden slide	Slide number of hidden slide+Enter
Change pen to arrow	Ctrl+A
Change arrow to pen	Ctrl+P
End slide show	Esc, Ctrl+Break (the Break key doubles as the Pause key), or – (minus)

Table 6-2	Mouse Tricks for Your Slide Show
To Do This	**Do This**
Display next slide	Click.
Move through slides	Roll the wheel on your mouse (if your mouse has a wheel).
Call up menu of actions	Right-click.
Display first slide	Hold down both mouse buttons for two seconds.
Use the laser pointer	Hold down the Ctrl key and then hold the left mouse button and move the mouse.
Doodle	Press Ctrl+P to change the mouse arrow to a pen and then draw onscreen like John Madden.

Using Presentation Tools

Presentation View has several icons that are useful during your presentation, as described in the following sections.

Using the Laser Pointer

The Laser Pointer feature displays a bright red dot on the screen, which you can move around by moving the mouse. It's not quite as good as using a real laser pointer, but if you don't happen to have one, the PowerPoint laser pointer will do. Figure 6-4 shows the laser pointer in action.

Laser pointer

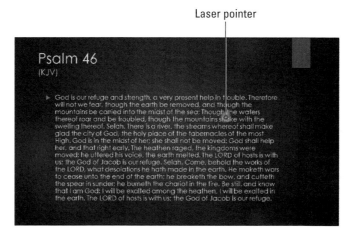

Figure 6-4: Using the laser pointer.

You can activate the laser pointer in two ways:

✔ The first is to click the Pen and Laser Pointer button in Presenter View (shown in the margin) and then choose Laser Pointer. Then, use your mouse to move the laser pointer around on the slide.

✔ The second way to activate the laser pointer is to hold down the Ctrl key, then click and hold the left mouse button and move the mouse. The laser pointer will appear on the screen and move as you move the mouse.

When you release the left mouse button, the laser pointer disappears.

Scribbling on Your Slides

You can doodle on your slides to draw your audience's attention to a particular part of the slide. For example, Figure 6-5 shows a slide on which I've drawn two circles to indicate the parts of the Psalm 46 that show Shakespeare's name.

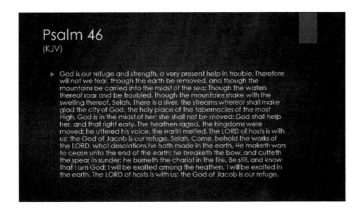

Figure 6-5: Using the pen tool.

To use the pen tool to draw on a slide, click the Pen and Laser Pointer button in Presenter View (shown in the margin) and select the Pen tool. Then, use your mouse to draw on the slide, holding down the left button and dragging the mouse around as best you can to leave your mark.

Here are some additional thoughts worth mentioning:

- Instead of a solid pen, you can also use a transparent highlighter. Just choose the Highlighter tool instead of the Pen tool, then use the mouse to mark on the slide. Note that the Highlighter tool works best on slides that have a light background.

- If you wish, you can change the color of the marks left by the pen tool. Click the Pen and Laser Pointer button, and then choose Ink Color and select the color you'd like to use.

- When you finish your presentation, you are given the option to keep your doodles as annotations in your presentation. Then, you won't have to redraw the doodles next time.

Rehearsing Your Slide Timings

You can use the PowerPoint Rehearsal feature to rehearse your presentation. The Rehearsal feature lets you know how long your presentation takes, and it can even set slide timings so that the slides automatically advance based on the timings you set during the rehearsal.

Rehearse
Timings

To rehearse a slide show, click the Rehearse Timings button in the Set Up section of the Slide Show Ribbon tab (shown in the margin). This starts the slide show, with a special Recording dialog box visible, as shown in Figure 6-6.

Figure 6-6: Rehearsing a slide show.

Now rehearse your presentation. Click or use keyboard shortcuts to advance slides. As you rehearse, the Rehearse dialog box keeps track of how long you display each slide and the total length of your presentation.

When you end the presentation, PowerPoint displays a dialog box that gives you the option of applying or ignoring the timings recorded during the rehearsal to the slides in the presentation. If you were satisfied with the slide timings during the rehearsal, click Yes.

If you mess up during a rehearsal, click the Repeat button. Clicking this button restarts the rehearsal from the beginning.

Using Custom Shows

The Custom Shows feature in PowerPoint lets you create several similar slide shows stored in a single presentation file. For example, suppose that you're asked to give presentations about company benefits to management and non-management staff. You can create a presentation containing slides for all the company benefits and then create a custom show containing only those slides describing benefits that are available to non-management staff. (This custom slide show can leave out slides such as "Executive Washrooms," "Golf Days," and "Boondoggles.") You may then show the complete presentation to management but show the custom show to non-management staff.

A presentation can contain as many custom shows as you want. Each custom show is simply a subset of the complete presentation — comprised of selected slides from the complete presentation.

Creating a custom show

To create a custom show, follow these steps:

Custom Slide
Show ▾

1. **On the Slide Show tab on the Ribbon, click Custom Slide Show (located in the Start Slide Show group) and then choose Custom Shows from the menu that appears.**

   This displays the Custom Shows dialog box.

2. **Click the New button.**

   The Define Custom Show dialog box appears, as shown in Figure 6-7.

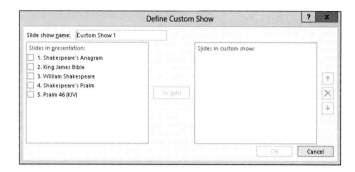

Figure 6-7: Defining a custom show.

3. **Type a name for the custom show in the Slide Show Name field.**

4. **Add the slides that you want to appear in the custom slide show.**

   All the slides available in the presentation are listed in the list box on the left side of the Define Custom Show dialog box. To add a slide to the custom show, select the slide that you want to add and then click Add. The slide appears in the list box on the right side of the Define Custom Show dialog box.

   You don't have to add slides to the custom show in the same order that the slides appear in the original presentation. Slides for a custom show can appear in any order you want. You can also include a slide from the original presentation more than once in a custom show.

   To remove a slide that you've added by mistake, deselect the slide that you want to remove in the list box on the right side of the Define Custom Show dialog box, and then click Remove.

   You can use the up and down arrows near the right edge of the Define Custom Show dialog box to change the order of the slides in the custom show.

5. **Click OK.**

   You return to the Custom Shows dialog box.

6. **Click Close to dismiss the Custom Shows dialog box.**

Showing a custom show

To show a custom show, first open the presentation that contains the custom show. Then open the Slide Show tab on the Ribbon, click the Custom Slide Show button, then choose Custom Shows from the menu that appears. This displays the Custom Shows dialog box, which lists any custom shows in the presentation. You can then select the custom show you want and start the show by clicking the Show button.

Hiding slides

Hide
Slide

If you don't want to go to all the trouble of creating a custom show, but you want to exclude a few slides from a presentation, you don't have to delete the slides. Instead, you can hide them. To hide a slide, select the slide and then click Hide Slide in the Slide Show Ribbon tab. To unhide a slide, select the slide and click the button again. (You can determine which slides have been hidden by looking at the slide in the Slides tab on the left. If the slide number has a slash through it, the slide is hidden.)

Showing Your Presentation Online

PowerPoint 2013 includes a new online presentation feature that makes it ridiculously easy to share your presentation with other people remotely over the Internet. To use it, simply follow these steps:

Present
Online ▾

1. **Click the Present Online button in the Slide Show Ribbon tab (shown in the margin).**

   Doing this brings up the Present Online dialog box, shown in Figure 6-8.

Figure 6-8: Showing a presentation online.

2. **Click Connect.**

3. **If prompted, enter your Windows Live username and password.**

   If you don't have a Windows Live account, sign up for one at `http://signup.live.com`.

   After you are connected, the dialog box shown in Figure 6-9 is shown.

Figure 6-9: Sharing the presentation address.

4. **To send an e-mail to your meeting participants, click Send in Email. Next, complete the e-mail by adding recipients and any other text you wish to add and send the e-mail.**

   Your participants can then click the link to open the presentation in their web browsers.

   You can also click Copy Link to copy the presentation link to the clipboard. You can then paste the link into an e-mail to distribute to your meeting participants.

5. **When everyone is ready to view the presentation, click Start Presentation.**

   This starts the presentation. Your participants can follow the presentation in their web browsers, as shown in Figure 6-10.

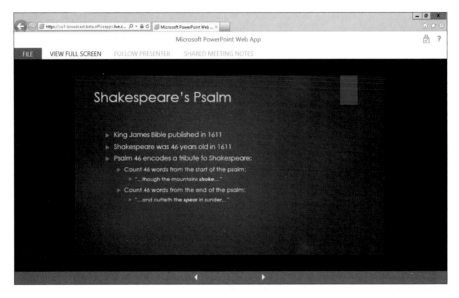

Figure 6-10: Sharing the presentation.

Part II

Creating Great-Looking Slides

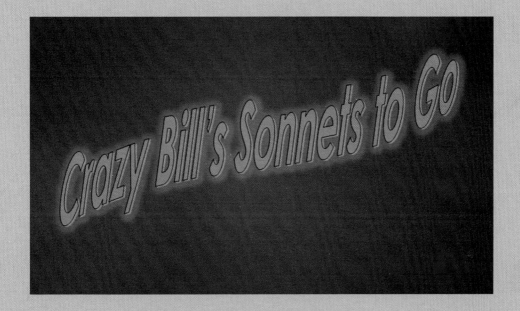

See how to add recurring text or other elements to each of your PowerPoint slides at www.dummies.com/extras/powerpoint2013.

In this part . . .

- ✔ Find out how to stun your audience and receive ooohs and aaahs from the crowd by formatting text and giving your slides a spectacular appearance.

- ✔ Get familiar with PowerPoint themes that allow you to create good-looking slides in minutes.

- ✔ Explore how to use slide transitions and animations to make even the dullest content look amazing.

- ✔ Discover how to utilize Masters, the surefire way to add something to every slide.

- ✔ See how to add recurring text or other elements to each of your PowerPoint slides at www.dummies.com/extras/powerpoint2013.

All about Fonts and Text Formatting

In This Chapter

▶ Using bold, italics, underlining, and other character effects

▶ Changing the text font, size, and color

▶ Using bullets and numbers

▶ Tabbing and indenting

▶ Spacing out lines of text

▶ Aligning text

▶ Making fanciful text with the WordArt feature

A good presentation is like a fireworks show: At every new slide, the audience gasps, "O-o-o-h. A-a-a-h." The audience is so stunned by the spectacular appearance of your slides that no one really bothers to read them.

This chapter gets you on the road toward ooohs and aaahs by showing you how to format text. If you use PowerPoint templates as the basis for your presentations, your text is already formatted acceptably. To really pull out the pyrotechnic stops, however, you have to know a few basic formatting tricks.

Many PowerPoint text-formatting capabilities work the same as in Microsoft Word. If you want to format text a certain way and you know how to do it in Word, try formatting the same way in PowerPoint. Odds are good that it works.

Changing the Look of Your Text

The theme that's applied to your presentation determines the basic look of the presentation's text. However, you'll often want to change that look, sometimes subtly and sometimes dramatically.

You can control the most commonly used font settings by using the Font group in the Home tab on the Ribbon, as shown in Figure 7-1.

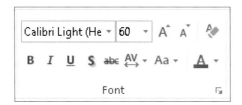

Figure 7-1: The Font group on the Home tab on the Ribbon.

If the Font group in the Home tab doesn't provide enough options for formatting your text, you can call up the Font dialog box for additional options. To summon this dialog box, just select the dialog launcher for the Font group. (The dialog launcher is the cursor at the bottom-right corner of the group.) Figure 7-2 shows this dialog box.

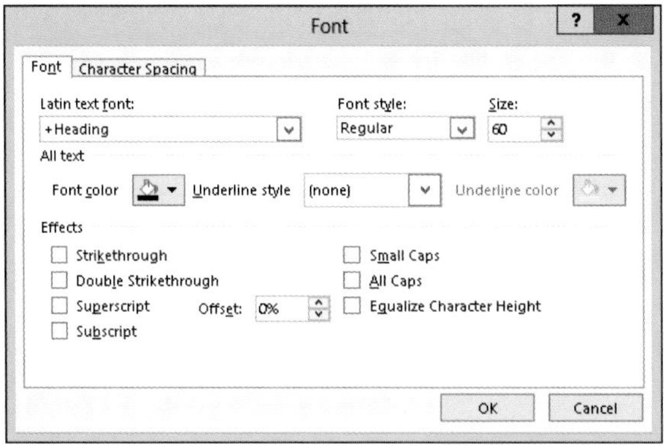

Figure 7-2: The Font dialog box.

Many font formatting options also have handy keyboard shortcuts. Table 7-1 lists the formatting commands along with their Ribbon buttons and equivalent keyboard shortcuts.

Table 7-1	Character-Formatting Commands	
Button	*Keyboard Shortcut*	*Formatting Command*
Calibri Light (He ▾)	(none)	Font
60 ▾	(none)	Size
A▲	Ctrl+Shift+>	Increase font size
A▼	Ctrl+Shift+<	Decrease font size
A✥	Ctrl+spacebar	Clear all formatting
B	Ctrl+B	Bold
I	Ctrl+I	Italic
U	Ctrl+U	Underline
S	(none)	Text shadow
abc	(none)	Strikethrough
AV↔	(none)	Character spacing
Aa ▾	Shift+F3	Change case
A ▾	(none)	Font color

It's true — PowerPoint has many keyboard shortcuts for character formatting. You don't have to know them all, though. The only ones I know and use routinely are the shortcuts for bold, italic, underline, and clear all formatting. Study these and you'll be in good shape. You get the added bonus that these keyboard shortcuts are the same as the shortcuts that many other Windows programs use. If you're mouse-happy and keyboard-annoyed, click away for goodness' sake. What matters most is that you can easily find and use what you need.

Two ways to apply formatting

You can format text in two basic ways:

- **To format existing text,** highlight the text that you want to format. Then, click the toolbar button or use the keyboard shortcut for the format that you want. For example, to make existing text bold, highlight it and then click the Bold button or press Ctrl+B.

- **To type new text using a fancy format,** click the toolbar button or use the keyboard shortcut for the format. Then, type away. The text that you type is given the format you selected. To return to normal formatting, click the button or use the keyboard shortcut again. Or press Ctrl+spacebar.

Changing the size of characters

Whether text is difficult to read or you simply want to draw attention to it, you can make part of the text bigger than the surrounding text. The easiest way to change the size of your text is to use the Font Size drop-down list that appears next to the font name in the Font group on the Home tab. Just choose among the sizes that appear in the Font Size drop-down list or click in the Font Size box and type whatever size you want to use.

You can also change the size of your text by using the Increase Font Size or Decrease Font Size buttons, or by using the Ctrl+Shift+> or Ctrl+Shift+< keyboard shortcuts. These commands increase or decrease the font size in steps, respectively.

If you type more text than will fit in a text placeholder, PowerPoint will automatically make your text smaller so that the text will fit within the placeholder.

Choosing text fonts

If you don't like the looks of a text font, you can switch easily to a different font. To change the font for existing text, select the text. Then click the arrow next to the Font control (found in the Font group of the Home tab) and choose the font that you want to use. If you're allergic to the mouse, you can get to the font list by pressing Ctrl+Shift+F. Then you can use the up- or down-arrow keys to choose the font you want to use.

Here are a gaggle of additional points to ponder concerning fonts:

- ✔ Although you can change the font from the Font dialog box, the Font control on the Ribbon has one major advantage over the Font dialog box: It displays each of your fonts by using the font itself, so you can see what each font looks like before you apply it to your text. In contrast, the Font dialog box displays the name of each font by using the standard Windows system font.

- ✔ If you want to change the font for all the slides in your presentation, switch to Slide Master View and then change the font. Details on how to do so are covered in Chapter 10.

- ✔ PowerPoint automatically moves the fonts that you use the most to the head of the font list. This feature makes picking your favorite font even easier.

- ✔ Don't overdo it with fonts! Just because you have many different font choices doesn't mean that you should try to use them all on the same slide. Don't mix more than two or three typefaces on a slide, and use fonts consistently throughout the presentation.

- ✔ If you want to set a font that is used consistently throughout a presentation, the best way to do so is to set the font for the presentation's theme. For more information, see Chapter 8.

Adding color to your text

Color is an excellent way to draw attention to text in a slide. To change text color, first select the text whose color you want to change. Then click the Font Color button and choose the color that you want to use from the color menu that appears.

If you don't like any color that the Font Color button offers, click More Colors. A bigger dialog box with more color choices appears. If you still can't find the right shade of teal, click the Custom tab and have at it. Check out Chapter 9 if you need further help with colors.

If you want to change the text color for your entire presentation, do so in the Slide Master View (see Chapter 10 for details). And you can refer to Chapter 8 for information about changing font colors by using the theme.

Adding shadows

Adding a shadow behind your text can make the text stand out against its background, which makes the entire slide easier to read. For that reason, many of the templates supplied with PowerPoint use shadows.

You can apply a shadow to any text by first selecting the text and then clicking the Text Shadow button, found in the Font section of the Home tab. If you want all the text on a slide to be shadowed, however, you should use the Slide Master View to create the shadow format. For more information, peek ahead to Chapter 10.

Big Picture Text Formatting

The Paragraph group on the Home tab on the Ribbon, as shown in Figure 7-3, has several buttons that apply formats to entire paragraphs. The following sections describe the most common uses for the buttons in this group.

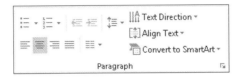

Figure 7-3: The Paragraph group on the Home tab on the Ribbon.

Biting the bulleted list

Most presentations have at least some slides that include a bulleted list, which is a series of paragraphs accented by special characters lovingly known as *bullets.* In the old days, you had to add bullets one at a time. Nowadays, PowerPoint comes with a semi-automatic bullet shooter that is illegal in 27 states.

PowerPoint lets you create fancy bullets that are based on bitmap pictures rather than simple dots and check marks. Before you go crazy with picture bullets, take a look at the basic way to bite the bullet.

To add bullets to a paragraph or series of paragraphs, take aim and fire, like so:

1. **Highlight the paragraphs to which you want to add bullets.**

   To add a bullet to just one paragraph, you don't have to highlight the entire paragraph. Just place the cursor anywhere in the paragraph.

2. **Click the Bullets button found in the Paragraph group of the Home tab.**

   PowerPoint adds a bullet to each paragraph that you select.

The Bullets button works like a toggle: Press it once to add bullets and press it again to remove bullets. To remove bullets from previously bulleted text, therefore, you select the text and click the Bullets button again.

If you don't like the appearance of the bullets that PowerPoint uses, you can select a different bullet character, picture, or even a motion clip by clicking the down arrow at the right side of the Bullets button. This action reveals a list of choices for various types of bullets.

If none of the bullets in this list are acceptable, you can bring up the Bullets and Numbering dialog box by clicking the arrow at the right of the Bullets button and then choosing Bullets and Numbers. This step summons the Bullets and Numbering dialog box, as shown in Figure 7-4. From this dialog box, you can choose a different bullet character, change the bullet's color, or change its size relative to the text size.

Figure 7-4: The Bullets and Numbering dialog box.

The following paragraphs point out some important tidbits to keep in mind when you use bullets:

✔ **Customize bullet characters:** You can choose from among several collections of bullet characters that are available. If you don't like any of the bullet characters displayed for you in the dialog box, click Customize in the lower-right corner of the dialog box. This brings up a dialog box that lists a variety of useful alternative bullet characters, such as pointing fingers, a skull and crossbones, and a time bomb. Pick the bullet that you want to use and then click OK. If you can't find a bullet that suits your fancy, choose a different font in the Font control drop-down list.

✔ **Change the size of bullet characters:** If the bullet characters don't seem large enough, increase the size in the Bullets and Numbering dialog box. The size is specified as a percentage of the text size.

✔ **Change the color of bullet characters:** To change the bullet color, use the Color drop-down list to choose the color that you want to use. Colors from the current color scheme appear in the drop-down menu that appears. For additional color choices, choose More Colors to call up a dialog box that offers a complete range of color choices. (For more information about using colors, see Chapter 8.)

✔ **Use images for your bullet characters:** To use a picture bullet, click the Picture button located in the lower right of the Bullets and Numbering dialog box. This click brings up the dialog box shown in Figure 7-5, which lets you choose from several sources for a picture to use as a bullet.

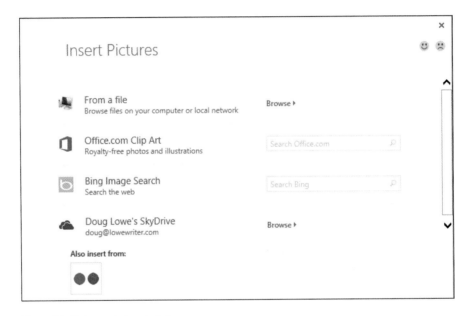

Figure 7-5: Using a picture bullet.

Creating numbered lists

If you want your slide to include a numbered list, use the Numbering button, which appears next to the Bullets button on the Home tab. When you click the Numbering button, PowerPoint adds simple numbers to the selected paragraphs.

If you want to change the numbering format, click the arrow next to the Numbering button to display a list of number style choices. Then you can select the style that suits your fancy.

If none of the styles in the list are right, choose Bullets and Numbering to reveal the numbering options shown on the Numbered tab of the Bullets and Numbering dialog box. See Figure 7-6.

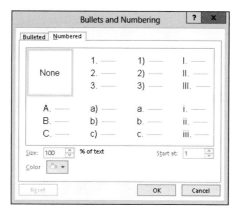

Figure 7-6: More ways to format numbers.

Normally, the starting number for each list reverts to 1 for each new slide. What if you have a list that has more items than can fit on one slide, such as a David Letterman-style Top Ten list? In that case, you can type the first half of the list on one slide and then type the second half of the list on a second slide. Next, right-click the first item on the second slide and choose Bullets and Numbering from the menu that appears. Then, change the Start At value to the number at which you want the second part of the list to begin. For example, if the first slide has five numbered items, change the Start At value for the first item on the second slide to 6.

Setting tabs and indents

PowerPoint enables you to set tab stops to control the placement of text within a text object. For most presentations, you don't have to fuss with tabs. Each paragraph is indented according to its level in the outline, and the template that you use to create the presentation presets the amount of indentation for each outline level.

If you're stubborn about tabs, you can mess with the indent settings and tab stops — that is, if you're adventurous and have no real work to do today. Here's how you do it:

1. **Click the Slide button to switch to Normal View.**

   You can't mess with tabs or indents in Notes Page View or Slide Sorter View.

2. **If the rulers aren't visible, summon them by clicking the View tab on the Ribbon and then selecting the Ruler check box in the Show/Hide group.**

Rulers appear above and to the left of the presentation window and show the current tab and indentation settings.

3. **Select the text object whose tabs or indents you want to change.**

   Each text object has its own tabs and indents settings. After you click a text object, the ruler shows that object's tabs and indents.

4. **Click the ruler to add a tab stop.**

   Move the cursor to the ruler location where you want to add a tab stop and then click. A tab stop appears.

5. **Grab the indentation doohickey and then drag it to change the indentation.**

   The indentation doohickey (that's not its official name) is the control that looks like an hourglass sitting on a little box, normally positioned at the left side of the ruler. It actually consists of three parts: the top upside-down triangle sets the indentation for the first line of the paragraph, the middle triangle sets the indentation for the remaining lines of the paragraph, and the box at the bottom sets the indentation for the paragraph. Try dragging the different parts of the indentation doohickey to see what happens. Have fun. Good luck.

Each text object is initially set up with default tab stops set at every inch. When you add a tab stop, any default tab stops located to the left of the new tab stop disappear.

To remove a tab stop, use the mouse to drag the tab stop off the ruler. (For instance, click the tab stop, drag it off the ruler, and then release the mouse button.)

Spacing out

Feeling a little spaced out? Try tightening the space between text lines. Feeling cramped? Space out the lines a little. These steps show you how to do it all:

1. **Highlight the paragraph — or paragraphs — whose line spacing you want to change.**

2. **Click the Line Spacing button and then select the amount of line spacing you want.**

   The Line Spacing button displays the most common line spacing options: 1.0, 1.5, 2.0, 2.5, and 3.0. If you want to set the line spacing to a value that's not shown on the Line Spacing button, select Line Spacing Options to display the Paragraph dialog box, as shown in Figure 7-7.

Don't even bother with this stuff about tab types

PowerPoint isn't limited to just boring left-aligned tabs. In all, it has four distinct types of tabs: left, right, center, and decimal. The square button that appears at the far-left side of the ruler when you select text tells you which type of tab is added when you click the ruler. Click this button to cycle through the four types of tabs:

✔ **Standard left-aligned tab:** Press Tab to advance the text to the tab stop.

✔ **Right-aligned tab:** Text is aligned flush right with the tab stop.

✔ **Centered tab:** Text lines up centered over the tab stop.

✔ **Decimal tab:** Numbers line up with the decimal point centered over the tab stop.

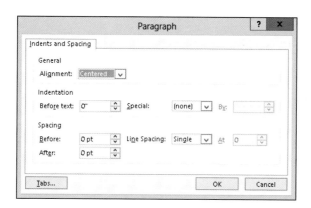

Figure 7-7: Change the line spacing.

Lining things up

PowerPoint enables you to control the way your text lines up on the slide. You can center text, line it up flush left or flush right, or justify it. You can change these alignments by using the alignment buttons in the Paragraph group on the Home tab. You can also use the keyboard shortcuts described in Table 7-2.

Table 7-2	Paragraph Alignment Commands	
Button	*Keyboard Shortcut*	*Alignment*
	Ctrl+L	Align Left
	Ctrl+E	Center
	Ctrl+R	Align Right
	Ctrl+J	Justify

Here are some semirandom thoughts on aligning paragraphs:

- **Centered text lines up right down the middle of the slide.** Actually, text lines up down the middle of the text object that contains the text; a text line appears centered on the slide only if the text object is centered on the slide.

- **Bulleted lists look best when left-aligned.** Otherwise, the bullets don't line up.

Making columns

Most slides place all their text in a single column. However, you can easily create multiple columns by using the Columns button, found in the Paragraph section of the Home tab. To create a one-, two-, or three-column layout, just click the Columns button and then choose one, two, or three columns from the menu that appears. If you want more than three columns, select the More Columns command and then choose the number of columns you want to use.

Creating Fancy Text with WordArt

Previous versions of PowerPoint included a feature called *WordArt* that let you insert special objects that could incorporate fancy text effects, such as gradient fills or curved paths. For PowerPoint 2013, Microsoft has integrated

WordArt into PowerPoint, so that you can apply WordArt formatting to any bit of text in your presentation just by highlighting the text and applying the WordArt formats. Figure 7-8 is an example of what you can do with WordArt in just a couple of minutes.

Figure 7-8: You, too, can create fancy text effects like this using WordArt.

Follow these steps to transform mundane text into something worth looking at:

1. **Select the text you want to apply WordArt formatting to.**

   The text can be anywhere in your presentation. For example, you can apply WordArt formatting to a slide title or body text.

2. **Click the Drawing Tools Format tab.**

   The Drawing Tools Format tab includes a WordArt Styles group, shown in Figure 7-9. As you can see, this Ribbon group includes several pre-configured WordArt styles as well as buttons that let you control the text fill, outline style, and text effects such as shadows and glowing.

Figure 7-9: The WordArt Styles group on the Drawing Tools Format tab.

3. **Click the More button found at the bottom of the scroll bar to the right of the predefined WordArt styles.**

   The WordArt Quick Styles gallery appears, as shown in Figure 7-10.

4. **Select the WordArt style that most closely resembles the formatting you want to apply.**

   Don't worry if none of the gallery choices exactly match the effect you want; you can tweak the text's appearance later.

5. **Fool around with other WordArt controls in the WordArt Styles group of the Drawing Tools Format tab.**

   Table 7-3 describes the other controls in the WordArt Styles group. Experiment with these controls as much as you want until you get the text to look just right.

Figure 7-10: The WordArt Quick Styles gallery.

Table 7-3	**Buttons on the WordArt Drawing Tools Format Tab**	
Control	*What It's Called*	*What It Does*
A	Text Fill	Sets the fill color. The fill can be a simple color, a gradient (which blends two or more colors), a picture, a pattern, or a texture.
A	Text Outline	Sets the properties of the text outline. You can select a color, a pattern, and a thickness.
	Text Effects	Lets you apply fancy text effects such as shadows, reflections, glowing text, beveled text, 3-D rotations, and transforms.

The Text Effects button is the key to creating fancy logos, such as text that wraps around circles or text that has a three-dimensional look. When you click this button, a menu with various text formatting options appears. Table 7-4 lists the formatting options available on this menu.

Table 7-4	Formatting Options on the Text Effects Menu	
Control	*What It's Called*	*What It Does*
A	Shadow	Adds a shadow to the text. The shadow can be directly behind the text, or it can appear beneath the text, which creates the impression that the text is floating above an invisible surface.
A	Reflection	Creates a faint reflection on an invisible surface beneath the text.
A	Glow	Adds a glowing effect to the text.
A	Bevel	Adds a beveled effect to the text, which creates the impression that the text has been chiseled from a solid object.
A	3-D Rotation	Rotates the text around three dimensions.
abc	Transform	Transforms the overall shape of the text.

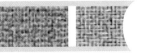

8

Designing Your Slides

*O*ne of the most bothersome tasks of putting together a good PowerPoint presentation is making the presentation look good. Always wanting to be helpful in such matters, Microsoft has endowed PowerPoint with a feature called *themes* that lets you create good-looking slides in minutes. One of the best features of themes is that they work not only in PowerPoint, but also in Word and Excel. Thus, you can use themes to create PowerPoint presentations, Word documents, and Excel spreadsheets that have a consistent appearance.

The main access to PowerPoint themes is from the Design tab on the Ribbon. This entire chapter is devoted to this Design tab. To keep things simple, I approach this most useful tab from left to right even though that's not always the order in which you use the controls it contains.

Looking at the Design Tab

To get things started, Figure 8-1 shows the Design tab on the Ribbon. As you can see, the Design tab contains several groups of controls that let you set various aspects of the slide design used within your presentation. You can summon the Design tab by clicking it on the Ribbon or by using the handy keyboard shortcut Alt+G.

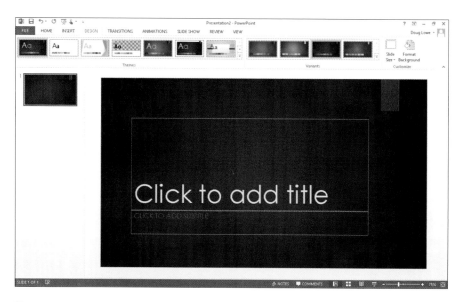

Figure 8-1: The Design tab.

The following list describes the general purpose of each group of controls on the Design tab:

- **Themes:** Lets you apply a theme to the presentation. This is the group you work with most while you play with the design of your slides.

- **Variants:** Lets you choose from several minor variants of a given theme.

- **Customize:** Lets you change the slide size and background appearance.

Working with Themes

The Themes group of the Design tab lets you select a theme to apply to your slides. PowerPoint 2013 comes with a ton of carefully crafted themes that give a professional look to your presentations. If you're somewhat artsy, you can design your own themes, as well.

A *theme* is a set of design elements that are applied to one or more slides in a presentation. Each theme includes several basic components:

- A set of **colors** that work well together. Each theme has four colors that can be used for text or backgrounds and six colors that can be used for accents.

- A set of **fonts** that looks good when used together. Each theme has a font used for headings and a font used for regular text.

    ✔ A set of **background styles,** which are a combination of background colors and effects such as patterns or gradient fills.

    ✔ A set of **design effects,** such as line and fill styles and line styles.

Office ships with 21 predefined themes. These themes are named as follows:

Office Theme	Slice	Mesh
Facet	Wisp	Metropolitan
Integral	Banded	Parallax
Ion	Basis	Quotable
Ion Boardroom	Celestial	Savon
Organic	Dividend	View
Retrospect	Frame	Wood Type

Each of these 21 themes is available in for color variations, which yields a total of 84 distinct theme variants you can apply to your slides.

Applying themes

To apply a theme to an entire presentation, simply click the theme you want to apply in the Themes group on the Design tab. If the theme you want to apply isn't visible, use the scroll buttons on the right side of the Themes group to display additional themes.

When you have selected a theme in the Themes group, variations on the theme will appear in the Variants group. You can then click on one of the variants you want to use.

To see a preview of how your presentation will appear with a particular theme, hover the mouse over that theme in the gallery. After a moment, the current slide momentarily appears formatted with the theme. If you move the mouse off the theme without actually clicking the theme, the current slide reverts to its previous formatting.

You can click the down arrow in the scroll bars in the Theme gallery, which displays an expanded list of themes, as shown in Figure 8-2. As you can see, this window displays PowerPoint's built-in themes and also includes links that let you browse for additional themes. A link even lets you save the current combination of theme elements as a new theme.

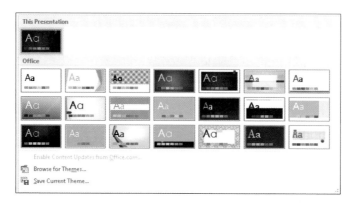

Figure 8-2: The Theme gallery.

Not all the slides in a presentation have to follow the same theme. To apply a theme to a single slide — or a set of slides — select the slide(s). Then, right-click the theme you want to apply and choose Apply to Selected Slides.

Using theme colors

Each PowerPoint theme includes a built-in *color scheme,* which consists of sets of colors chosen by color professionals. Microsoft paid these people enormous sums of money to debate the merits of using mauve text on a teal background. You can use these professionally designed color schemes, or you can create your own if you think that you have a better eye than the Microsoft-hired color guns.

As far as I'm concerned, the color schemes in PowerPoint themes are the best things to come along since Peanut M&Ms. Without color schemes, people like me are free to pick and choose from among the 16 million or so colors that PowerPoint lets you incorporate into your slides. The resulting slides can easily appear next to Cher and Lindsay Lohan in *People* magazine's annual "Worst Dressed of the Year" issue.

Each color scheme has 12 colors, with each color designated for a particular use, as shown in this list:

 ✓ **Four Text/Background colors:** These four colors are designed to be the primary colors for the presentation. One from each pair is used for text, and the other for the background. (You could use the same color for both, but that would make the slides impossible to read!)

 ✓ **Six accent colors:** These colors are used for various bits and pieces of your slides that complement the basic text and background colors.

 ✓ **Two hyperlink colors:** These colors are used only when your presentation includes hyperlinks.

When you apply a theme, the color scheme for that theme is applied along with the other elements of the theme. However, PowerPoint lets you change the color scheme from the scheme that comes with the theme. For example, you can apply a theme such as Opulent but then change the color scheme to the scheme from the Verve theme.

Applying a color scheme

To change the standard color scheme used for your slides, you must first switch to Slide Master view. You find out more about working with Slide Masters in Chapter 10, but for now just realize that a Slide Master controls the overall appearance of one or more slides. To switch to Slide Master view, open the View tab in the Ribbon and click the Slide Master button. In the Background group, you'll find a Colors button, which you can click to reveal the drop-down list shown in Figure 8-3. Then you can choose the color scheme you want to apply.

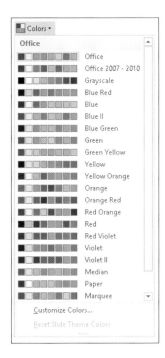

Figure 8-3: The Colors drop-down list.

Creating your own color scheme

If you don't like any color schemes that come with the built-in themes, you can create your own color scheme. Here are the steps:

1. **Select a color scheme that's close to the one you want to use.**

   Be warned that after you deviate from the preselected color scheme combinations, you'd better have some color sense. If you can't tell chartreuse from lime, you should leave this stuff to the pros.

2. **Click the Theme Colors button and then choose Create New Theme Colors.**

   The Create New Theme Colors dialog box appears, as shown in Figure 8-4.

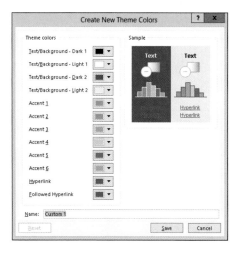

Figure 8-4: Creating new theme colors.

3. **Click the button for the color you want to change.**

   For example, to change the first accent color, click the Accent 1 button. You then see a gallery of color choices, as shown in Figure 8-5.

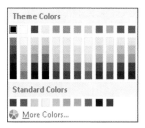

Figure 8-5: Changing a color.

4. **Pick a color you like.**

   As you can see, a plethora of color choices are available. This gallery reminds me of the shelf of paint color chips in the paint section of a hardware store.

5. **If you don't like any of the choices, click the More Colors button.**

   Doing this brings up the Colors dialog box, as shown in Figure 8-6. As you can see, PowerPoint displays what looks like a tie-dyed version of Chinese checkers. (Note that this dialog box comes up with the Standard tab selected. If you used the Custom tab the last time you used this dialog box, the Custom tab will be selected instead.)

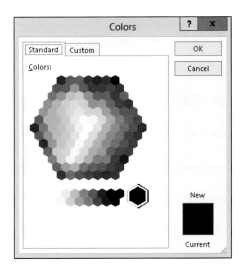

Figure 8-6: A wonderful world of color.

6. **Click the color that you want and then click OK.**

   After you click OK, you're whisked back to the Create New Theme Colors dialog box.

7. **(Optional) Repeat Steps 3 through 6 for any other colors you want to change.**

8. **Click Save.**

   The new color scheme is saved.

The Standard tab of the Colors dialog box (refer to Figure 8-6) shows 127 popular colors, plus white, black, and shades of gray. If you want to use a color that doesn't appear in the dialog box, click the Custom tab. This step draws forth the custom color controls, as shown in Figure 8-7. From this tab in the dialog box, you can construct any of the 16 million colors that are theoretically possible with PowerPoint. You need a PhD in physics to figure out how to adjust the Red, Green, and Blue controls, though. Mess around with this stuff if you want, but you're on your own.

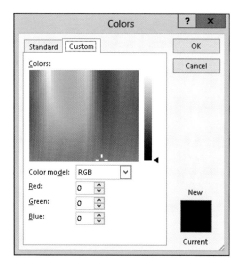

Figure 8-7: PowerPoint offers 16 million colors from which you can choose.

Using theme fonts

Theme fonts are similar to theme colors, but theme fonts have fewer choices. Although there are 12 colors per theme, there are only two fonts: one for headings, the other for body text.

If you don't want to use the fonts associated with the theme you've chosen for your presentation, you can use the Theme Fonts button at the right side of the Themes group on the Design tab on the Ribbon to choose fonts from a different theme. Then the fonts you select are applied throughout your presentation.

Note that changing the theme font is not the same as changing the font via the Font controls found in the Font group of the Home tab. When you use the Font controls on the Home tab, you're applying *direct formatting*. Direct formatting temporarily overrides the font setting specified by the theme. As a general rule, you should use theme fonts to set the fonts used throughout a presentation. Use direct formatting sparingly — when you want to create a word or two in a font that differs from the rest of the presentation.

You can change the font used in a theme by clicking the Theme Fonts button and then choosing Customize Fonts. Doing this brings up the Create New Theme Fonts dialog box, as shown in Figure 8-8. Here you can change the font used for headings and body text.

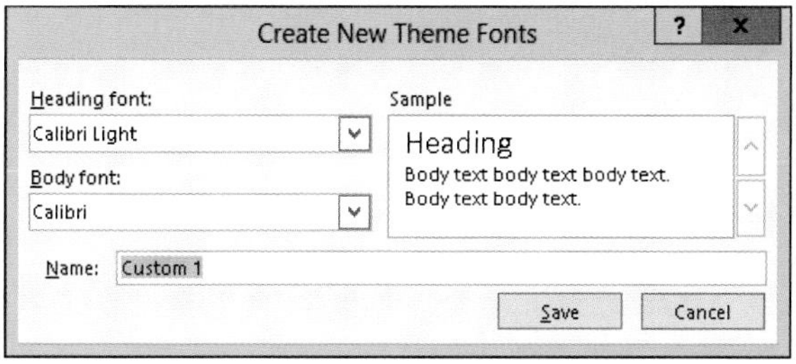

Figure 8-8: Changing theme fonts.

Applying theme effects

Another major component of PowerPoint themes are the *theme effects,* which apply subtle variations to the graphical look of your presentations. Theme effects are applied automatically whenever you apply a theme. However, you can apply theme effects from a different theme by clicking the Effects button at the right side of the Themes group on the Design tab on the Ribbon. This brings up the Theme Effects gallery, as shown in Figure 8-9. You can choose any of the theme effects listed.

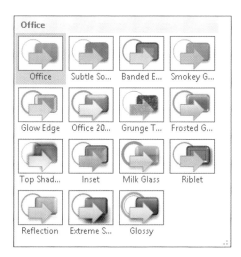

Figure 8-9: Changing theme effects.

Changing the Slide Size

The Customize group of the Design ribbon tab includes a Slide Size control that lets you change the size of the slide from standard to widescreen. You should use widescreen only if you plan on showing the presentation on a projector that displays in widescreen format.

Besides standard and widescreen formats, you can also click the Slide Size button and then choose Customize Slide Size. Doing this brings up the Slide Size dialog box, as shown in Figure 8-10. This dialog box gives you extra control over your presentation's page setup.

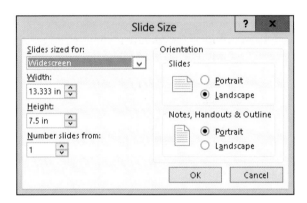

Figure 8-10: The Slide Size dialog box.

The following list describes the controls in this dialog box:

 ✓ **Slides Sized For:** This drop-down list lets you set the size of your slides based on how you plan to present them. The most common is to present the slides on a standard computer screen, which has an aspect ratio of 4:3. (*Aspect ratio* is the ratio of the screen's width to its height. Although 4:3 is a common aspect ratio, many newer computers use widescreen displays, which usually have an aspect ratio of 16:10.) Other options on this drop-down list include different screen ratios (suitable for widescreen displays), standard sized paper, and even 35mm slides. A Custom option even lets you set whatever width and height you want for your slides.

 ✓ **Width:** Lets you set a custom width for your slides.

 ✓ **Height:** Lets you set a custom height for your slides.

 ✓ **Number Slides From:** If your slides include numbers, this option lets you set the number for the first slide. The default is 1.

 ✓ **Orientation:** Lets you set the orientation to *portrait* (tall and skinny) or *landscape* (short and fat). You can set the setting separately for your slides, handouts, and notes. The most common setting is for the slides to use landscape orientation and the notes and handouts to use portrait.

Using Background Styles

A *background style* is a combination of a background color chosen from a theme color scheme and a background fill effect. The color scheme always includes four colors that can be used for the background — two light colors and two dark colors. In addition, you can choose from three background fill effects. These three fills are Subtle, Moderate, and Intense. For example, the Subtle fill might be a solid color, the Moderate fill might be a gentle pattern applied to the color, and the Intense fill might be a bold gradient fill.

Each combination of the four background colors and three background fills is a *background style.* Thus, each theme provides a total of 12 background styles.

To apply one of the theme's background styles to your presentation, use the Background Styles control in the Background group on the Design tab. This control reveals the Background Styles gallery, as shown in Figure 8-11.

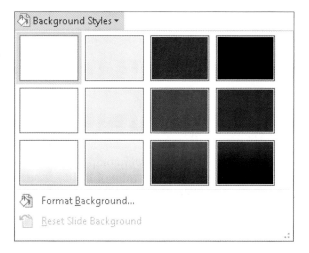

Figure 8-11: Changing the background style.

Using a gradient fill

You may have noticed that the slide background used in many PowerPoint templates is not a solid color. Instead, the color is gradually shaded from top to bottom. This type of shading — *gradient fill* — creates an interesting visual effect. For example, look at the slide shown in Figure 8-12. This slide was based on the standard Office Theme that comes with PowerPoint 2013. The background is light pink in the center and fades to darker pink on the edges.

Figure 8-12: Using a gradient fill to create an interesting background.

You can create your own custom gradient fill by following these steps:

1. **Choose the slide that you want to shade.**

   This step isn't necessary if you want to apply the shading to all slides in the presentation.

2. **Click the Background Styles button in the Background group of the Design tab on the Ribbon.**

   The Background Styles gallery appears.

3. **Click Format Background.**

   Doing this brings up the Format Background pane that appears to the right of the slide, as shown in Figure 8-13.

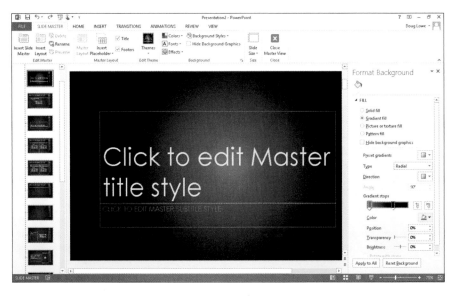

Figure 8-13: The Format Background pane.

4. **Select the Gradient Fill radio button if it isn't already selected.**

5. **Set the gradient fill options the way you want them.**

   You have to play with the controls until you get a feel for how they work. Start by selecting the present colors, which let you choose one of several predefined fill patterns. Then play with the controls until you get the fill to look the way you want. You can choose the colors to use for the fill, the transparency level, the direction, and several variants for each option.

6. **Click OK.**

Using other background effects

Besides gradient fills, you can use the Format Background dialog box to create several other interesting types of backgrounds. For example, you can assign a picture of your choosing, or you can use one of several predefined patterns supplied with PowerPoint.

To use a texture, select the Picture or Texture Fill radio button. Then click the Texture button to reveal the Texture gallery, as shown in Figure 8-14.

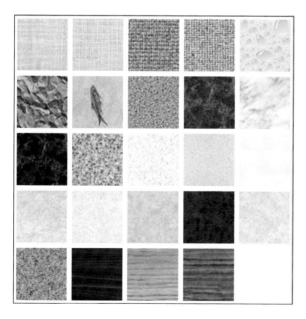

Figure 8-14: Using a textured background.

You can also use the Picture or Texture Fill radio button to select an image file of your own. Just click the File button and then select the file you want to use. Or, you can import an image from the Clipboard or select a clip art image. The remaining controls on this dialog box let you further tweak the appearance of the picture or text you select.

9

Animating Your Slides

*I*f you plan to run your presentation on your computer's screen or on a computer projector, you can use (or abuse) a bagful of exciting onscreen PowerPoint animations. The audience members probably won't be fooled into thinking that you hired Disney to create your slides, but they'll be impressed all the same. Animations are just one more example of how PowerPoint can make even the dullest content look spectacular.

This chapter begins with slide transitions, which are not technically animations because they don't involve movement of individual items on a slide. However, slide transitions are usually used in concert with animations to create presentations that are as much fun to watch as they are informative.

Using Slide Transitions

A *transition* is how PowerPoint gets from one slide to the next during an onscreen slide show. The normal way to segue from slide to slide is simply cutting to the new slide — effective, yes, but also boring. PowerPoint enables you to assign any of the more than 50 different special effects to each slide transition. For example, you can have the next slide scoot over the top of the current slide from any direction, or you can have the current slide scoot off the screen in any direction to reveal the next slide. You can have slides fade out, dissolve into each other, open up like Venetian blinds, or spin in like spokes on a wheel.

You can control slide transitions by using the Transitions tab of the Ribbon, as shown in Figure 9-1.

Figure 9-1: The Transitions tab.

The Transitions tab consists of three groups of controls, as described in the following list:

- **Preview:** This group includes a single control — a Preview — that displays a preview of the transition effect you selected for the current slide.

- **Transition to This Slide:** This group lets you select the transition effect that will be used to display the current slide.

- **Timing:** This group lets you select options that affect how the transition effect is applied to the slide, such as how quickly the transition occurs and whether it's triggered by a mouse click or automatically after a time delay.

To create a slide transition, follow these steps:

1. **Move to the slide to which you want to apply the transition.**

   Note that the transition applies when you come to the slide you apply the transition to, not when you go to the next slide. For example, if you apply a transition to slide 3, the transition is displayed when you move from slide 2 to slide 3, not when you move from slide 3 to slide 4.

   If you want to apply the animation scheme to all your slides, you can skip this step because it won't matter which slide you start from.

   If you want to apply different transitions to different slides, you may prefer to work in Slide Sorter View (click the Slide Sorter View button near the bottom-right corner of the screen), which allows you to see more slides at once. If you're going to use the same transition for all your slides, though, no benefit comes from switching to Slide Sorter View.

2. **Select the transition you want to apply from the Transition to This Slide section of the Transitions tab on the Ribbon.**

   If you want, you can display the complete gallery of transition effects by clicking the More button at the bottom right of the mini-gallery of transition effects displayed within the Ribbon. Figure 9-2 shows the complete Transitions gallery.

   Note that when you select a transition, PowerPoint previews the transition by animating the current slide. If you want to see the preview again, just click the transition again.

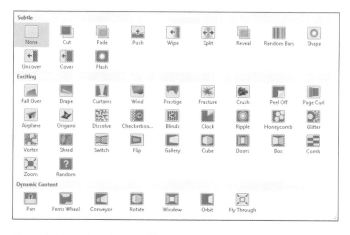

Figure 9-2: The Transitions gallery.

3. **Use the Effect Options drop-down list to select a variation of the transition effect you selected in Step 2.**

The available variations depend on the transition you've chosen. For example, if you choose the Wipe transition, the following variations are available:

- From Right
- From Left
- From Top
- From Bottom
- From Top-Right
- From Bottom-Right
- From Top-Left
- From Bottom-Left

4. **If you want, use the Sound drop-down list to apply a sound effect.**

The Sound drop-down list lists a collection of standard transition sounds, such as applause, a cash register, and the standard *whoosh*. You can also choose Other Sound to use your own .wav file.

5. **Use the Duration drop-down list to control how fast the transition should proceed.**

The default is 1 second, but you can specify a slower or faster speed if you want.

6. Use the On Mouse Click or After options to indicate how the transition should be triggered.

If you want to control the pace of the slide show yourself, select the On Mouse Click check box. Then, the slide will remain visible until you click the mouse. If you want the slide to advance automatically after a delay, select the After check box and specify the time delay.

To apply the animation to the entire presentation, click Apply to All. This applies the animation to all the slides in the presentation.

Here are some additional points to keep in mind when using slide transitions:

- ✒ **Consider computer speed:** Transition effects look better on faster computers, which have more raw processing horsepower to implement the fancy pixel dexterity required to produce good-looking transitions. If your computer is a bit slow, change the speed setting to Fast so the transition won't drag.

- ✒ **Select sets of transitions:** Some of the transition effects come in matched sets that apply the same effect from different directions. You can create a cohesive set of transitions by alternating among these related effects from slide to slide. For example, set up the first slide with Wipe Right, the second slide with Wipe Left, the third with Wipe Down, and so on.

- ✒ **Preview transitions:** When you work in Slide Sorter View, you can click the little star icon beneath each slide to preview the transition for that slide. Also, the automatic slide timing is shown beneath the slide if you set the slide to advance automatically.

Using the Animations Tab

Besides slide transitions, the most common type of animation in PowerPoint is adding entrance and exit effects to the text that appears on the slide. This effect is especially useful for bullet lists because it lets you display the list one item at a time. You can have each item appear out of nowhere, drop from the top of the screen, march in from the left or right, or do a back somersault followed by two cartwheels and a double-twist flip (talc, please!).

This type of animation is often called a *build effect* because it lets you build your points one by one. It's easy to apply this type of animation using the Animations tab of the Ribbon, shown in Figure 9-3.

Figure 9-3: The Animations tab.

The Animations tab consists of four groups of controls, as described in the following list:

- **Preview:** This group includes a single control — a Preview button — that displays a preview of the animation effects you selected for the current slide.

- **Animation:** This group lets you select one of several predefined animations for the selected object.

- **Advanced Animation:** The controls in this group let you create custom animations with features that the basic animations provided by using the Animation group. For more information, see the section "Customizing Your Animation," later in this chapter.

- **Timing:** This group lets you set the timing of the animation. For more information, see the section "Timing your animations," later in this chapter.

To apply an animation effect, first select the text box that you want to animate. Then, choose the animation style from the Animation gallery on the Animations tab.

Like other PowerPoint galleries, the Animation gallery includes a More button (at the bottom right) that summons the complete gallery, as shown in Figure 9-4.

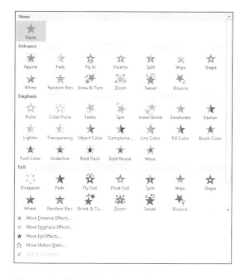

Figure 9-4: The Animation gallery.

After you apply a basic animation, you can use the Effect Options drop-down list to select one of several variations of the animation. For example, if you choose the Fly In animation, the Effect Options drop-down list lets you pick the direction from which the object will fly on to the slide.

Notice that there are several *More...* menu items at the bottom of the Animation gallery. You can click any of these buttons to reveal even more preanimation types.

For more complex animations, you need to use custom animations as described in the next section, "Customizing Your Animation."

Customizing Your Animation

Custom animation is the nitty-gritty of PowerPoint animation. Custom animation is the only way to apply text animation that's more complicated than the predefined Fade, Wipe, or Fly In styles of the Animate drop-down list. In addition to animating text, custom animation lets you animate other objects on your slides, such as pictures, shapes, and charts.

Understanding custom animation

Before I get into the details of setting up custom animation, you need to understand some basic concepts. Don't worry — this won't get too technical. But you need to know this stuff before you start creating custom animations.

For starters, you can apply custom animations to any object on a slide, whether it's a text placeholder, a drawing object such as an AutoShape or a text box, or a clip art picture. For text objects, you can apply the animation to the text object as a whole or to individual paragraphs within the object. You can also specify whether the effect goes all at once, word by word, or letter by letter. And you can indicate whether the effect happens automatically or whether PowerPoint waits for you to click the mouse or press Enter to initiate the animation.

Custom animation lets you create four basic types of animation effects for slide objects:

- **Entrance effect:** This is how an object enters the slide. If you don't specify an entrance effect, the object starts in whatever position that you placed it on the slide. If you want to be more creative, though, you can have objects appear by using any of the 52 different entrance effects, such as Appear, Blinds, Fade, Descend, Boomerang, Bounce, Sling, and many others.

- **Emphasis effect:** This effect lets you draw attention to an object that's already on the slide. PowerPoint offers 31 different emphasis effects, including Change Fill Color, Change Font Size, Grow/Shrink, Spin, Teeter, Flicker, Color Blend, Blast, and many more.

✔ **Exit effect:** This is how an object leaves the slide. Most objects don't have exit effects, but if you want an object to leave, you can apply one of the 52 different effects — which are similar to the entrance effects — Disappear, Blinds, Peek Out, Ease Out, Spiral Out, and so on.

✔ **Motion path:** Motion paths are the most interesting types of custom animation. A motion path lets you create a track along which the object travels when animated. PowerPoint provides you with 64 predefined motion paths, such as circles, stars, teardrops, spirals, springs, and so on. If that's not enough, you can draw your own custom path to make an object travel anywhere on the slide you want it to go.

If the motion path begins off the slide and ends somewhere on the slide, the motion path effect is similar to an entrance effect. If the path begins on the slide but ends off the slide, the motion path effect is like an exit effect. And if the path begins and ends on the slide, it is similar to an emphasis effect. In that case, when the animation starts, the object appears, travels along its path, and then zips off the slide.

To draw a custom motion path, click the Add Effect button in the Custom Animation pane, choose Motion Paths Draw, and then choose Draw Custom Path and select one of the motion path drawing tools from the menu that appears. The tools include straight lines, curves, freeform shapes, and scribbles. You can then draw your motion path using the tool you selected.

You can create more than one animation for a given object. For example, you can give an object an entrance effect, an emphasis effect, and an exit effect. That lets you bring the object onscreen, draw attention to it, and then have it leave. If you want, you can have several emphasis or motion path effects for a single object. You can also have more than one entrance and exit effect, but in most cases, one will do.

Each effect that you apply has one or more property settings that you can tweak to customize the effect. All the effects have a Speed setting that lets you set the speed for the animation. Some effects have an additional property setting that lets you control the range of an object's movement. (For example, the Spin effect has an Amount setting that governs how far the object spins.)

If you want, you can create a *trigger* that causes an animation effect to operate when you click an object on the slide. For example, you might create a trigger so that all the text in a text placeholder pulsates in when you click the slide title. To do so, first add the animation effect to the text. Then, click Trigger in the Advanced Animation group and choose On Click Of. A list of all objects on the slide that can be clicked is displayed; select the Title placeholder. (You can also trigger an animation when a specific location is reached during playback of a video file. For more information, refer to Chapter 15.)

Using the Animation pane

The Animation pane is a task pane that appears to the right of the slide and displays important information about the animations you have added to your slides. The Custom Animation task pane is hidden by default, but I recommend you turn it on before you start adding custom animations to your slides. To turn on the Custom Animation task pane, just click the Animation Pane button (shown in the margin) in the Advanced section of the Animation Ribbon tab.

Figure 9-5 shows how the Animation pane appears for a slide that has not yet had any animations added to it.

In the sections that follow, you find out how to use the Animation pane as you create custom animations.

Figure 9-5: The Animation pane.

Adding an effect

To animate an object on a slide, follow these steps:

1. **In Normal View, call up the slide that contains the object you want to animate and then click the object to select it.**

   For example, to animate text paragraphs, select the text placeholder that holds the text.

2. **If you haven't already done so, click the Animation Pane button.**

   This step opens the Custom Animation task pane.

3. **Click the Animations tab on the Ribbon.**

4. **Click the Add Animation button and then select the effect you want to create from the menu that appears.**

   Clicking the Add Animation button menu reveals a menu that lists the four types of effects: Entrance, Emphasis, Exit, and Motion Path. In this example, I chose the Bounce entrance effect.

   The entrance effect you selected is added to the Animation pane, as shown in Figure 9-6.

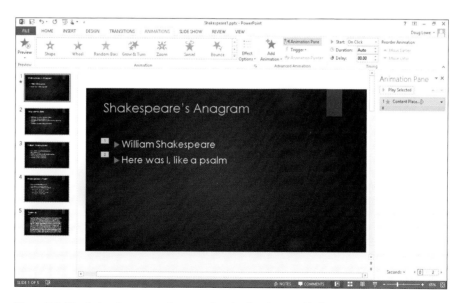

Figure 9-6: The Animation pane after an animation has been added.

Note that each of the paragraphs in the text placeholder has been assigned the number 1 or 2 to indicate the sequence in which the paragraphs will be animated. In the Custom Animation pane, the animation that was added in Step 4 is given the single number 1; number 2 doesn't appear in the pane. That's because although this animation is applied to two separate paragraphs, it is treated as a single animation in the Custom Animation pane.

However, if you click the double-down arrow beneath the animation, the two separate paragraph animations will be listed individually, as shown in Figure 9-7.

Figure 9-7: Text paragraphs can be listed separately in the Custom Animation pane.

5. **(Optional) Use the Effect Options control to select additional options for the effect.**

   For example, if you choose a Fly In effect, you can use the Effect Options control to specify the direction from which you want the text to fly.

6. **To preview the animation, click the Play button at the bottom of the Custom Animation task pane.**

   Or, if you prefer, just run the slide show to see how the animation looks. If nothing happens, click the mouse button to start the animation.

If you add more than one effect to a slide, the effects are initiated one at a time by mouse clicks, in the order you create them. You can drag effects up or down in the custom animation list to change the order of the effects. For more information about changing the order or setting up automatic effects, see the "Timing your animations" section, later in this chapter.

You can further tweak an effect by clicking the down arrow that appears next to the effect in the custom animation list and then choosing Effect Options. Doing this brings up a dialog box similar to the one shown in Figure 9-8. This dialog box has settings that let you add a sound to the animation, change the color of the object after the animation completes, and specify how you want text animated (All at Once, One Word at a Time, or One Letter at a Time). Depending on the type of effect, additional controls might appear in this dialog box.

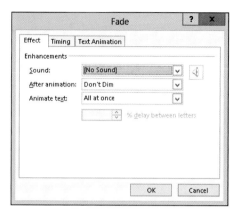

Figure 9-8: The settings dialog box for an animation effect.

More about animating text

The most common reason for animating text is to draw attention to your text one paragraph at a time while you show your presentation. One way to do this is to create an entrance effect for the text placeholder and then adjust the effect settings so that the entrance effect is applied one paragraph at a time. When you do that, your slide initially appears empty except for the title. Click once, and the first paragraph appears. Talk about that paragraph for a while and then click again to bring up the second paragraph. You can keep talking and clicking until all the paragraphs have appeared. When you click again, PowerPoint calls up the next slide.

Another approach is to use an emphasis effect instead of an entrance effect. This sort of effect allows all the paragraphs to display initially on the slide. When you click the mouse, the emphasis effect is applied to the first paragraph — it changes colors, increases in size, spins, whatever. Each time you click, the emphasis effect is applied to the next paragraph in sequence.

Either way, you must first add the effect for the text placeholder and then call up the Effect Settings dialog box by clicking the down arrow next to the effect in the custom animation list and then choosing Effect Settings. Doing this summons the settings dialog box for the text object. Click the Text Animation tab to see the animation settings, shown in Figure 9-9.

The Group Text setting, found on the Text Animation tab of the Animation Settings dialog box, controls how paragraphs appear when you click the mouse during the show, based on the paragraph's outline level. If you have only one outline level on the slide, grouping By 1st Level Paragraphs will do. If you have two or more levels, grouping text By 1st Level Paragraphs causes each paragraph to be animated along with any paragraphs that are subordinate to it. If you'd rather animate the second-level paragraphs separately, group your text By 2nd Level Paragraphs instead.

Figure 9-9: Animating text.

The other controls on this tab let you animate each paragraph automatically after a certain time interval or display the paragraphs in reverse order. (David Letterman, if you're reading this, you can use this feature when you present your Top Ten lists.)

Timing your animations

Most animations are initiated by mouse clicks. However, you can set up several animations to activate automatically — in sequence or all at the same time. To do so, you must use PowerPoint's Animation Timing features.

The first trick to controlling animation timing is to get the effects listed in the custom animation list in the correct order. Effects are added to the list in the order you create them. If you plan carefully, you might be able to create the effects in the same order that you want to animate them. More likely, you'll need to change the order of the effects. Fortunately, you can do that easily enough by dragging the effects up or down in the Custom Animation task pane.

After you get the effects in the right order, choose an option from the Start drop-down list that's near the top of the Custom Animation task pane to set the Start setting for each effect. This setting has three options:

- ✔ **Start On Click:** Starts the effect when you click the mouse or press Enter

- ✔ **Start With Previous:** Starts the effect when the effect immediately above it starts

  Use this option to animate two or more objects simultaneously.

- ✔ **Start After Previous:** Starts the effect as soon as the preceding effect finishes

Starting with the first effect in the list, click each effect to select it and then choose the Start setting for the effect. If all the effects except the first are set to With Previous or After Previous, the entire slide's animations run automatically after you start the first effect by clicking the mouse.

For example, Figure 9-10 shows a slide with three polygons drawn to resemble pieces of a puzzle. You can animate this puzzle so that the three pieces come together at the same time.

If you want to find out how to draw the shapes that are animated in this illustration, you can look ahead to Chapter 12.

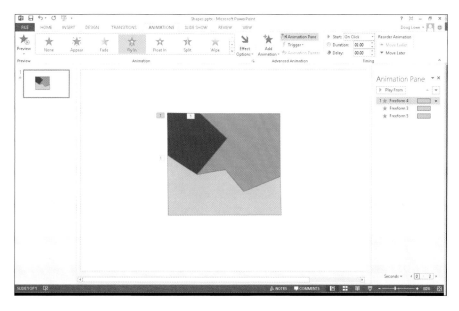

Figure 9-10: An animated puzzle.

Follow these steps to set up an animated puzzle like the one shown in Figure 9-10:

1. **Add a Fly In entrance effect for the top-left piece with the following settings:**

   - *Start:* On Click

   - *Direction:* From Top-Left

   - *Duration:* 2 Seconds

2. **Add a Fly In entrance effect for the top-right piece with the following settings:**

   - *Start:* With Previous

- *Direction:* From Top-Right

- *Duration:* 2 Seconds

3. **Add a Fly In entrance effect for the bottom piece with the following settings:**

- *Start:* With Previous

- *Direction:* From Bottom

- *Duration:* 2 Seconds

For even more control over an effect's timings, click the down arrow to the right of the effect and then choose Timing. A dialog box similar to the one in Figure 9-11 appears. Here's the lowdown on the timing settings:

- **Start:** This is the same as the Start setting in the Custom Animation task pane.

- **Delay:** This lets you delay the start of the animation by a specified number of seconds.

- **Duration:** This is the same as the Speed setting in the Custom Animation task pane.

- **Repeat:** This lets you repeat the effect so that the object is animated several times in succession.

- **Rewind When Done Playing:** Certain effects leave the object in a different condition than the object was when you started. For example, the object might change color or size or move to a new position on the slide. If you select the Rewind When Done Playing option, the object is restored to its original condition when the animation finishes.

Figure 9-11: Establishing the timing settings.

Making Text Jiggle

One of my favorite cute little animations is to make text — especially a short heading — jiggle. Not a lot, but just a little. The effect works best if the text has a funny typeface, such as Cosmic or Jokerman. By using a very small motion path and setting the timing options to repeat until the end of the slide, you can make the text jiggle just a little bit the entire time the slide is onscreen:

1. **Type the text that you want to jiggle and use the Font drop-down list to choose an appropriately silly typeface.**

   Jokerman is a favorite font for jiggling text.

2. **Use the Zoom control at the bottom-right corner of the screen to zoom in to 400%.**

   You want to zoom way in so that you can draw a very small motion path.

3. **On the Animation tab, click Add Animation and then choose Custom Path from the Motion Paths section of the gallery. (You probably have to scroll the gallery to see this option.)**

   The cursor changes to a little pencil.

4. **Draw a tightly knit scribble pattern directly in the center of the text.**

   Just wiggle the pencil cursor back and forth and up and down in an area of just a few pixels. Go back and forth quite a few times to make the jiggle effect appear to be random.

5. **Zoom back out to normal size.**

6. **In the Custom Animation task pane, click the arrow next to the animation you just created and then choose Timing.**

   This step brings up the dialog box that lets you set the timing options.

7. **Change the speed to 2 seconds and the Repeat drop-down to Until End of Slide. Then click OK.**

8. **Run the slide show to check the effect.**

You might have to try this several times before you get an effect you like, adjusting the random scribbles or the duration of the animation. Don't be afraid to experiment!

Using the Animation Painter

The Animation Painter makes it easy to copy a complete animation effect from one object to another. To use the Animation Painter, follow these steps:

1. **Use the techniques presented throughout this chapter to apply an animation effect to one of the objects in your slide show.**

2. **Select the object you have animated.**

3. **In the Custom Animation group of the Animation Ribbon tab, click the Animation Painter button.**

   The mouse pointer changes to a little paintbrush.

4. **Click the object you want to apply the animation to.**

   The animation that you created for the object selected in Step 2 is applied to the object you clicked on in this step.

If you want to apply the animation to more than one object, double-click the Animation Painter button in Step 3. Then, you can repeat Step 4 as many times as you wish to copy the animation to multiple objects. When your animation frenzy has come to a close, press the Esc key.

10

Masters of the Universe Meet the Templates of Doom

*W*ant to add a bit of text to every slide in your presentation? Or maybe add your name and phone number at the bottom of your audience handouts? Or place a picture of Rush Limbaugh at the extreme right side of each page of your speaker notes?

Masters are the surefire way to add something to every slide. No need to toil separately at each slide. Add something to the Master, and it shows up automatically on every slide. Remove it from the Master, and — poof! — it disappears from every slide. Very convenient.

Masters govern all aspects of a slide's appearance: background color, objects that appear on every slide, text that appears on all slides, and more.

Working with Masters

In PowerPoint, a Master governs the appearance of all the slides or pages in a presentation. Each presentation has at least three Masters:

✔ **Slide Master:** Dictates the format of your slides

You work with this Master most often when you tweak your slides to cosmetic perfection.

✔ **Handout Master:** Controls the look of printed handouts

✔ **Notes Master:** Determines the characteristics of printed speaker notes

Each Master specifies the appearance of text (font, size, and color, for example), slide background color, animation effects, and any additional text or other objects that you want to appear on each slide or page.

In addition, each Master can contain one or more *layouts* that provide different arrangements of text and other elements on the slide. For example, a typical Slide Master might contain a Title layout and several Text layouts for various types of body text slides.

One interesting — and often useful — aspect of Slide Masters is that any elements you add to the Master itself are also included in each layout that's associated with the Master. For example, if you set the background color for the Slide Master, that color is used for each layout. Likewise, if you add a big blue rectangle in the top-left corner of the Slide Master, that rectangle is visible in the top-left corner of each layout.

However, you can also add elements to an individual layout. Then, the element is present only for that layout. For example, you may want to add more graphical elements to the Title layout. Then, those elements appear only on slides that use the Title layout.

Here are a few other points to ponder while you lie awake at night thinking about Slide Masters:

✔ Masters aren't optional. Every presentation has them. You can, however, override the formatting of objects contained in the Master for a particular slide. This capability enables you to vary the appearance of slides when necessary.

✔ PowerPoint allows you to create more than one Slide Master in a single presentation, so you can mix two or more slide designs in your presentations. That's why I say a presentation has *at least* three Masters. If you have more than one Slide Master, a presentation will have more than three Masters altogether. Note, however, that you can still have only one Handout or Notes Master in each presentation. For more information about using more than one Slide Master, see the section, "Yes, You Can Serve Two Masters," at the end of this chapter.

✔ If you've used previous versions of PowerPoint, you might be wondering what happened to the Title Master. In the old days, there was actually a separate Master for title slides. However, in PowerPoint 2013, title slides don't have their own Masters. Instead, the format of title slides is controlled by a Title Slide layout that belongs to a particular Slide Master.

Modifying the Slide Master

If you don't like the layout of your slides, call up the Slide Master and do something about it, as shown in these steps:

1. **Open Slide Master View by opening the View tab on the Ribbon and then clicking the Slide Master button, found in the Presentation Views group.**

   Alternatively, you can hold down the Shift key and then click the Normal View button near the bottom right of the screen.

2. **Behold the Slide Master in all its splendor.**

   Figure 10-1 shows a typical Slide Master. You can see the placeholders for the slide title and body text. Although none are visible in this example, the Master can also contain background colors and other elements that are present on each slide.

   The Slide Master includes placeholders for three objects that appear at the bottom of each slide: the Date area, Footer area, and Number area. These special areas are described later in this chapter under the heading, "Using Headers and Footers."

   A thumbnail of each Slide Master as well as the layouts for each Master are shown on the left side of the screen.

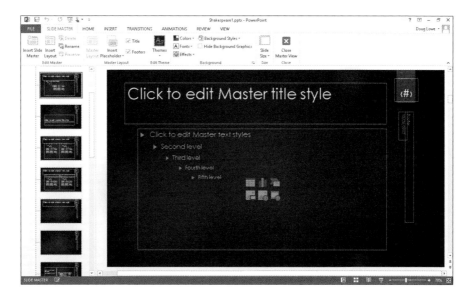

Figure 10-1: Slide Master View.

3. **Make any formatting changes that you want.**

   Select the text you want to apply a new style to and make your formatting changes. If you want all the slide titles to be in italics, for example, select the title text and then press Ctrl+I or click the Italic button on the Formatting toolbar.

   Make sure the Slide Master itself is selected — not one of its layouts. That way, any changes you make apply to all the layouts associated with the Slide Master.

4. **(Optional) To add elements that are specific to one of the layouts, select the layout and then add your changes.**

   For example, you may want to add more graphical elements or select different fonts for your title slides. To do that, select the Title Slide layout and make your changes.

5. **Click the Normal View button near the bottom right of the window to return to Normal View.**

   You're done!

Notice that the body object contains paragraphs for five outline levels formatted with different point sizes, indentations, and bullet styles. If you want to change the way an outline level is formatted, this is the place to do so.

You can type all you want in the title or object area placeholders, but the text that you type doesn't appear on the slides. The text that appears in these placeholders is provided only so that you can see the effect of the formatting changes you apply. (To insert text that appears on each slide, see the upcoming section, "Adding recurring text or other elements.")

You can edit any other object on the Master by clicking it. Unlike the title and object area placeholders, any text that you type in other Slide Master objects appears exactly as you type it on each slide.

Working with the Slide Master and Edit Master tabs

When you switch to Slide Master View, an entirely new tab appears on the Ribbon. This new tab — appropriately called Slide Master — is shown in Figure 10-2.

Figure 10-2: The Slide Master tab.

Throughout this chapter, I show you how to use many of the controls on this tab. For now, here's a quick overview of each group on this tab and the controls found in them:

- **Edit Master:** The controls in this group let you edit the Slide Master. You can use the Insert Slide Master button to create a new Slide Master, or you can use the Insert Layout button to add a new layout to an existing Master. You can also use the Delete and Rename buttons to delete or rename Masters or layouts. For information about the Preserve button, see the section "Preserving your masters," later in this chapter.

- **Master Layout:** The controls in this group let you edit a layout by adding or removing placeholders, the title, and footer elements.

- **Edit Theme:** The controls in this group let you apply a theme to a Master or a layout. For more information about themes, flip to Chapter 8.

- **Background:** The controls in this group let you set the background for a Master or a layout. Refer to Chapter 8 for more information.

- **Page Setup:** The control in this group lets you change the orientation for a page. (Unfortunately, PowerPoint doesn't allow you to have Masters with different orientations in a single presentation. When you change the orientation of a Slide Master or a layout, the orientation of all Masters and layouts in the presentation is changed.)

- **Size:** The control in this group lets you select Standard, Widescreen, or a custom slide size.

- **Close:** This group contains a Close Master View button that returns you to Normal View.

Adding recurring text or other elements

To add recurring text to each slide, follow this procedure:

1. **Call up the Slide Master (by clicking Slide Master in the Presentation Views group of the Views tab) if it's not displayed already.**

2. **Add a text box to the Slide Master by selecting the Insert tab on the Ribbon and then clicking the Text Box button (found in the Text group).**

   Click where you want to add the text.

3. **Type the text that you want to appear on each slide.**

   For example, **Call 1-800-555-NERD today! Don't delay! Operators are standing by!**

4. **Format the text however you want.**

   For example, if you want bold, press Ctrl+B or click the Bold button on the Formatting toolbar. (See Chapter 7 for more on text formatting.)

5. Click the Normal View button to return to your presentation.

Now's the time to gloat over your work. Lasso some co-workers and show 'em how proud you are that you added some text that appears on each slide in your presentation.

You can add other types of objects to the Slide Master, too. You can add clip art, pictures, or even a video or sound clip. Anything that you can add to an individual slide can be added to the Slide Master.

After you place an object on the Slide Master, you can grab it with the mouse and move it or resize it in any way you want. The object appears in the same location and size on each slide.

To delete an object from the Slide Master, click it and press Delete. To delete a text object, you must first click the object and then click again on the object frame. Then press Delete.

Applying themes to your Masters

You can use the Edit Theme group in the Slide Master tab on the Ribbon to change the theme applied to a Slide Master. ***Note:*** All the layouts that belong to a given Master use the same theme. So, it doesn't matter whether the Slide Master itself or one of its layouts is selected when you change the theme; either way, the entire Slide Master is changed.

To change the theme for a Slide Master, follow these steps:

1. Choose View➪Presentation Views➪Slide Master or Shift+click the Normal View button at the bottom right of the PowerPoint window to summon the Slide Master.

2. Use the Themes drop-down list on the Slide Master tab to select the theme you want to apply to the Slide Master.

3. (Optional) Use the Colors, Fonts, and Effects controls to modify the color scheme, fonts, and effects used for the theme.

Treat yourself to a bag of Cheetos if it works the first time. If it doesn't work, have a bag of Cheetos anyway. Then rub all that orange gunk that sticks to your fingers on the computer screen. That will apply the Cheetos Orange color scheme to your Slide Master — at least temporarily.

PowerPoint themes are hefty enough that I've devoted an entire chapter to them. Go to Chapter 8 if you need to know how they work.

If you want to adjust the slide background, use the Background Styles control. Chapter 8 walks you through this feature.

Adding new layouts

If you don't like the standard layouts that come with PowerPoint's built-in Slide Master, you can add a layout and customize it any way you want. To add your own layout, just follow these steps:

1. **Switch to Slide Master View by choosing View⇨Presentation Views⇨Slide Master or Shift+click the Normal View button near the bottom right of the window.**

2. **On the Slide Master tab on the Ribbon, click Insert Layout in the Edit Master group.**

   A new, blank layout is inserted in the current Slide Master.

3. **Use the Insert Placeholder drop-down list in the Master Layout group on the Slide Master tab on the Ribbon to insert whatever placeholders you want to add to the new layout.**

   This control reveals a list of placeholder types you can insert. The options are Content, Text, Picture, Chart, Table, Diagram, Media, and Clip Art.

4. **Play with the layout until you get it just right.**

   You can move and resize the placeholders to your heart's content, and you can apply any formatting or other options you want for the layout.

5. **When you're happy, click the Close Master View button to switch back to Normal View.**

Adjusting the Handout and Notes Masters

Like the Slide Master, the Handout and Notes Masters contain formatting information that's applied automatically to your presentation. This section tells you how you can modify these Masters.

Changing the Handout Master

Follow these simple steps to change the Handout Master:

1. **Choose View⇨Presentation Views⇨Handout Master or hold down the Shift key while clicking the Slide Sorter View button.**

   The Handout Master rears its ugly head, as shown in Figure 10-3. Notice that it includes a special Handout Master tab on the Ribbon.

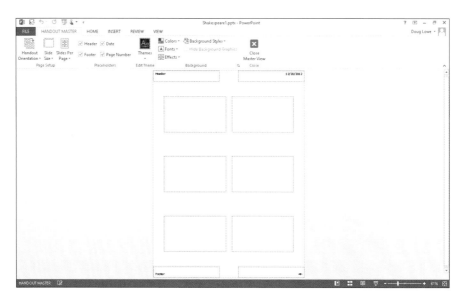

Figure 10-3: The Handout Master.

2. **Mess around with it.**

   The Handout Master shows the arrangement of handouts for slides printed two, three, four, six, or nine per page, plus the arrangement for printing outlines. You can switch among these different handout layouts by using the Slides-Per-Page control in the Page Setup group on the Handout Master tab.

   Unfortunately, you can't move, resize, or delete the slide and outline placeholders that appear in the Handout Master. You *can,* however, add or change elements that you want to appear on each handout page, such as your name and phone number, a page number, and maybe a good lawyer joke.

3. **Click the Close Master View button on the Handout Master tab on the Ribbon.**

   PowerPoint returns to Normal View.

4. **Print a handout to see whether your changes worked.**

   Handout Master elements are invisible until you print them, so you should print at least one handout page to check your work.

When you print handout pages, the slides are formatted according to the Slide Master. You can't change the appearance of the slides from the Handout Master.

Changing the Notes Master

Notes pages consist of a reduced image of the slide, plus any notes that you type to go along with the slide. For more information about creating and using Notes Pages, see Chapter 5.

When printed, notes pages are formatted according to the Notes Master. To change the Notes Master, follow these steps:

1. **Choose View⇨Presentation Views⇨Notes Master.**

   The Notes Master comes to life, as shown in Figure 10-4.

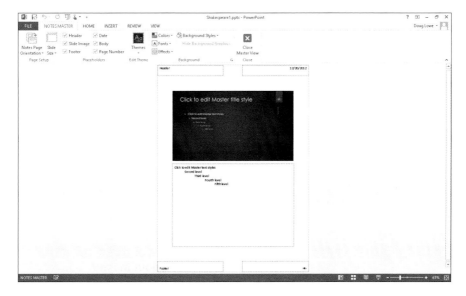

Figure 10-4: The Notes Master.

2. **Indulge yourself.**

   The Notes Master contains two main placeholders — one for your notes and the other for the slide. You can move or change the size of either of these objects, and you can change the format of the text in the notes placeholder. You also can add or change elements that you want to appear on each handout page. Also notice the convenient placement of the header, footer, date, and page number blocks.

3. **Click the Close Master View button.**

   PowerPoint returns to Normal View.

4. **Print your notes to see whether your changes worked.**

At the very least, add page numbers to your speaker notes. That way, if you drop a stack of notes pages, you can use the page numbers to quickly sort them back into order.

If public speaking gives you severe stomach cramps, add the text "Just picture them naked" to the Notes Master. It works every time for me.

Using Masters

You don't have to do anything special to apply the formats from a Master to your slide; all slides automatically pick up the Master format unless you specify otherwise. So this section really should be titled "Not Using Masters" because it talks about how to *not* use the formats provided by Masters.

Overriding the Master text style

To override the text style specified by a Slide Master, simply format the text however you want while you're working in Normal View. The formatting changes you make apply only to the selected text. The Slide Masters aren't affected.

The only way to change one of the Masters is to do it directly by switching to the appropriate Master View. Therefore, any formatting changes you make while in Slide View affect only that slide.

If you change the layout or formatting of text elements on a slide (for example, if you move the title placeholder or change the title font) and then decide that you liked it better the way it was, you can quickly reapply the text style from the Slide Master. Right-click the slide in the Slide Preview pane (on the left side of the screen) and then choose Reset Slide from the menu that appears.

Hiding background objects

Slide Masters enable you to add background objects that appear on every slide in your presentation. You can, however, hide the background objects for selected slides. You can also change the background color or effect used for an individual slide. These steps show you how:

1. **Display the slide that you want to show with a plain background.**

2. **Click the Design tab on the Ribbon and then select the Hide Background Graphics check box found in the Background group.**

Hiding background objects or changing the background color or effect applies only to the current slide. Other slides are unaffected.

If you want to remove some but not all the background objects from a single slide, try this trick:

1. **Hide the background graphics from the slide.**

   To hide a background object, choose Design⇨Background⇨Hide Background Objects.

2. **Call up the Slide Master by choosing View⇨Presentation Views⇨Slide Master.**

3. **Hold down the Shift key and then click each of the background objects that you want to appear.**

4. **Press Ctrl+C to copy these objects to the Clipboard.**

5. **Return to Normal View by clicking the Normal button at the bottom of the screen.**

6. **Press Ctrl+V to paste the objects from the Clipboard.**

7. **Click the Design tab on the Ribbon and then click the Send to Back button (in the Arrange group) if the background objects obscure other slide objects or text.**

Note that if you paste objects in this way, those objects are no longer tied to the Slide Master. Thus, if you later change the objects on the Slide Master, the change won't be reflected on the slides with the pasted copies of the objects.

Using Headers and Footers

Headers and footers provide a convenient way to place repeating text at the top or bottom of each slide, handout, or notes page. You can add the time and date, slide number or page number, or any other information that you want to appear on each slide or page, such as your name or the title of your presentation.

The PowerPoint Slide Masters include three placeholders for such information:

- The **Date area** can be used to display a date and time.
- The **Number area** can be used to display the slide number.
- The **Footer area** can be used to display any text that you want to see on each slide.

In addition, Handout and Notes Masters include a fourth placeholder, the *Header area,* which provides an additional area for text that you want to see on each page.

Although the Date, Number, and Footer areas normally appear at the bottom of the slide in the Slide Masters, you can move them to the top by switching to Slide View or Slide Master View and then dragging the placeholders to the top of the slide.

Adding a date, number, or footer to slides

To add a date, slide number, or footer to your slides, follow these steps:

1. **Click the Insert tab on the Ribbon and then click the Header and Footer button (found in the Text group).**

   The Header and Footer dialog box appears, as shown in Figure 10-5. (If necessary, click the Slide tab so that you see the slide footer options as shown in the figure.)

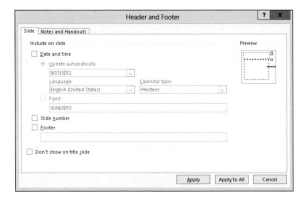

Figure 10-5: The Header and Footer dialog box.

2. **To display the date, select the Date and Time check box. Then select the date format that you want in the list box beneath the Update Automatically radio button.**

   Alternatively, you can select the Fixed radio button and then type any text that you want in the Fixed text box. The text that you type appears in the Date area of the Slide Master.

3. **To display slide numbers, select the Slide Number check box.**

4. **To display a footer on each slide, select the Footer check box and then type the text that you want to appear on each slide in the Footer text box.**

   For example, you may type your name, your company name, a subliminal message, or the name of your presentation.

5. **If you want the date, number, and footer to appear on every slide except for the title slide, select the Don't Show on Title Slide check box.**

6. **Click Apply to All.**

If you're going to give a presentation on a certain date in the future (for example, at a sales conference or a trade show), type the date that you'll be giving the presentation directly into the Fixed text box. You can use the same technique to postdate presentations that you never really gave but need to supply to your legal counsel to back up your alibi. (You can also type any other type of text you want to appear here.)

If you want to change the Footer areas for just one slide, click Apply instead of Apply to All. This option comes in handy for those occasional slides that contain a graphic or a block of text that crowds up against the footer areas. You can easily suppress the footer information for that slide to make room for the large graphic or text.

Adding a header or footer to notes or handouts pages

To add header and footer information to notes or handouts pages, follow the steps described in the preceding section, "Adding a date, number, or footer to slides," except click the Notes and Handouts tab after the Header and Footer dialog box appears. Clicking this tab displays a dialog box that's similar to the Header and Footer dialog box for Slide, except that it gives you an additional option to add a header that appears at the top of each page. After you indicate how you want to print the Date, Header, Number, and Footer areas, click the Apply to All button.

Editing the header and footer placeholders directly

If you want, you can edit the text that appears in the header and footer placeholders directly. First, display the appropriate Master — Slide, Handout, or Notes. Then click the date, number, footer, or header placeholder and start typing.

You may notice that the placeholders include special codes for the options that you indicated in the Header and Footer dialog box. For example, the date placeholder may contain the text *<date,time>* if you indicated that the date should be displayed. You can type text before or after these codes, but you should leave the codes themselves alone.

Yes, You Can Serve Two Masters

In spite of the Biblical edict, Microsoft has endowed PowerPoint with the capability to have more than one Slide Master. This feature lets you set up two or more Slide Masters and then choose which Master you want to use for each slide in your presentation.

The following sections explain how to use the multiple Masters feature.

Creating a new Slide Master

To add a new Master to a presentation, follow these steps:

1. **Switch to Slide Master View.**

   From the View tab on the Ribbon, click the Slide Master button (found in the Presentation Views group). Or if you prefer, hold down the Shift key and click the Normal View button near the lower-right corner of the screen.

2. **In the Slide Master tab on the Ribbon, click the Insert Slide Master button in the Edit Master group.**

   A new Slide Master appears, as shown in Figure 10-6. Notice that a thumbnail for the new Slide Master is added to the list of thumbnails on the left side of the screen, and that the new Slide Master uses PowerPoint's default settings (white background, black text, and so forth).

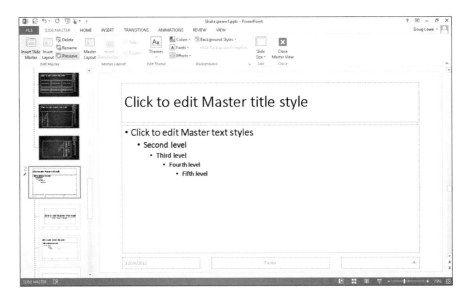

Figure 10-6: Creating a new Slide Master.

3. **Modify the new Slide Master to your liking.**

   You can make any formatting changes you want: Change the background color and text styles, add background objects, and so on.

4. **Click the Close Master View button on the Slide Master tab on the Ribbon to return to Normal View.**

   You can now begin using the new Master that you created. (See the section, "Applying Masters," later in this chapter, for more information.)

 Another way to create a new Slide Master is to duplicate one of your presentation's existing Slide Masters. When you do that, the new Slide Master inherits the formatting of the original one. This inheritance can save you a lot of work, especially if you want to create a new Slide Master that varies from an existing one in only a minor way, such as having a different background color.

To duplicate a Slide Master, click the Master that you want to duplicate in the thumbnails on the left of the screen and then press Ctrl+D.

To delete a Slide Master, click the Master that you want to delete. Then click the Delete Master button in the Slide Master tab on the Ribbon (located in the Edit Master group). Or, just press Delete.

Applying Masters

If you have created multiple Masters for a presentation, you can select which Master to use for each slide in your presentation. To apply a Master to one or more slides, follow these steps:

1. **Select the slide or slides to which you want to apply the alternate Slide Master.**

   The easiest way to do this is to click the slide that you want in the thumbnails area on the left of the screen. To select more than one slide, hold down the Ctrl key and click each slide that you want to select.

2. **Click the Home tab on the Ribbon and then click the Layout button (in the Slides group).**

   This action summons the gallery, shown in Figure 10-7. Here, you can see all the layouts for all the Slide Masters contained in the presentation.

3. **Select the Slide Master layout you want to apply to the slides you selected.**

   The Slide Master is applied to the selected slides.

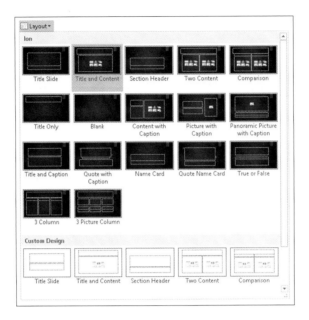

Figure 10-7: Choosing a layout.

Preserving your masters

PowerPoint has a bad habit of deleting Slide Masters when they're no longer used in your presentation. For example, if you create a new Slide Master and then apply it to all the slides in your presentation, PowerPoint assumes that you no longer need the original Slide Master. So, the original is deleted. Poof! Your presentation is now one pickle short of a full jar.

You can prevent this from happening with the Preserve Master option for your Slide Masters. Any new Slide Masters that you create automatically get the Preserve Master option, so they won't be deleted. However, the Slide Masters that your presentations start off with don't have the Preserve Master option, so you may want to set it yourself.

To preserve a Master, switch to Slide Master View, click the thumbnail for the Master that you want to preserve, and then click the Preserve button on the Slide Master tab on the Ribbon (found in the Edit Master group). A little pushpin icon appears next to the Master's thumbnail to show that the Master will be preserved.

Don't click the Preserve button indiscriminately! If you click it for a Master that already has the Preserve Master setting, Preserve Master is removed for that Master. Then the Master is subject to premature deletion.

Restoring Lost Placeholders

If you've played around with your Masters too much, you may inadvertently delete a layout placeholder that you wish you could get back. For example, suppose that you delete the footer placeholder from a Master and now you want it back. No problem! Just follow these steps:

1. **Switch to Slide Master View.**

2. **Call up the Master with the missing placeholder.**

3. **In the Slide Master tab on the Ribbon, click the Master Layout button (in the Master Layout group).**

   This step calls up the Master Layout dialog box, as shown in Figure 10-8.

Figure 10-8: The Master Layout dialog box.

The Master Layout dialog box is one of the strangest dialog boxes you encounter. If you summon it for a Master that still has all its placeholders, all the check boxes on the Master Layout dialog box are grayed out. So, all you can do is look at the controls, grunt, scratch your head, and then click OK to dismiss the seemingly useless dialog box. However, if you *have* deleted one or more placeholders, the check boxes for the missing placeholders are available.

4. **Select the check boxes for the placeholders that you want to restore.**

5. **Click OK.**

   The missing placeholders reappear.

Note that the preceding procedure works only for actual masters, not for individual layouts. If you delete a placeholder from a layout, you must re-create it by using the Insert Placeholder command as described in the section "Adding new layouts," earlier in this chapter.

Working with Templates

If you had to create every presentation from scratch, starting with a blank slide, you would probably put PowerPoint back in its box and use it as a bookend. Creating a presentation is easy, but creating one that looks good is a different story. Making a good-looking presentation is tough even for the artistically inclined. For left-brained, nonartistic types, it's next to impossible.

Thank heavens for themes and templates. A *theme* is simply a PowerPoint presentation with predefined Slide Masters. A *template* is similar to a theme, but also includes boilerplate text. Because they are so similar, I refer to both themes and templates simply as *templates* throughout the rest of this section.

Templates jump-start the process of creating good-looking presentations. You can create your own templates, but fortunately PowerPoint comes with a ton of them designed by professional artists who understand color combinations, balance, and all that other artsy stuff. Have a croissant and celebrate.

Templates use the special file extension `.potx`, but you can also use ordinary PowerPoint presentation files (PPT) as themes or templates. You can, therefore, use any of your own presentations as a template. If you make extensive changes to a presentation's Masters, you can use that presentation as a template for other presentations that you create. Or, you can save the presentation as a template by using the `.potx` file extension.

Because a template is a presentation, you can open it and change it if you want.

Creating a new template

If none of the templates that come with PowerPoint appeals to you, you can easily create your own. All you have to do is create a presentation with the Masters, and the color scheme set up just the way you want, and then save it as a template. Here are a few points to remember about templates:

- ✓ If you want to make minor modifications to one of the supplied templates, open the template by using the Open command. Then, make your changes and use the Save As command to save the template under a new name.

- ✓ You can also create your own presentation templates. Just create the template as a normal presentation and add however many slides that you want to include.

- ✓ Choose a location to store all your templates. You need to know the path to this location to create new presentations based on your templates.

Creating a presentation based on a template

To create a new presentation based on a template you have created yourself, you must first configure PowerPoint to look for personal templates. To do so, choose File⇨Options, click Save, enter the path to your templates folder in the Default Personal Templates Location box, and click OK.

Once you have configured the template location, you can create a new presentation based on one of your templates by choosing File⇨New, then clicking on Personal to display a list of your personal templates. See Figure 10-9.

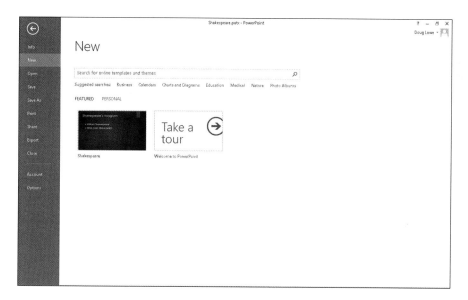

Figure 10-9: Creating a new presentation.

Working with Presentation Sections

Sections let you divide a presentation into two or more groups of slides called *sections.* Sections are designed to be used with large presentations that contain a large number of slides that can easily be grouped into logical groupings.

Using sections couldn't be easier. To create a new section in your presentation, just select the first slide that you want in the new section, switch to the Home tab, click the Section button (found in the Slides group), and then choose Add Section. The new section appears in the Slide thumbnail area with the name *Untitled Section,* as shown in Figure 10-10.

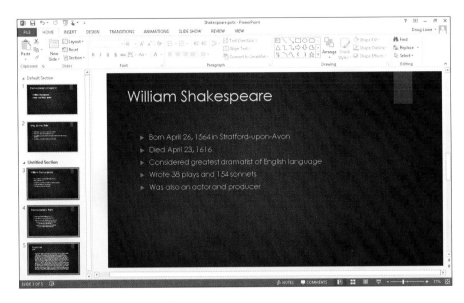

Figure 10-10: Creating a new section.

After you've created one or more sections in your presentation, you can do several interesting things with the sections:

✔ You can select all the slides in a section by clicking the section header in the Slide Thumbnail pane.

✔ You can collapse or expand the sections in the Slide Thumbnail pane by clicking the arrow at the left of the section header.

✔ You can rename a section by right-clicking the section header and choosing Rename Section.

✔ You can move all the slides in a section by dragging the section header to a new location in the Slide Thumbnail pane.

✔ You can delete the slides in a section, as well as the section itself, by clicking the section header to select the section and then pressing the Delete key.

✔ You can remove a section without deleting its slides by right-clicking the section header and choosing Remove Section.

✔ During a slide show, you can go to the first slide in any section by clicking the Menu icon in the bottom-left corner of the slide, then choosing Go To Section and selecting the section you want to go to.

Part III
Embellishing Your Slides

Find out how to hyperlink your slide to summon another slide, another presentation, or some other type of document (such as a Word document or an Excel spreadsheet) at www.dummies.com/extras/powerpoint2013.

In this part . . .

- ✔ Get familiar with about the different types of computer pictures, how you can insert them into a PowerPoint slide, and how you can fiddle with them to get them to look better.

- ✔ Find out about the powerful drawing tools of PowerPoint 2013.

- ✔ Understand how to add a chart to your presentation and get it to look the way you want.

- ✔ Learn to add all sorts of embellishments to your slides, including one of the coolest ways to embellish your slides — adding special diagrams called *SmartArt*.

- ✔ Discover how to include and edit video and sound elements in your slide show, thus giving you the power to craft some impressive high-tech presentations.

- ✔ Know how to insert tables, WordArt, hyperlinks, and actions into your presentations.

- ✔ Find out how to hyperlink your slide to summon another slide, another presentation, or some other type of document (such as a Word document or an Excel spreadsheet) at www.dummies.com/extras/powerpoint2013.

Inserting Pictures

*F*ace it: Most of us weren't born with even an ounce of artistic ability. Some day (soon, hopefully), the genetic researchers combing through the billions and billions of genes strung out on those twisty DNA helixes will discover the Artist Gene. Then, in spite of protests from the da Vincis, van Goghs, and Monets among us (who fear that their NEA grants will be threatened), doctors will splice the little gene into our DNA strands so that we can all be artists. Of course, this procedure won't be without its side effects: Some will develop an insatiable craving for croissants, and others will inexplicably develop French accents and whack off their ears. But artists we shall be.

Until then, we have to rely on clip art pictures, pictures we've found on the Internet, or pictures that we scanned into the computer with a scanner or took with a digital camera.

In this chapter, you find out about the different types of computer pictures and how you can insert them into a PowerPoint slide. Then, after you get your pictures into PowerPoint, you discover how you can fiddle with them to get them to look better.

Exploring the Many Types of Pictures

The world is awash with many different picture file formats. Fortunately, PowerPoint works with almost all these formats. The following sections describe the two basic types of pictures that you can work with in PowerPoint: bitmap pictures and vector drawings.

Bitmap pictures

A *bitmap picture* is a collection of small dots that compose an image. Bitmap pictures are most often used for photographs and for icons and other buttons used on web pages. You can create your own bitmap pictures with a scanner, a digital camera, or a picture-drawing program, such as Adobe Photoshop. You can even create crude bitmap pictures with Microsoft Paint, which is the free painting program that comes with Windows.

The dots that make up a bitmap picture are called *pixels*. The number of pixels in a given picture depends on two factors: the picture's resolution and its size. *Resolution* refers to the number of pixels per inch. A typical computer monitor displays 72 pixels per inch, though many monitors can display at higher resolutions. At 72 pixels per inch, a 1-inch square picture requires 5,184 pixels (72 x 72). Photographs that will be printed on an inkjet or laser printer usually have a much higher resolution, often 300 pixels per inch or more. At 300 pixels per inch, a 4-x-6-inch photograph requires more than two million pixels.

The amount of color information stored for the picture — also referred to as the picture's *color depth* — affects how many bytes of computer memory the picture requires. The color depth determines how many different colors the picture can contain. Most pictures have one of two color depths: 256 colors or 16.7 million colors. Most simple charts, diagrams, cartoons, and other types of clip art look fine at 256 colors. Photographs usually use 16.7 million colors.

Pictures with 16.7 million colors are also known as *True Color* pictures or *24-bit color* pictures.

A 4-x-6-inch photograph, which has more than 2 million pixels, requires about 2MB to store with 256 colors. With True Color, the size of the picture jumps to a whopping 6.4MB. Fortunately, bitmap pictures can be compressed to reduce their size without noticeably distorting the image. Depending on the actual contents of the picture, a 6MB picture might be reduced to 250KB or less.

Bitmap picture files usually have filename extensions such as `.bmp`, `.gif`, `.jpg`, `.png`, or `.pcx`. Table 11-1 lists the bitmap file formats that PowerPoint supports.

If you have a choice in the matter, I recommend you use JPEG format images for photographs that you want to include in PowerPoint presentations because JPEG's built-in compression saves hard drive space.

Table 11-1	PowerPoint's Bitmap Picture File Formats
Format	*What It Is*
BMP	Garden variety Windows bitmap file, used by Windows Paint and many other programs
GIF	Graphics Interchange Format, a format commonly used for small Internet pictures
JPEG	A common format for photographs that includes built-in compression
PCD	Kodak Photo CD format
PCT	Macintosh PICT files
PCX	A variant type of bitmap file
PNG	Portable Network Graphics file, an image format designed for Internet graphics
TGA	Targa files
TIFF	Tagged Image Format file, another bitmap program most often used for high-quality photographs

Victor, give me a vector

Besides bitmap pictures, you can also use vector drawing with PowerPoint. A *vector drawing* is a picture file that contains a detailed definition of each shape that makes up the image. Vector drawings are usually created with high-powered drawing programs, such as Adobe Illustrator.

PowerPoint supports all the most popular vector drawing formats, as described in Table 11-2.

Table 11-2	PowerPoint's Vector File Formats
Format	*What It Is*
CDR	Format for CorelDRAW!, a popular, upper-crust drawing program
CGM	Computer Graphics Metafiles
DRW	Format for Micrografx Designer or Micrografx Draw, two popular ooh-aah drawing programs
EMF	An Enhanced Windows MetaFile picture
EPS	Encapsulated PostScript, a format used by some high-end drawing programs
WMF	Windows MetaFile, a format that many programs recognize (note that WMF files can hold bitmap as well as vector data)
WPG	A WordPerfect drawing

Using Pictures

Are you sitting down? Whether you buy PowerPoint by itself or get it as a part of Microsoft Office, you also get access to an online collection of thousands of clip art pictures that you can drop directly into your presentations.

Don't overdo the pictures. One surefire way to guarantee an amateurish look to your presentation is to load it down with three cheesy clip art pictures on every slide. Judicious use is much more effective.

Dropping in a picture

The following steps explain how to insert picture art into your presentation:

1. **Move to the slide on which you want to plaster the picture.**

   If you want the same picture to appear on every slide, move to Slide Master View.

2. **On the Ribbon, choose Insert⇨Online Pictures.**

   After a brief moment's hesitation, the Insert Pictures dialog box appears, as shown in Figure 11-1.

Figure 11-1: The Insert Pictures dialog box.

3. **Type a keyword in the Search Office.com text box and then press Enter.**

   For example, to search for pictures of William Shakespeare, type **Shakespeare** in the Search For text box and then press Enter.

   PowerPoint searches through the Office.com picture collection to locate the picture you're looking for, and then it displays thumbnails of the pictures it finds, as shown in Figure 11-2.

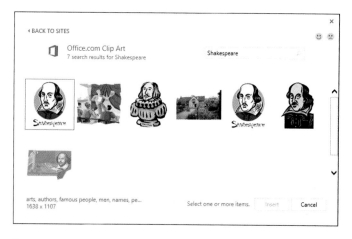

Figure 11-2: Office.com has several pictures of William Shakespeare.

4. Click the picture that you want to use, then click Insert.

The picture is inserted on the current slide, as shown in Figure 11-3. Notice that a special Picture Tools tab with tools for working with pictures has appeared. This Picture Tools tab appears whenever you select a picture object.

5. Drag and resize the picture as needed.

To find out how, see the following section.

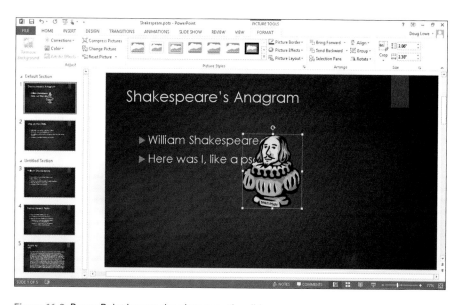

Figure 11-3: PowerPoint inserts the picture on the slide.

Office.com contains only a limited selection of clip art images, and many of those are a bit too cartoonish for my tastes. You may have better results if you search for Bing images rather than Office.com images. To search Bing, just type your keyword in the Search Bing text box instead of the Search Office.com text box. Figure 11-4 gives a sampling of the results generated when I searched for "Shakespeare" on Bing.

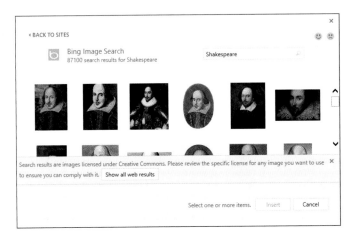

Figure 11-4: Bing often has better images than Office.com.

Note that some of the images displayed by Bing's image search may be copyrighted, so you must ensure that you have permission from the copyright holder before using images found on Bing.

Moving, sizing, and stretching pictures

Because PowerPoint chooses an arbitrary position on the slide to insert pictures, you undoubtedly want to move the clip art to a more convenient location. You probably also want to change the size of the picture if it's too big or too small for your slide.

Follow these steps to force your inserted clip art into full compliance:

1. **Click the picture and drag it wherever you want.**

   You don't have to worry about clicking exactly the edge of the picture or one of its lines; just click anywhere in the picture and drag it around.

2. **Notice the eight handles. Drag one of them to resize the picture.**

   You can click and drag any of these handles to adjust the size of the picture. When you click one of the corner handles, you can change the height and width of the picture at the same time. When you drag one of the edge handles (top, bottom, left, or right) to change the size of the picture in just one dimension, you distort the picture's outlook as you go.

When you resize a picture, the picture changes its position on the slide. As a result, you can count on moving it after you resize it. If you hold down the Ctrl key while dragging a handle, however, the picture becomes anchored at its center point as you resize it. Therefore, its position is unchanged, and you probably don't have to move it.

Stretching a clip art picture by dragging one of the edge handles can dramatically change the picture's appearance. For example, you can stretch an object vertically to make it look tall and thin or horizontally to make it look short and fat.

Inserting Pictures from a File

If you happen to already have an image file on your computer that you want to insert into a presentation, PowerPoint lets you insert the file. These steps show you how:

1. **Move to the slide on which you want to splash a picture.**

2. **Open the Insert tab on the Ribbon and then click the Pictures button in the Illustrations group.**

   This step summons the Insert Picture dialog box, shown in Figure 11-5.

Figure 11-5: The Insert Picture dialog box.

3. **Dig through the bottom of your hard drive until you find the file that you want.**

   The picture you want might be anywhere. Fortunately, the Insert Picture dialog box has all the controls you need to search high and low until you find the file. Just click the icons at the left side of the box and you're halfway there.

4. **Click the file and then click Insert.**

   You're done! Figure 11-6 shows how a picture appears when it has been inserted on a slide.

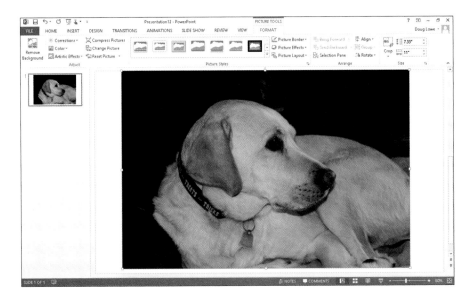

Figure 11-6: What a good boy!

As you can see in Figure 11-6, PowerPoint scales your pictures so that they fill as much of the slide as possible. You need to resize the picture if you want it to be smaller. Just select the picture and then drag one of the size handles in the corner of the picture.

You also can paste a picture directly into PowerPoint by way of the Clipboard. Anything that you can copy to the Clipboard can be pasted into PowerPoint. For example, you can doodle a sketch in Paintbrush, copy it, and then zap over to PowerPoint and paste it. *Voilà* — instant picture!

Cropping a Picture

Sometimes you want to cut off the edges of a picture so that you can include just part of the picture in your presentation. For example, you might have a picture of two people, only one of whom you like. You can use PowerPoint's cropping feature to cut off the other person. (Note that you can crop bitmap images, but not vector pictures.)

To crop a picture, select the picture and click the Crop button located near the right side of the Format tab on the Ribbon, in the group labeled Size. The selection handles change to special crop marks. You can then drag the crop marks around to cut off part of the picture. When you're satisfied, press the Esc key. Figure 11-7 shows the picture that was inserted in Figure 11-6 after it has been cropped and resized.

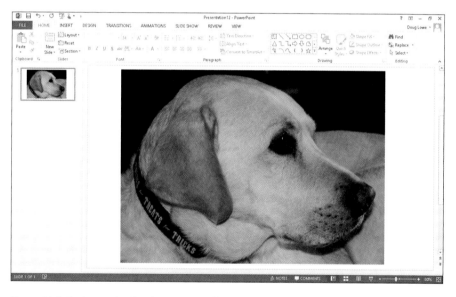

Figure 11-7: A picture that has been cropped.

If you decide later that you don't like the cropping, you can right-click the picture and choose Format Picture from the menu that appears. Then click the Reset button.

When you crop a picture, the picture still retains a basic rectangular shape. If you prefer to remove the background from an irregular shape in the picture, refer to the section "Removing Picture Backgrounds," later in this chapter.

Adding Style to Your Pictures

PowerPoint enables you to draw attention to your pictures by adding stylistic features such as borders, shadows, and reflections. Figure 11-8 shows a slide with several copies of a picture, each with a different style applied.

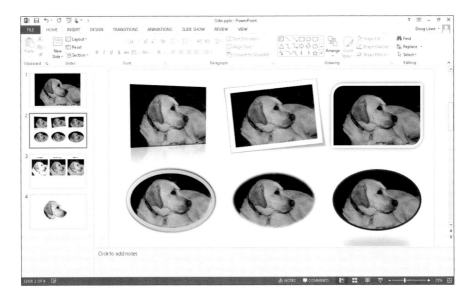

Figure 11-8: Pictures with style.

To add a style effect to a picture, select the picture and open the Picture Tools tab on the Ribbon. Then, simply select the picture style you want to apply.

PowerPoint comes with 28 predefined picture styles, shown in the gallery pictured in Figure 11-9. Each of these styles is simply a combination of three types of formatting you can apply to pictures: Shape, Border, and Effects. If you want, you can apply these formats individually as described in the following sections.

Note that if you use one of these predefined picture styles, the picture will be updated automatically if you later change the presentation's theme. As a result, you should use one of the predefined styles whenever possible.

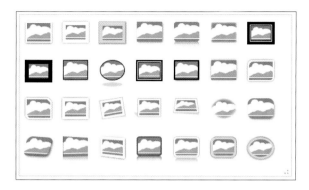

Figure 11-9: The Picture Style gallery.

Applying a picture border

You can apply a border to a picture by opening the Picture Tools➪Format tab and clicking Picture Border in the Picture Styles group. This reveals the Picture Border menu, which lets you choose the border color, weight (the width of the border lines), and the pattern of dashes you want to use.

Note that if you have applied a shape to the picture, the border is applied to the shape.

Applying picture effects

The Picture Effects button in the Picture Styles group (located on the Format tab) lets you apply several interesting types of effects to your pictures. When you click this button, a menu with the following effect options is displayed:

- **Shadow:** Applies a shadow to the picture. You can select one of several predefined shadow effects or call up a dialog box that lets you customize the shadow.

- **Reflection:** Creates a reflected image of the picture beneath the original picture.

- **Glow:** Adds a glowing effect around the edges of the picture.

- **Soft Edges:** Softens the edges of the picture.

- **Bevel:** Creates a 3-D beveled look.

- **3-D Rotation:** Rotates the picture in a way that creates a three-dimensional effect.

The best way to figure out how to use these effects is to experiment with them to see how they work.

Correcting Sharpness, Brightness, and Contrast

Sometimes, in spite of your best efforts, your pictures just don't come out quite right. They may be too bright or too dim, faded or too contrasty, or a bit out of focus.

PowerPoint's new Corrections command can help you out in those situations. This command, found on the Picture Tools Format tab, lets you adjust a picture's sharpness, brightness, and contrast.

To change a picture's sharpness, contrast, or brightness, click the Corrections button and choose one of the preset options from the gallery of choices that appears. Or, choose the Picture Correction Options command from the bottom of the Corrections menu to reveal the Picture Corrections controls in the task pane to the right of the slide, as shown in Figure 11-10. You can use these controls to individually adjust the sharpness, brightness, and contrast adjustments.

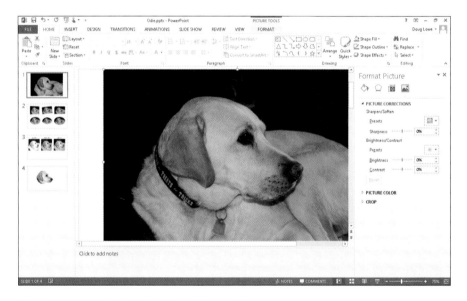

Figure 11-10: Setting the Picture Corrections options.

Adjusting Color

The Color button on the Picture Tools Format tab lets you adjust the color of your pictures. You can adjust the following aspects of a picture's color:

- ✒ **Saturation:** Controls the overall amount of color in the picture
- ✒ **Color Tone:** Controls the overall "warmth" of the picture's color
- ✒ **Recolor:** Lets you change the primary color visible in the picture

To change a picture's color, click the Color button on the Picture Tools Format tab and choose one of the options from the gallery of preset choices. Or, choose the Picture Color Options command at the bottom of the Color menu. Doing this brings up the color controls shown in Figure 11-11. As you can see, in this figure I've used the color controls to render the picture in black and white.

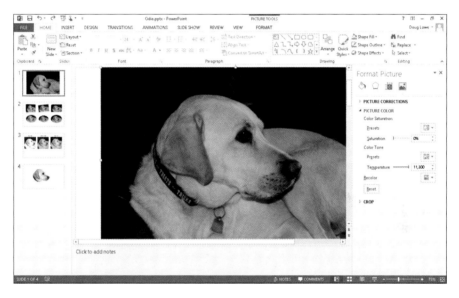

Figure 11-11: Setting the Color options for a picture.

Applying Artistic Effects

The Artistic Effects command applies one of several special filters to your picture in an effort to make the picture look like it was created by an artist rather than photographed with a $60 digital camera. Depending on the nature of the original picture, the results may or may not be convincing; the only way to find out is to try.

Here is a list of the artistic effects that are available on the Artistic Effects button:

- Marker
- Pencil Grayscale
- Pencil Sketch
- Line Drawing
- Chalk Sketch
- Paint Strokes
- Paint Brush
- Glow Diffused
- Blur
- Light Screen
- Watercolor Sponge

- Film Grain
- Mosaic Bubbles
- Glass
- Cement
- Texturizer
- Crisscross Etching
- Pastels Smooth
- Plastic Wrap
- Cutout
- Photocopy
- Glow Edges

To apply one of these effects, simply double-click the picture, click the Artistic Effects button on the Picture Tools Format tab, and choose the effect you want from the gallery.

To give you an idea of what these effects can accomplish, Figure 11-12 shows how the photograph originally shown in Figure 11-7 appears with the Pencil Sketch, Watercolor Sponge, and Plastic Wrap filters applied.

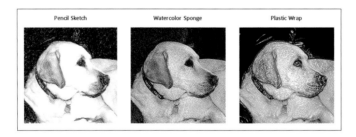

Figure 11-12: Artistic effects can dramatically change the appearance of a picture.

Compressing Your Pictures

Adding pictures to your slide show can dramatically increase the size of your presentation's file on disc. This is especially true if you insert a bunch of pictures taken with a modern digital camera. For example, pictures taken with digital cameras are often half a megabyte or more each. Insert 50 such pictures into your slide show and the file will grow accordingly.

However, it turns out that the amount of detail contained in your average digital photograph is mostly wasted in a PowerPoint slide show. That's because digital cameras are designed to create pictures that can be printed on high-resolution printers. However, most computer monitors (and projectors) have a much lower resolution.

To compensate for this, PowerPoint includes a Compress Pictures command that can eliminate the extraneous detail in your images and thereby reduce the size of your presentation files. To save even more space, the Compress Pictures command also removes any parts of your pictures that have been cropped.

You can use this command to compress just a single picture or to compress all the pictures in your presentation at once. I recommend that you compress all your pictures by following these steps:

1. **Double-click any picture in the presentation to bring up the Picture Tools Format tab.**

   The dialog box shown in Figure 11-13 appears.

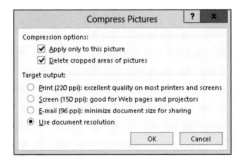

Figure 11-13: Compressing pictures.

2. **Deselect the Apply Only to This Picture option.**

   If you leave this option checked, only the selected picture will be compressed. Deselect this option to compress all the pictures in the presentation.

3. **Select Screen for the Target Output option.**

   This step sets the compression so that image quality will still be good when the pictures are displayed on a computer screen or projector.

4. **Click OK.**

The images are compressed. Note that if you have a lot of pictures in your presentation, this step may take a few moments.

5. **Save your presentation.**

The images won't actually be compressed in the presentation file until you save the file.

Removing Picture Backgrounds

One final bit of picture editing wizardry provided by PowerPoint 2013 is the capability to remove the background from a picture. For example, Figure 11-14 shows a picture of my dog Odie with the background removed.

Figure 11-14: Odie with the background removed.

To accomplish this bit of photo-editing magic, follow these steps:

1. **Double-click the picture whose background you want to remove.**

2. **Click the Remove Background button in the Picture Tools Format tab.**

When you do, PowerPoint attempts to determine which part of your picture is the subject of the picture and which part is the background. The background is then displayed in purple. In addition, a special Background Removal tab appears on the Ribbon. See Figure 11-15.

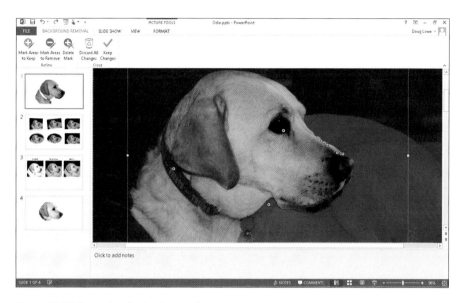

Figure 11-15: Removing the background.

3. **Use the Mark Areas to Keep and Mark Areas to Remove buttons to refine the location of the picture's background.**

   For example, if an area that's part of the subject is shown as background, click the Mark Areas to Keep button. Then, either click in the area you want included or click and drag a line across a large portion of the area to be included. PowerPoint will attempt to discern which part of the picture you marked and include that area in the picture's subject.

   Similarly, if PowerPoint has mistaken part of the background for the subject, click the Mark Areas to Remove button and click or draw a line within the area that should be removed.

   If PowerPoint misinterprets your mark, press Ctrl+Z to undo your action. Or, click the Delete Mark button and then click the mark you want to delete.

4. **Repeat Step 3 until you've successfully removed the picture's background.**

5. **Click the Keep Changes button.**

   The slide returns to normal, with the background of your picture removed.

12

Drawing on Your Slides

In This Chapter

▶ Using the PowerPoint drawing tools
▶ Using predefined shapes
▶ Drawing polygons or curved lines
▶ Changing colors and line types
▶ Creating 3-D objects
▶ Flipping and rotating objects
▶ Using advanced tricks

"Chim-chiminey, chim-chiminey, chim-chim cheroo, I draws what I likes and I likes what I drew. . . ."

Art time! Get your crayons and glue and don an old paint shirt. You're going to cut out some simple shapes and paste them on your PowerPoint slides so that people either think that you're a wonderful artist or scoff at you for not using clip art.

This chapter covers the drawing features of PowerPoint 2013. Once upon a time, PowerPoint had but rudimentary drawing tools — the equivalent of a box of crayons — but PowerPoint now has powerful drawing tools that are sufficient for all but the most sophisticated aspiring artists.

Some General Drawing Tips

Before getting into the specifics of using each PowerPoint drawing tool, the following sections describe a handful of general tips for drawing pictures.

Zooming in

When you work with the PowerPoint drawing tools, you might want to increase the zoom factor so that you can draw more accurately. I often work at 200, 300, or even 400 percent when I'm drawing. To change the zoom factor, use the zoom slider located in the bottom-right corner of the screen.

Before you change the zoom factor to edit an object, select the object that you want to edit. This way, PowerPoint zooms in on that area of the slide. If you don't select an object before you zoom in, you might need to scroll around to find the right location.

Displaying the ruler, gridlines, and guides

PowerPoint provides three onscreen features that can help you line up your drawings:

- ✔ **Ruler:** Horizontal and vertical rulers appear at the top of and to the left of the slide.

- ✔ **Gridlines:** A grid of evenly spaced dots appears directly on the slide.

- ✔ **Guides:** A pair of horizontal and vertical lines intersect on your slide like crosshairs in a target.

You can activate any or all of these features by clicking the View tab on the Ribbon and selecting the Ruler, Gridlines, or Guides check box. Figure 12-1 shows PowerPoint with the rulers, gridlines, and guides displayed.

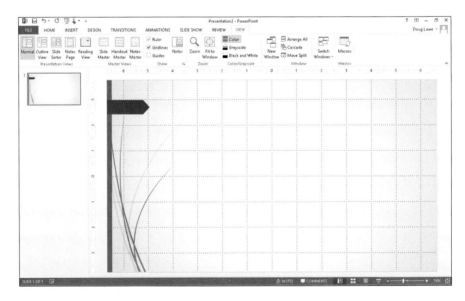

Figure 12-1: PowerPoint with the rulers, gridlines, and guides on.

When you work with drawing objects, the ruler is positioned so that zero is at the middle of the slide. When you edit a text object, the ruler changes to a text ruler that measures from the margins and indicates tab positions.

For more information about using the gridlines or guides, see the section "Using the grids and guides," later in this chapter.

Sticking to the color scheme

You can assign individual colors to each object that you draw, but the purpose of the PowerPoint color schemes (described in Chapter 8) is to talk you out of doing that. If possible, let solid objects default to the color scheme's fill color, or, if you must change the fill color, change it to one of the alternative colors provided by the scheme. The beauty of doing this is that if you change the color scheme later, the fill color for objects changes to reflect the new fill color. After you switch to a color that's not in the theme, however, the object ignores any subsequent changes to the theme.

Saving frequently

Drawing is tedious work. You don't want to spend two hours working on a particularly important drawing only to lose it all just because a comet strikes your building or an errant Scud lands in your backyard. You can prevent catastrophic loss from incidents such as these by pressing Ctrl+S or by frequently clicking the Save button as you work. And always wear protective eyewear.

Remembering Ctrl+Z

In my opinion, Ctrl+Z — the ubiquitous Undo command — is the most important keyboard shortcut in any Windows program, and PowerPoint is no exception. Remember that you're never more than one keystroke away from erasing a boo-boo. If you do something silly — like forgetting to group a complex picture before trying to move it — you can always press Ctrl+Z to undo your last action. Ctrl+Z is my favorite and most frequently used PowerPoint key combination. (For left-handed mouse users, Alt+Backspace does the same thing.) And if you aren't ready to climb on a chair shrieking at the first sign of a mouse, try clicking the handy Undo button on the Quick Access Toolbar.

Drawing Simple Objects

To draw an object on a slide, first call up the Insert tab on the Ribbon. Then click the Shapes button (located in the Illustrations group) to reveal a gallery of shapes you can choose from, as shown in Figure 12-2. Finally, select the shape you want to draw from the Shapes gallery.

Figure 12-2: The Shapes gallery.

You find detailed instructions for drawing with the more important tools in the Shapes gallery in the following sections. Before I get to that, though, I want to give you some pointers to keep in mind:

- **Choosing a location:** Before you draw an object, move to the slide on which you want to draw the object. If you want the object to appear on every slide in the presentation, display the Slide Master by choosing Slide Master in the Master Views section of the View tab on the Ribbon or by Shift+clicking the Normal View button.

- **Fixing a mistake:** If you make a mistake while drawing a shape, the Undo command on the Quick Access Toolbar can usually correct the mistake for you.

- **Holding down the Shift key:** If you hold down the Shift key while drawing a shape, PowerPoint forces the shape to be "regular." That is, rectangles are squares, ellipses are circles, and lines are constrained to horizontal or vertical, or 45-degree diagonals.

Drawing straight lines

You can use the Line button to draw straight lines on your slides. Here's the procedure:

1. **Click the Line button in the Shapes group on the Insert tab.**
2. **Point the cursor to where you want the line to start.**
3. **Click and drag the cursor to where you want the line to end.**
4. **Release the mouse button when you reach your destination.**

After you've drawn the shape, the Ribbon displays the Drawing Tools tab, as shown in Figure 12-3. You can then use the controls in the Shape Styles group to change the fill, outline, and effects applied to the line.

Figure 12-3: The Drawing Tools tab.

After you've drawn a line, you can adjust it by clicking it and then dragging the handles that appear on each end of the line.

Remember that you can force a line to be perfectly horizontal or vertical by holding down the Shift key while you draw. If you hold the Shift key and drag diagonally while you draw the line, the line will be constrained to perfect 45-degree angles.

Drawing rectangles, squares, ovals, and circles

To draw a rectangle, follow these steps:

1. **On the Insert tab, click the Shape buttons (in the Illustrations group), then click the Rectangle button.**
2. **Point the cursor to where you want one corner of the rectangle to be positioned.**
3. **Click and drag to where you want the opposite corner of the rectangle to be positioned.**
4. **Release the mouse button.**

The steps for drawing an oval are the same as the steps for drawing a rectangle except that you click the Oval button rather than the Rectangle button. To draw a square or perfectly round circle, select the Rectangle button or the Oval button but hold down the Shift key while you draw.

You can adjust the size or shape of a rectangle or circle by clicking it and dragging any of its love handles (the small circles you see at the corners of the shape).

Creating Other Shapes

Rectangles and circles aren't the only two shapes that PowerPoint can draw automatically. The Shapes gallery includes many other types of shapes you can draw, such as pentagons, stars, and flowchart symbols.

The Shapes gallery (refer to Figure 12-2) organizes shapes into the following categories:

- **Recently Used Shapes:** The top section of the gallery lists as many as 24 of the shapes you've used most recently. The shapes found in this section change each time you draw a new shape.

- **Lines:** Straight lines, curved lines, lines with arrowheads, scribbly lines, and free-form shapes that can become polygons if you want. The free-form shape is useful enough to merit its own section, "Drawing a polygon or free-form shape," later in this chapter.

- **Rectangles:** Basic rectangular shapes, including not just a regular rectangle but also rectangles with corners lopped off.

- **Basic Shapes:** Squares, rectangles, triangles, crosses, happy faces, lightning bolts, hearts, clouds, and more.

- **Block Arrows:** Fat arrows pointing in various directions.

- **Equation Shapes:** Shapes for drawing simple math equations.

- **Flowchart:** Various flowcharting symbols.

- **Stars and Banners:** Shapes that add sparkle to your presentations.

- **Callouts:** Text boxes and speech bubbles like those used in comic strips.

- **Action Buttons:** Buttons that you can add to your slides and click during a slide show to go directly to another slide or to run a macro.

Drawing a shape

The following steps explain how to draw a shape:

1. **Click the Shapes button in the Illustrations group of the Insert tab.**

   The Shapes gallery appears.

2. **Select the shape you want to insert.**

   When you select one of the shapes, the Shapes gallery disappears and PowerPoint is poised to draw the shape you selected.

3. **Click the slide where you want the shape to appear and then drag the shape to the desired size.**

   Hold down the Shift key while drawing the Shape to create an evenly proportioned shape.

   When you release the mouse button, the Shape object takes on the current fill color and line style.

4. **(Optional) Start typing if you want the shape to contain text.**

   After you've typed your text, you can use PowerPoint's formatting features to change its typeface, size, color, and so on. For more information, refer to Chapter 8.

Some shapes — especially the stars and banners — cry out for text. Figure 12-4 shows how you can use a star shape to add a jazzy burst to a slide.

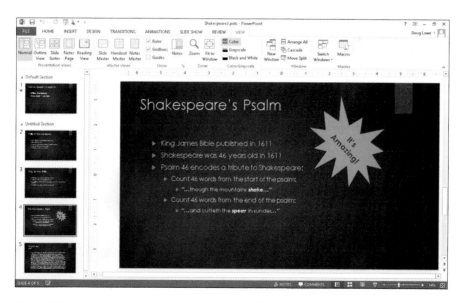

Figure 12-4: Use a star shape to make your presentation look like a late-night infomercial.

You can change an object's shape at any time. First, select the shape. Then, open the Drawing Tools tab on the Ribbon, look in the Insert Shapes group, click the Edit Shape button, and choose Change Shape from the menu that appears.

Many shape buttons have an extra handle shaped like a yellow diamond that enables you to adjust some aspect of the object's shape. For example, the block arrows have a handle that enables you to increase or decrease the size of the arrowhead. The location of these handles varies depending on the shape you're working with. Figure 12-5 shows how you can use these extra handles to vary the shapes produced by six different shapes. For each of the six shapes, the first object shows how the shape is initially drawn; the other two objects drawn with each shape show how you can change the shape by dragging the extra handle. (Note that the yellow handles aren't shown in this figure. When you select a shape that has one of these adjustment handles, the handles will appear.)

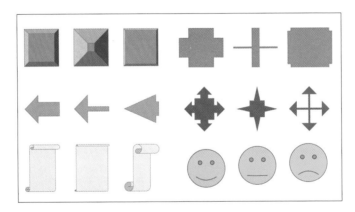

Figure 12-5: You can create interesting variations by grabbing the extra handles on these shapes.

Drawing a polygon or free-form shape

Mr. Arnold, my seventh-grade math teacher, taught me that a *polygon* is a shape that has many sides and has nothing to do with having more than one spouse. (One is certainly enough for most people.) Triangles, squares, and rectangles are polygons, but so are hexagons, pentagons, and any unusual shapes whose sides all consist of straight lines. Politicians are continually inventing new polygons when they revise the boundaries of congressional districts.

One of the most useful shapes in the Shapes gallery is the Freeform Shape tool. It's designed to create polygons, but with a twist: Not all the sides have to be straight lines. The Freeform Shape tool lets you build a shape whose sides are a mixture of straight lines and free-form curves. Figure 12-6 shows three examples of shapes that I created with the Freeform Shape tool.

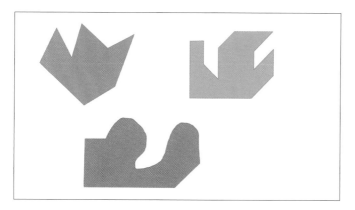

Figure 12-6: Three free-form shapes.

Follow these steps to create a polygon or free-form shape:

1. **Select the Freeform shape (shown in the margin) from the Shapes gallery.**

   You can find the Shapes gallery in the Shapes group on the Insert tab. When you select the Freeform Shape tool, the cursor changes to a cross-hair pointer.

2. **Click where you want to position the first corner of the object.**

3. **Click where you want to position the second corner of the object.**

4. **Keep clicking wherever you want to position a corner.**

5. **(Optional) To draw a free-form side on the shape, hold down the mouse button when you click a corner and then drag to draw the free-form shape. When you get to the end of the free-form side, release the mouse button.**

   You can then click again to add more corners. Shape 3 in Figure 12-6 has one free-form side.

6. **To finish the shape, click near the first corner — the one that you created in Step 2.**

   You don't have to be exact. If you click anywhere near the first corner that you put down, PowerPoint assumes that the shape is finished.

You're finished! The object assumes the line and fill color from the slide's color scheme.

You can reshape a polygon or free-form shape by double-clicking it and then dragging any of the love handles that appear on the corners.

If you hold down the Shift key while you draw a polygon, the sides are constrained to 45-degree angles. Shape 2 in Figure 12-6 was drawn in this manner. How about a constitutional amendment requiring Congress to use the Shift key when it redraws congressional boundaries?

You also can use the Freeform Shape tool to draw a multisegmented line called an *open shape.* To draw an open shape, you can follow the steps in this section, except that you skip Step 6. Instead, double-click or press Esc when the line is done.

Drawing a curved line or shape

Another useful tool is the Curve Shape tool, which lets you draw curved lines or shapes. Figure 12-7 shows several examples of curved lines and shapes drawn with the Curve Shape tool.

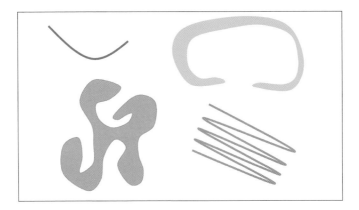

Figure 12-7: Examples of curved lines and shapes.

Here's the procedure for drawing a curved line or shape:

1. **Select the Curve shape tool from the Shapes gallery.**

   You can find the Shapes gallery in the Shapes group on the Insert tab. When you select this tool, the cursor changes to a cross-hair pointer.

2. **Click where you want the curved line or shape to begin.**

3. **Click where you want the first turn in the curve to appear.**

   The straight line turns to a curved line, bent around the point where you clicked. As you move the mouse, the bend of the curve changes.

4. **Click to add turns to the curve.**

   Each time you click, a new bend is added to the line. Keep clicking until the line is as twisty as you want.

5. **To finish a line, double-click where you want the end of the curved line to appear. To create a closed shape, double-click over the starting point, where you clicked in Step 2.**

Creating a text box

A text box is a special type of shape that's designed to place text on your slides. To create a text box, call up the Insert tab, select the Text Box button in the Text group, and then click where you want one corner of the text box to appear and drag to where you want the opposite corner, just like you're drawing a rectangle. When you release the mouse button, you can type text.

You can format the text that you type in the text box by highlighting the text and using the usual PowerPoint text formatting features, most of which are found on the Home tab. For more information about formatting text, see Chapter 7.

You can format the text box itself by using Shape Fill, Shape Outline, Shape Effects, and other tools available on the Drawing Tools tab, as described in the next section. By default, text boxes have no fill or line color, so the box itself is invisible on the slide — only the text is visible.

Most shapes also function as text boxes. If you want to add text to a shape, just click the shape and start typing. The text appears centered over the shape. (The only shapes that don't accept text are lines and connectors.)

Styling Your Shapes

The center section of the Drawing Tools tab is called Shape Styles. It lets you control various stylistic features of your shapes. For example, you can set a fill color, set the outline, and add effects such as shadows or reflections.

You can set these styles individually, or you can choose one of the preselected shape styles that appears in the Shape Styles group. Note that the styles that appear in the Shape Styles group vary depending on the type of shape you've selected and the theme used for the presentation. For example, if you select a line, various predefined line styles are displayed. But if you select a rectangle, the styles appropriate for rectangles are displayed.

Setting the shape fill

The Shape Fill control (in the Shape Styles group of the Drawing Tools tab) lets you control how shapes are filled. The simplest type of fill is a solid color. But you can also use a picture, a gradient fill, or a pattern to fill the shape.

Working with shape fills is similar to working with background and theme colors. For more information on backgrounds and themes, check out Chapter 8.

Setting the shape outline

The Shape Outline control (in the Shape Styles group of the Drawing Tools tab) lets you change the style of line objects or the border for solid shape objects. You can change the following settings for the outline:

- ✔ **Color:** Sets the color used for the outline.

- ✔ **Weight:** Sets the thickness of the line.

- ✔ **Dashes:** The dashing pattern used for the lines that outline the object. The default uses a solid line, but different patterns are available to create dashed lines.

- ✔ **Arrows:** Lines can have an arrowhead at either or both ends. Arrowheads are used mostly on line and arc objects.

For maximum control over the outline style, choose the More command from the menu that appears when you click the Fill, Outline, or Effects button. Doing this brings up the Format Shape task pane shown in Figure 12-8. From here, you can control all aspects of a line's style: its color, width, dash pattern, and cap type (various arrowheads can be applied).

Figure 12-8: Formatting the line style.

Applying shape effects

The Shape Effects button on the Drawing Tools tab on the Ribbon lets you apply several interesting types of effects to your shapes. When you click this button, a menu with the following effect options is displayed:

- **Shadow:** Applies a shadow to the picture. You can select one of several predefined shadow effects, or you can call up a dialog box that lets you customize the shadow.

- **Reflection:** Creates a reflected image of the picture beneath the original picture.

- **Glow:** Adds a glowing effect around the edges of the picture.

- **Soft Edges:** Softens the edges of the picture.

- **Bevel:** Creates a beveled effect.

- **3-D Rotation:** Rotates the picture in a way that creates a three-dimensional effect.

The best way to discover how to use these effects is to experiment with them to see how they work.

Flipping and Rotating Objects

To *flip* an object means to create a mirror image of it. To *rotate* an object means to turn it about its center. PowerPoint lets you flip objects horizontally or vertically, rotate objects in 90-degree increments, or freely rotate an object to any angle.

Rotation works for text boxes and Shape text. Therefore, you can use rotation to create vertical text or text skewed to any angle you want. However, flipping an object doesn't affect the object's text.

Flipping an object

PowerPoint enables you to flip an object vertically or horizontally to create a mirror image of the object. To flip an object, follow these steps:

1. **Select the object that you want to flip.**

2. **Open the Drawing Tools tab, click the Rotate button on the Arrange group, and then choose Flip Horizontal or Flip Vertical.**

Rotating an object 90 degrees

You can rotate an object in 90-degree increments by following these steps:

1. **Choose the object that you want to rotate.**

2. **Open the Drawing Tools tab, click the choose Rotate button on the Arrange group, and then choose Rotate Right or Rotate Left.**

3. **To rotate the object 180 degrees, click the appropriate Rotate button again.**

Using the rotate handle

Remember how all the bad guys' hideouts were slanted in the old *Batman* TV show? The rotate handle lets you give your drawings that same kind of slant. With the rotate handle, you can rotate an object to any arbitrary angle just by dragging it with the mouse.

The rotate handle is the green handle that appears when you select an object that can be rotated. The rotate handle appears above the object, connected to the object by a line, as shown in Figure 12-9. You can rotate an object to any angle simply by dragging the rotate handle.

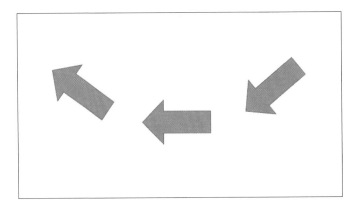

Figure 12-9: The rotate handle lets you rotate an object to any arbitrary angle.

The following steps show you how to use the rotate handle:

1. **Click the object that you want to rotate.**

2. **Drag the rotate handle in the direction that you want to rotate the object.**

   As you drag, an outline of the object rotates around. When you get the object's outline to the angle you want, release the mouse button, and the object is redrawn at the new angle.

To restrict the rotation angle to 15-degree increments, hold the Shift key while dragging around the rotation handle.

Drawing a Complicated Picture

When you add more than one object to a slide, you might run into several problems. What happens when the objects overlap? How do you line up objects so that they don't look like they were thrown at the slide from a moving car? And how do you keep together objects that belong together?

The following sections show you how to use PowerPoint features to handle overlapped objects and how to align and group objects.

Changing layers

Whenever you have more than one object on a slide, the potential exists for objects to overlap one another. Like most drawing programs, PowerPoint handles this problem by layering objects like a stack of plates. The first object that you draw is at the bottom of the stack; the second object is on top of the first; the third is atop the second object; and so on. If two objects overlap, the one that's at the highest layer wins; objects below it are partially covered. (Note that PowerPoint's layers aren't nearly as powerful as layers in other programs, such as Adobe Illustrator or AutoCAD. All they really do is set the stacking order when objects are placed on top of one another.)

So far, so good — but what if you don't remember to draw the objects in the correct order? What if you draw a shape that you want to tuck behind a shape that you've already drawn, or what if you want to bring an existing shape to the top of the pecking order? No problem. PowerPoint enables you to change the stacking order by moving objects toward the front or back so that they overlap just the way you want.

The Drawing Tools tab provides two controls that let you move an object forward or backward in the layer order:

✓ **Bring to Front:** Brings the chosen object to the top of the stack. Note that this button has a down arrow next to it. If you click this down arrow, you reveal a menu with two subcommands: Bring to Front and Bring Forward. The Bring Forward command moves the object just one step closer to the top of the heap, whereas the Bring to Front command moves the object all the way to the top.

✓ **Send to Back:** Sends the chosen object to the back of the stack. Again, this button has a down arrow next to it. You can click this down arrow to access the Send Backward subcommand, which sends the object one level down in the layer order.

Layering problems are most obvious when objects have a fill color. If an object has no fill color, objects behind it are allowed to show through. In this case, the layering doesn't matter much.

To bring an object to the top of another, you might have to use the Bring Forward command several times. The reason is that even though the two objects appear to be adjacent, other objects might occupy the layers between them.

Line 'em up

Nothing looks more amateurish than objects dropped randomly on a slide with no apparent concern for how they line up with each other. The Drawing Tools tab includes an Align button that brings up a menu with the following commands:

- Align Left
- Align Center
- Align Right
- Align Top
- Align Middle
- Align Bottom
- Distribute Horizontally
- Distribute Vertically

The first three commands (Align Left, Center, and Right) align items horizontally; the next three commands (Align Top, Middle, and Bottom) align items vertically.

You can also distribute several items so that they're spaced evenly. Select the items that you want to distribute, click the Draw button, choose Align or Distribute, and then choose Distribute Horizontally or Distribute Vertically. PowerPoint then adjusts the spacing of the objects that appear between the two outermost objects selected.

Another quick way to align one item to another is to simply drag the first item until it is close to the alignment you want. When the item reaches the correct alignment, a magic guideline will appear to indicate that you have found the correct alignment. If you release the mouse button while this magic guideline is visible, the object will be snapped into alignment.

Using the grids and guides

To help you create well-ordered slides, PowerPoint lets you display a grid of evenly spaced lines over the slide. These lines aren't actually a part of the slide, so your audience won't see them when you give your presentation. They exist simply to make the task of lining things up a bit easier.

In addition to the grid, PowerPoint also lets you use guides. The guides are two lines — one horizontal, the other vertical — that appear onscreen. Although the gridlines are fixed in their location on your slides, you can move the guides around as you want. Any object that comes within a pixel's breadth of one of these guidelines snaps to it. Like the grid, the guides don't show up when you give your presentation. They appear only when you're editing your slides. Guides are a great way to line up objects in a neat row.

To display the grid or guides, click the dialog box launcher in the bottom-right corner of the Show section of the View tab on the Ribbon. This click summons the Grid and Guides dialog box, shown in Figure 12-10.

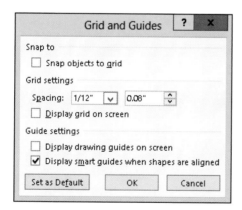

Figure 12-10: The Grid and Guides dialog box.

To activate the grid, select the Snap Objects to Grid check box and then adjust the grid spacing to whatever setting you want. If you want to actually see the grid onscreen, select the Display Grid on Screen check box.

To fire up the guides, select the Display Drawing Guides on Screen check box. After the guides are visible, you can move them around the slide by clicking and dragging them.

You can also uncheck Display Smart Guides When Shapes Are Aligned to disable the guidelines that appear when you move shapes into alignment with each other. This is a useful feature, however; so I recommend that you leave this option selected.

Group therapy

A *group* is a collection of objects that PowerPoint treats as though they were one object. Using groups properly is one key to putting simple shapes together to make complex pictures without becoming so frustrated that you have to join a therapy group. ("Hello, my name is Doug, and PowerPoint drives me crazy.")

To create a group, follow these steps:

1. **Choose all objects that you want to include in the group.**

   You can do this by holding down the Shift key and clicking each of the items or by clicking and dragging the resulting rectangle around all the items.

2. **Right-click one of the selected objects and then choose Group⇨Group from the menu that appears.**

You can also find the Group command on the Drawing Tools tab, but it's much easier to find by right-clicking.

To take a group apart so that PowerPoint treats the objects as individuals again, follow these steps:

1. **Right-click the group you want to break up.**

2. **Choose Group⇨Ungroup.**

If you create a group and then ungroup it so that you can work on its elements individually, you can easily regroup the objects. These steps show you how:

1. **Right-click one of the objects that was in the original group.**

2. **Choose Group⇨Regroup.**

   PowerPoint remembers which objects were in the group and automatically includes them.

PowerPoint enables you to create groups of groups. This capability is useful for complex pictures because it enables you to work on one part of the picture, group it, and then work on the next part of the picture without worrying about accidentally disturbing the part that you've already grouped. After you have several such groups, select them and group them. You can create groups of groups of groups and so on, ad nauseam.

COVENTRY UNIVERSITY LONDON CAMPUS
East India House,
109-117 Middlesex Street, London, E1 7JF
Tel: 020 7247 3666 | Fax: 020 7375 3048
www.coventry.ac.uk/londoncampus

Charting for Fun and Profit

*O*ne of the best ways to prove a point is with numbers, and one of the best ways to present numbers is in a chart. With PowerPoint, adding a chart to your presentation is easy. And getting the chart to look the way you want is usually easy, too. It takes a little bit of pointing and clicking, but it works. This chapter shows you how.

Understanding Charts

If you've never attempted to add a chart to a slide, the process can be a little confusing. A *chart* is simply a series of numbers rendered as a graph. You can supply the numbers yourself, or you can copy them from a separate file, such as an Excel spreadsheet. You can create all kinds of different charts, ranging from simple bar charts and pie charts to exotic doughnut charts and radar charts. Very cool, but a little confusing to the uninitiated.

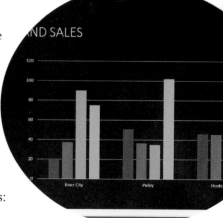

The following list details some of the jargon that you have to contend with when you're working with charts:

▶ **Graph or chart:** Same thing. These terms are used interchangeably. A graph or chart is nothing more than a bunch of numbers turned into a picture. After all, a picture is worth a thousand numbers.

▶ **Chart type:** PowerPoint supports several chart types: bar charts, column charts, pie charts, line charts, scatter charts, area charts, radar charts, Dunkin' Donut charts, and others. You can even create cone charts that look like something that fell off a Fembot in an Austin Powers movie. Different types of charts are better suited to displaying different types of data.

✐ **Chart Layout:** A predefined combination of chart elements, such as headings and legends, that lets you easily create a common type of chart.

✐ **Chart Style:** A predefined combination of formatting elements that controls the visual appearance of a chart.

✐ **Datasheet:** Supplies the underlying data for a chart. After all, a chart is nothing more than a bunch of numbers made into a picture. Those numbers come from the datasheet, which is actually an Excel spreadsheet. When you create a chart, PowerPoint automatically starts Excel (if it isn't already running) and uses Excel to hold the numbers in the datasheet.

✐ **Series:** A collection of related numbers. For example, a chart of quarterly sales by region might have a series for each region. Each series has four sales totals, one for each quarter. Each series is usually represented by a row on the datasheet, but you can change the datasheet so that each column represents a series. Most chart types can plot more than one series. Pie charts can plot only one series at a time, however. The name of each series can be displayed in a legend.

✐ **Axes:** The lines on the edges of a chart. The *X-axis* is the line along the bottom of the chart; the *Y-axis* is the line along the left edge of the chart. The X-axis usually indicates categories. Actual data values are plotted along the Y-axis. Microsoft Graph automatically provides labels for the X- and Y-axes, but you can change them.

✐ **Legend:** A box used to identify the various series plotted on the chart. PowerPoint can create a legend automatically if you want one.

The most interesting thing to know about charting in PowerPoint 2013 is that it is closely integrated with Excel 2013. When you insert a chart in PowerPoint, Excel is automatically started, and the data that you chart is placed in an Excel workbook. However, that Excel workbook isn't stored as a separate document. Instead, the chart and the datasheet workbook are stored within the PowerPoint document.

Adding a Chart to Your Presentation

To add a chart to your presentation, you have several options:

✐ Create a new slide by using a layout that includes a Content placeholder (an object that reserves space for content on the slide). Then click the Chart icon in the Content placeholder to create the chart.

✐ Use the Insert tab to insert a chart into any slide.

✔ Create the chart separately in Microsoft Excel and then paste the chart into PowerPoint. This is the most common method if the chart is based on data that's already stored in an Excel workbook.

Adding a new slide with a chart

The following procedure shows how to insert a new slide that contains a chart:

1. **Move to the slide that you want the new slide to follow.**

2. **Click the Home tab and then click the New Slide button in the Slides group.**

   This action reveals a list of slide layouts.

3. **Click one of the slide layouts that includes a Content placeholder.**

   Several slide types include a Content placeholder. When you click the one you want, a slide with the selected layout is added to your presentation, as shown in Figure 13-1. (In this case, I chose the "Title and Content" layout.)

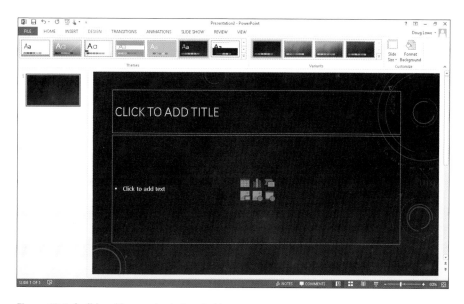

Figure 13-1: A slide with a content placeholder.

As you can see, the Content placeholder includes six little icons for inserting different types of content:

 • *Table:* Inserts a table, as described in Chapter 16.

- *Chart:* Inserts a chart.

- *SmartArt:* Inserts a SmartArt graphic, as described in Chapter 14.

- *Picture:* Inserts a picture, as described in Chapter 11.

- *Online Picture:* Inserts a picture from an online source, as described in Chapter 11.

- *Media:* Inserts a movie, as described in Chapter 15.

4. **Click the Chart icon in the middle of the Content placeholder.**

   The Chart icon is the one in the middle of the top row of icons. Clicking this icon summons the Insert Chart dialog box shown in Figure 13-2.

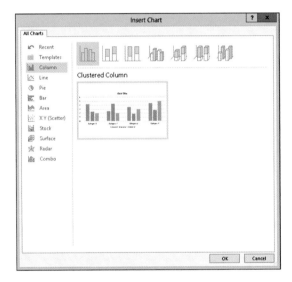

Figure 13-2: The Insert Chart dialog box.

5. **Select the type of chart you want to create.**

   You can select any of the following chart types:

   - *Column:* Data is shown as vertical columns. The columns can be displayed side by side or stacked, and you can pick various shapes for the columns including simple bars, 3-D blocks, cylinders, cones, and pyramids.

   - *Line:* The data is shown as individual points linked by various types of lines.

   - *Pie:* The data is shown as slices in a circular pie.

- *Bar:* The same as a column chart, except the columns are laid out horizontally instead of vertically.

- *Area:* Similar to a line chart, but the areas beneath the lines are shaded.

- *X Y (Scatter):* Plots individual points using two values to represent the X, Y coordinates.

- *Stock:* Plots high/low/close values.

- *Surface:* Similar to a line chart but represents the data as a three-dimensional surface.

- *Radar:* Plots data relative to a central point rather than to X, Y axes.

- *Combo:* Lets you combine different chart types in a single chart.

6. Click OK.

PowerPoint whirs and grinds for a moment and then inserts the chart into the slide, as shown in Figure 13-3. The reason for all the commotion is that to insert the chart, PowerPoint must find out whether Excel is already running. If not, PowerPoint launches Excel, as you can see in the figure.

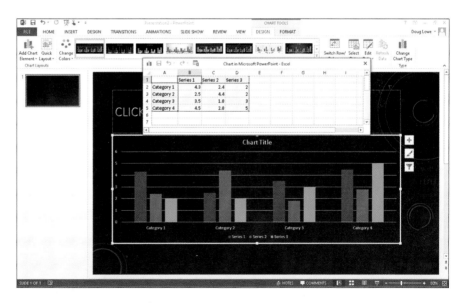

Figure 13-3: A chart after it has been inserted into PowerPoint.

7. Change the sample data to something more realistic.

As you can see, the data for the chart is shown in a separate spread-sheet window that resembles Excel, tiled alongside PowerPoint. You need to edit the data in this spreadsheet to provide the data you want to chart. Notice that any changes you make to the spreadsheet data are automatically reflected in the chart.

For more information, turn to the section "Working with Chart Data," later in this chapter.

8. **Customize the chart any way you want.**

For example, you can change the chart layout or style, as described later in this chapter. Figure 13-4 shows a finished chart.

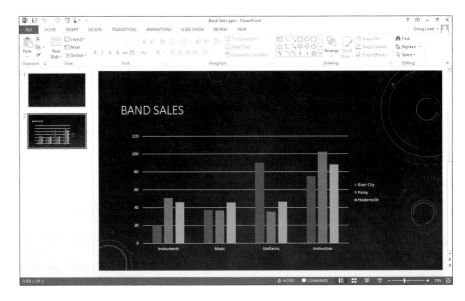

Figure 13-4: A slide with a finished chart.

Adding a chart to an existing slide

If you prefer, you can add a chart to an existing slide by following these steps:

1. **Move to the slide on which you want to place the chart.**

2. **Activate the Insert tab on the Ribbon. Click the Chart button in the Illustrations group.**

This step summons the Insert Chart dialog box (refer to Figure 13-2).

3. **Select the type of chart you want to create and then click OK.**

PowerPoint launches Excel (if it isn't already running) and inserts a chart based on sample data.

See the section "Changing the Chart Type," later in this chapter, for more information about chart types.

4. **Change the sample data to something more realistic.**

   For more information about working with chart data, check out the section "Working with Chart Data," later in this chapter.

5. **Finish the chart by setting the chart layout and style.**

   For more information, see the sections "Changing the Chart Layout" and "Changing the Chart Style," later in this chapter.

6. **Rearrange everything.**

   The chart undoubtedly falls on top of something else already on the slide. You probably need to resize the chart by selecting it and then dragging it by the love handles. You can move the chart like any other object: Just click and drag it to a new location. You might also need to move, resize, or delete other objects to make room for the chart or change the layer order of the chart or other surrounding objects. You can find information about these manipulations in Chapters 11 and 12.

Pasting a chart from Excel

If the data you want to chart already exists in an Excel workbook, the easiest way to chart it in PowerPoint is to first create the chart in Excel. Then copy the chart to the clipboard, switch over to PowerPoint, and paste the chart to the appropriate slide. When you do so, the chart appears in PowerPoint exactly as it did in Excel.

When you paste an Excel chart into PowerPoint, a smart tag appears near the bottom right of the chart. You can click this smart tag to reveal a menu that lets you indicate whether you want to keep the original formatting of the chart or use the theme in the PowerPoint presentation.

In addition, the smart tag lets you indicate whether the chart should be embedded or linked. If you embed the chart, PowerPoint creates a copy of the Excel data and stores it as a workbook object within your PowerPoint file. This effectively severs the chart in the PowerPoint presentation from the original workbook, so any changes you make to the data in the original workbook aren't reflected in the PowerPoint chart.

On the other hand, if you link the chart, PowerPoint copies the chart into the PowerPoint presentation but creates a link to the data in the original Excel workbook. Then any changes you make to the data in the original Excel workbook are reflected in the chart.

One final option on the smart tag lets you insert the chart as a picture. If you choose this option, PowerPoint converts the chart to a collection of PowerPoint shape objects, with no linkage to the original Excel chart or data.

Changing the Chart Type

PowerPoint enables you to create 14 basic types of charts. Each type conveys information with a different emphasis. Sales data plotted in a column chart might emphasize the relative performance of different regions, for example, and the same data plotted as a line chart might emphasize an increase or decrease in sales over time. The type of chart that's best for your data depends on the nature of the data and which aspects of it you want to emphasize.

Fortunately, PowerPoint doesn't force you to decide the final chart type up front. You can easily change the chart type at any time without changing the chart data. These steps show you how:

1. **Click the chart to select it.**

   When you select a chart, a set of three tabs called the Chart Tools is added to the Ribbon.

2. **Click the Design tab, as shown in Figure 13-5.**

Figure 13-5: The Chart Tools Design contextual tab.

Change
Chart Type

3. **Click the Change Chart Type button (shown in the margin).**

   PowerPoint displays a gallery of chart types.

4. **Click the chart type that you want.**

5. **Click OK, and you're done.**

Working with Chart Data

The data that provides the numbers plotted in a PowerPoint chart is stored in an Excel workbook. Depending on how you created the chart, this Excel workbook can either be a separate workbook document or be embedded within your PowerPoint document. Either way, you can work with Excel whenever you want to modify the chart data.

To change the data on which a chart is based, select the chart. A set of three tabs called the Chart Tools is automatically added to the Ribbon when you select the chart. Next, choose the Design tab. This tab includes a group called

Data, which provides four controls. These controls let you perform various tricks on the data, as described in the following sections.

Switching rows and columns

Switch Row/ Column

The first control in the Data group, shown in the margin, is called Switch Row/Column. It changes the orientation of your chart in a way that can be difficult to describe but easy to visualize. Look back at the chart in Figure 13-4. It's based on the following data:

	River City	*Pixley*	*Hootersville*
Instruments	20.4	50.6	45.9
Music	37.4	36.6	45.9
Uniforms	90	34.6	45
Instruction	75	102	88

As shown earlier in Figure 13-4, the rows are used to determine the data categories. Thus, the chart displays the data for Instruments, Music, Uniforms, and Instruction along the horizontal axis.

If you click the Switch Row/Column button, the chart changes, as shown in Figure 13-6. Here, the chart categorizes the data by city, so sales for River City, Pixley, and Hootersville are shown along the horizontal axis.

Figure 13-6: Swapping the row/column orientation of a chart.

Changing the data selection

Select
Data

The Select Data button in the Data group of the Design tab (shown in the margin) lets you change the selection of data that your chart is based on. When you click this button, you're escorted to Excel, and the dialog box shown in Figure 13-7 is displayed.

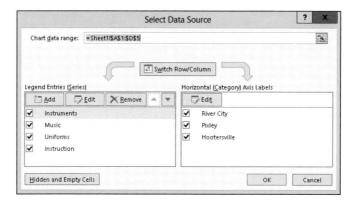

Figure 13-7: The Select Data Source dialog box.

This dialog box lets you do three basic tasks:

- **Change the range.** You can change the range of data that's used for the chart by using the Chart Data Range text box.

- **Switch row/column.** You can switch rows and columns by clicking the Switch Row/Column button. Doing this has the same effect as clicking the Switch Row/Column button back in PowerPoint.

- **Modify ranges and series.** You can play with the individual ranges that contain the data for each series. You can add a new series, edit the range used for an existing series, delete a series, or change the order in which the series are presented.

Editing the source data

Edit
Data ▾

To change the actual data values on which a chart is based, click the Edit Data button in the Data group of the Design tab (shown in the margin). This action launches Excel to display the chart data. You can then make any changes you want. When you return to PowerPoint (by clicking anywhere in the PowerPoint window), the chart is updated to reflect your changes.

Refreshing a chart

If a chart is linked to a separate Excel workbook, you can update the chart to reflect any changes that have been made to the underlying data. To do so, follow these steps:

1. **Click the chart to select it.**

   The Ribbon expands to include the Chart Tools tabs.

2. **Click the Design tab on the Ribbon.**

3. **Click the Refresh Data button in the Data group.**

   The chart is updated with the data from the underlying Excel workbook.

Changing the Chart Layout

A *chart layout* is a predefined combination of chart elements such as legends, titles, and so on. Microsoft studied thousands of charts and talked to chart experts to come up with galleries of the most common layouts for each chart type.

To change the layout for a chart, follow these steps:

1. **Click the chart to select it.**

   The Ribbon expands to include the Chart Tools tabs.

2. **Click the Design tab on the Ribbon.**

3. **Click the Quick Layout button.**

   Doing this opens the Quick Layout Gallery, as shown in Figure 13-8.

Figure 13-8: The Quick Layout Gallery for column charts.

4. **Click the layout you want to use.**

   The layout you select is applied to the chart. Figure 13-9 shows the Band Sales chart with a different layout applied.

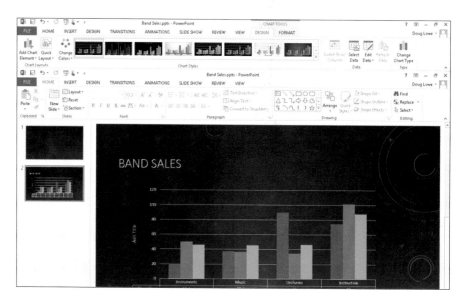

Figure 13-9: Changing the layout changes the appearance of a chart.

Changing the Chart Style

A *chart style* is a predefined combination of formatting elements such as colors and shape effects. Microsoft provides a large assortment of chart styles to choose from. For example, Figure 13-10 shows the Chart Style gallery for column charts.

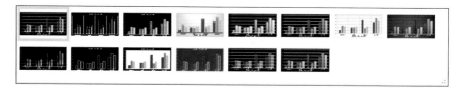

Figure 13-10: The Chart Style gallery for column charts.

To change the style for a chart, follow these steps:

1. **Click the chart to select it.**

The Ribbon expands to include the three Chart Tools tabs. (Refer to Figure 13-5.)

2. **Click the Design tab.**

3. **Select the style you want to use from the Chart Styles group.**

   The Chart Styles group displays the most commonly used styles for the chart type.

   If the style you want to use isn't visible in this group, you can click the More button to display a gallery of all available styles. (The More button is the down-arrow button at the bottom of the scroll bar that appears at the right side of the Chart Styles group.)

Embellishing Your Chart

PowerPoint enables you to embellish a chart in many ways: You can add titles, labels, legends, and who knows what else. The easiest way to add these elements is by selecting a chart layout, as described in the earlier section "Changing the Chart Layout." However, you can create your own unique chart layout by adding these elements individually.

To do that, select the chart and then click the Chart Elements button that appears next to the chart (shown in the margin). A list of chart elements appears, as shown in Figure 13-11. You can then select the chart elements you want to appear on your chart.

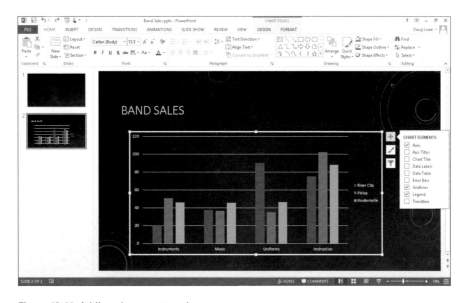

Figure 13-11: Adding elements to a chart.

The following paragraphs describe the elements you can add to your charts:

- **Axes:** Sometimes an axe is what you'd like to use to fix your computer. But in this case, *axes* refer to the X- and Y-axes on which chart data is plotted. The *X-axis* is the horizontal axis of the chart, and the *Y-axis* is the vertical axis. For 3-D charts, a third axis — *Z* — is also used. The Axes control lets you show or hide the labels used for each chart axis.

- **Axis titles:** These titles describe the meaning of each chart axis. Most charts use two axes titles: the Primary Horizontal Axis Title and the Primary Vertical Axis Title.

- **Chart titles:** A chart title describes the chart's contents. It normally appears at the top of the chart, but you can drag it to any location.

- **Data Labels:** Lets you add labels to the data points on the chart. For maximum control over the data labels, choose More Options to display the Format Data Labels task pane, as shown in Figure 13-12.

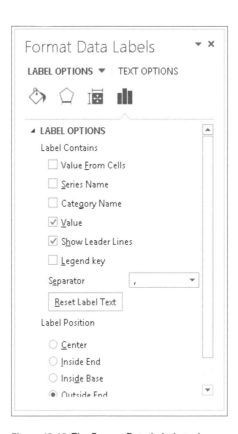

Figure 13-12: The Format Data Labels task pane.

For most slide types, data labels add unnecessary clutter without adding much useful information. Use labels only if you think that you must back up your chart with exact numbers.

✔ **Data Table:** The *data table* is a table that shows the data used to create a chart. Most charts do not include a data table, but you can add one if you think your audience will benefit from seeing the raw numbers. For example, Figure 13-13 shows a chart with a data table.

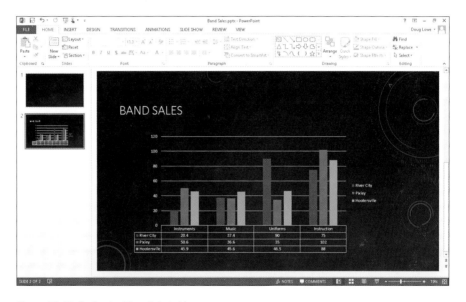

Figure 13-13: A chart with a data table.

✔ **Error Bars:** Adds a graphical element that indicates a range of values for each point rather than a single point. The size of the range can be calculated as a fixed value, a percentage of the point value, or a standard deviation.

✔ **Gridlines:** *Gridlines* are light lines drawn behind a chart to make it easier to judge the position of each dot, bar, or line plotted by the chart. You can turn gridlines on or off via the Gridlines button.

✔ **Legends:** A *legend* identifies the data series that appear in the chart. When you click the Legend button, a menu with several choices for the placement of the legend appears. You can also choose More Legend Options to display the Format Legend task pane, shown in Figure 13-14. From this dialog box, you can set the position of the legend as well as control various formatting options for the legend, such as the fill and border style. (Note that you can also drag the legend to move it to another location in the chart.)

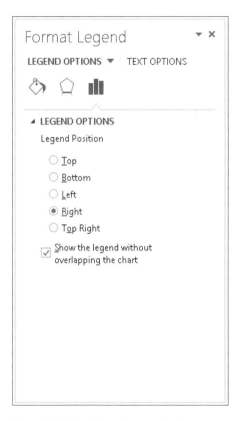

Figure 13-14: The Format Legend task pane.

PowerPoint enables you to create a legend, but you're on your own if you need a myth or fable.

✔ **Trendline:** Allows you to add line elements, which shows the trend of one or more data points, using one of several methods to calculate the trend. Figure 13-15 shows a chart with several trendlines added.

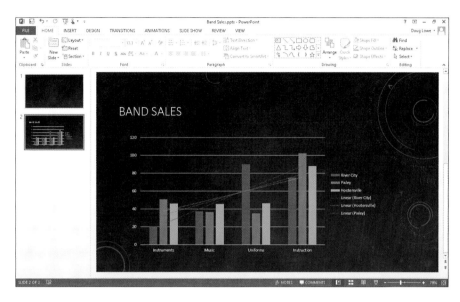

Figure 13-15: A chart with trendlines.

14

Working with SmartArt

*Y*ou'll hear nothing but yawns from the back row if your presentation consists of slide after slide of text and bulleted lists with an occasional bit of clip art thrown in for good measure. Mercifully, PowerPoint is well equipped to add all sorts of embellishments to your slides. This chapter shows you how to work with one of the coolest ways to embellish your slides — adding special diagrams called *SmartArt*.

Understanding SmartArt

PowerPoint includes a nifty little feature called SmartArt, which lets you add several different types of useful diagrams to your slides. With SmartArt, you can create List, Process, Cycle, Hierarchy, Relationship, Matrix, Pyramid, and Picture diagrams. And each of these basic diagram types has multiple variations. In all, you can choose from 185 variations.

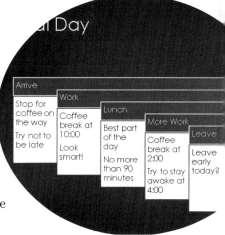

The diagrams created by SmartArt consist of multiple elements, such as shapes and lines. SmartArt itself takes care of drawing these elements in a coordinated fashion, so you don't have to draw the separate elements manually.

The basic idea behind SmartArt diagrams is to represent bullet lists as a diagram of interconnected shapes. Although many different types of SmartArt diagrams are available, they all work the same way. The only real difference among the various SmartArt diagram types is how they graphically represent the bullets. For example, consider the following bullet list:

✔ Arrive

✔ Work

✔ Lunch

✔ More work

✔ Leave

Figure 14-1 shows this list represented by a SmartArt diagram. All I did to create this diagram was select the text, right-click, and choose Convert to SmartArt, and then select the Descending Process SmartArt diagram type.

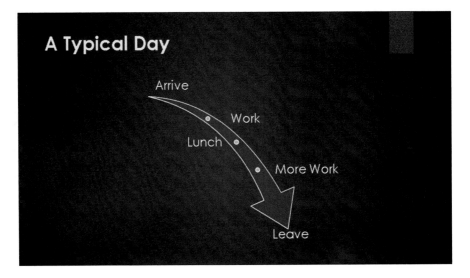

Figure 14-1: A simple SmartArt diagram.

Note that many of the SmartArt diagram types can display two or more outline levels in your bullet list. For example, suppose you have this list:

✔ Arrive

• Stop for coffee on the way

• Try not to be late

- ✔ Work
  - Coffee break at 10:00
  - Look smart!
- ✔ Lunch
  - Best part of the day!
  - No more than 90 minutes
- ✔ More work
  - Coffee break at 2:00
  - Try to stay awake at 4:00
- ✔ Leave
  - Leave early today?

Figure 14-2 shows how this list appears when formatted as an Increasing Arrows Process chart. As you can see, the second-level bullets are incorporated as text within the diagram.

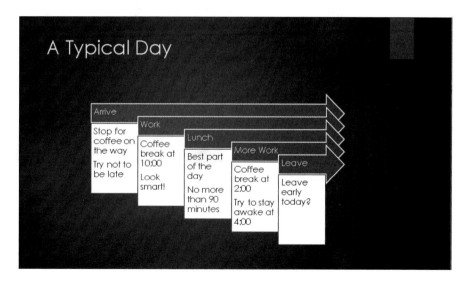

Figure 14-2: How second-level text is displayed in an Increasing Arrows Process chart.

One of the most useful aspects of SmartArt is that you can easily change from one type of diagram to another. Thus, if you decide that a diagram doesn't convey the message you intend, you can try changing the diagram type to see whether the message is clearer.

Creating a SmartArt Diagram

The easiest way to create a SmartArt diagram is to create a new slide and enter the bullet list as if you were going to display the list as normal text and then convert the text to SmartArt. Just follow these steps:

1. **Create a new slide with the Title and Content layout.**

2. **Type your bullet list.**

   Use one or two levels of bullets, but try to keep the list as short and concise as you can.

3. **Right-click anywhere in the list and choose Convert to SmartArt.**

   A menu of SmartArt diagram types appears, as shown in Figure 14-3.

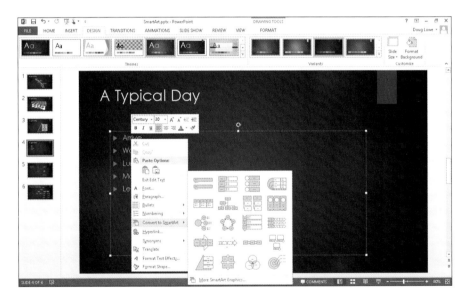

Figure 14-3: Converting text to SmartArt.

4. Select the SmartArt type you want to use.

If the SmartArt type doesn't appear in the menu, you can choose More SmartArt Graphics to display the Choose a SmartArt Graphic dialog box, as shown in Figure 14-4. As you can see, this dialog box lets you choose from about a million different SmartArt diagram types. PowerPoint offers eight basic categories of SmartArt diagrams; these diagram types are pictured and described in Table 14-1.

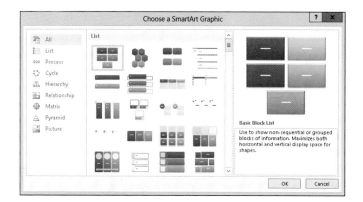

Figure 14-4: The Choose a SmartArt Graphic dialog box.

5. Click OK.

The diagram is created.

6. Modify the diagram however you see fit.

For more information, see the section "Tweaking a SmartArt Diagram," later in this chapter.

7. You're done!

Well, you're never really done. You can keep tweaking your diagram until the end of time to get it perfect. But at some point, you have to say, "Enough is enough," and call it finished.

Table 14-1	Types of Diagrams You Can Create	
Icon	*Diagram Type*	*Description*
List	List	Shows a simple list. Some of the list diagrams show information that doesn't have any particular organization; others display information in a way that implies a sequential progression, such as steps in a task.
Process	Process	Shows a process in which steps flow in a sequential fashion.
Cycle	Cycle	Shows a process that repeats in a continuous cycle.
Hierarchy	Hierarchy	Shows hierarchical relationships, such as organization charts.
Relationship	Relationship	Shows how items are conceptually related to one another. Included in this group are various types of radial and Venn diagrams.
Matrix	Matrix	Shows four items arranged into quadrants.
Pyramid	Pyramid	Shows how elements build upon one another to form a foundation.
Picture	Picture	Shows information in a variety of different formats that incorporate picture objects into the chart design. For more information about working with pictures, refer to Chapter 11.

Tweaking a SmartArt Diagram

After you've created a SmartArt diagram, you can adjust its appearance in many ways. The easiest is to change the SmartArt Style that's applied to the diagram. A SmartArt Style is simply a collection of formatting elements such as colors and shape effects that are assigned to the various elements of a SmartArt diagram.

Microsoft provides a large assortment of SmartArt styles to choose from. For example, Figure 14-5 shows the style gallery for Pyramid diagrams.

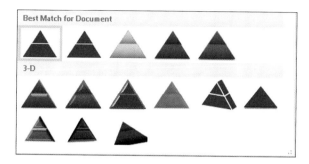

Figure 14-5: The SmartArt Style Gallery for pyramid diagrams.

To change the quick style for a SmartArt diagram, follow these steps:

1. **Click the diagram to select it.**

   Doing this adds the SmartArt tools to the Ribbon.

2. **Click the Design tab.**

   Figure 14-6 depicts the SmartArt Tools Design tab.

Figure 14-6: The SmartArt Tools Design tab.

3. **Select the style you want to use from the SmartArt Styles group.**

   The Quick Styles group displays the most commonly used styles for the diagram type. If the style you want to use isn't visible in this group, you can click the More button to display a gallery like the one shown in Figure 14-5.

Note that the SmartArt Tools Design tab also includes controls that let you modify the SmartArt diagram by adding additional shapes or bullet items or changing the chart type. You can also reset the diagram to its original appearance by clicking the Reset Graphic button found in the Reset group.

Flowcharts, anyone?

One type of diagram that people often want to create with PowerPoint is a flowchart. Although SmartArt doesn't have an option for creating flowcharts, you can easily create flowcharts by using PowerPoint's AutoShapes. For example, take a look at the following flowchart, which I created with just a few minutes' work.

To create a flowchart like this, follow these basic steps:

1. **Draw each flowchart shape by using basic shape objects as described in Chapter 12.**

   Use the shapes in the Flowchart section of the Shapes gallery to create the shapes for the flowchart, and use arrows to connect the shapes.

2. **Enter text into each flowchart shape by clicking the shape and typing.**

   If necessary, adjust the text font and size.

3. **Adjust the alignment of your shapes.**

   Here's where the flowcharting AutoShapes really shine: The connectors stay attached to the shapes even when you move the shapes around! Pretty slick, eh?

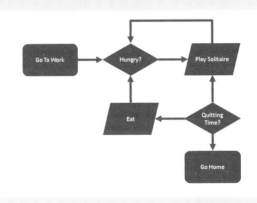

Editing the SmartArt Text

When you create a SmartArt diagram from an existing bullet list, the bullet text is replaced by the diagram. After you've converted the text to SmartArt, what do you do if you need to modify the text?

To modify SmartArt text, simply select the SmartArt diagram. Then click the little double-arrow icon that appears on the left edge of the diagram's selection box. This action reveals a fly-out window called the Text pane, in which you can edit the bullet points. See Figure 14-7.

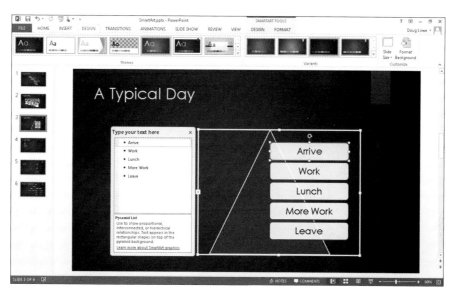

Figure 14-7: Editing SmartArt bullet text.

Working with Organization Charts

Organization charts — you know, those box-and-line charts that show who reports to whom, where the buck stops, and who got the lateral arabesque — are an essential part of many presentations.

The hierarchical SmartArt diagrams are ideal for creating organization charts. You can create diagrams that show bosses, subordinates, co-workers, and assistants. You can easily rearrange the chain of command, add new boxes or delete boxes, and apply fancy 3-D effects. Figure 14-8 shows a finished organization chart.

The bullet list I used to create this chart looked like this before I converted it to SmartArt:

✔ Doc

    • Sneezy

    • Grumpy

       •Sleepy

       •Happy

    • Bashful

Notice that Dopey isn't in this list. That's because Dopey is in a special kind of box on the chart, called an *Assistant.* You find out how to add Assistant boxes later in this chapter.

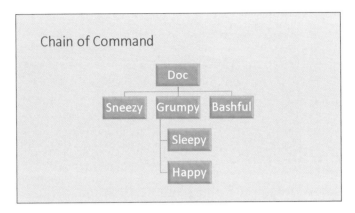

Chain of Command

Doc

Sneezy Grumpy Bashful

Sleepy

Happy

Figure 14-8: A finished organization chart.

Keep in mind that organization charts are useful for more than showing employee relationships. You also can use them to show any kind of hierarchical structure. For example, back when I wrote computer programs for a living, I used organization charts to plan the structure of my computer programs. They're also great for recording family genealogies, although they don't have any way to indicate that Aunt Milly hasn't spoken to Aunt Beatrice in 30 years.

Adding boxes to a chart

You can add a box to an organization chart by calling up the Text pane and editing the text. Refer to the section "Editing the SmartArt Text," earlier in this chapter, for tips on how to do that.

Alternatively, you can use the controls in the SmartArt Tools tab on the Ribbon to add boxes. One nice feature that these controls provide is the capability to add an *Assistant,* which is a box that appears outside of the hierarchical chain of command. Here are the steps:

1. **Click the box you want the new box to be below or next to.**

2. **Open the SmartArt Tools tab on the Ribbon.**

3. **Click the Add Shape button to reveal a menu of choices. Then select one of the following options:**

   - *Add Shape Before:* Inserts a new box at the same level as the selected box, immediately to its left.

   - *Add Shape After:* Inserts a new box at the same level as the selected box, immediately to its right.

   - *Add Shape Above:* Inserts a new box above the selected box.

   - *Add Shape Below:* Inserts a new box beneath the selected box.

   - *Add Assistant:* Inserts a new box beneath the selected box, but the new box is connected with a special elbow connector to indicate that the box is an Assistant, not a subordinate.

4. **Click the new box and then type whatever text you want to appear in the box.**

5. **If necessary, drag the box to adjust its location.**

Deleting chart boxes

To delete a box from an organization chart, select the box and press Delete. PowerPoint automatically adjusts the chart to compensate for the lost box.

When you delete a box from an organization chart, you should observe a moment of somber silence — or throw a party. It all depends on whose name was in the box, I suppose.

Changing the chart layout

PowerPoint lets you choose from four methods of arranging subordinates in an organization chart branch:

- **Standard:** Subordinate shapes are placed at the same level beneath the superior shape.

- **Both Hanging:** Subordinates are placed two per level beneath the superior with the connecting line between them.

- **Left Hanging:** Subordinates are stacked vertically beneath the superior, to the left of the connecting line.

- **Right Hanging:** Subordinates are stacked vertically beneath the superior, to the right of the connecting line.

Figure 14-9 shows an organization chart that uses all four of these layouts. Sneezy, Grumpy, and Bashful use Standard layout. Sleepy and Happy use Both Hanging layout. Groucho, Harpo, and Chico use Left Hanging layout, and Manny, Moe, and Jack use Right Hanging layout.

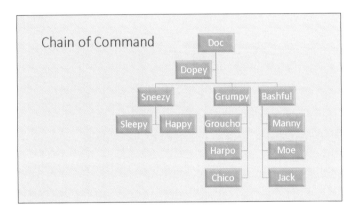

Figure 14-9: An organization chart that uses all four layout types.

To change the layout of a branch of your chart, first click the shape at the top of the branch, and then click the SmartArt Tools Design tab on the Ribbon. Then click the Layout button in the Create Graphic group and choose the layout type you want to use.

15

Lights! Camera! Action! (Adding Sound and Video)

In This Chapter

▶ Adding interesting sound effects to your presentation

▶ Spicing your presentation up with video

▶ Fiddling with audio and video settings

*O*ne of the cool things about PowerPoint is that it lets you create slides that contain not only text and pictures but also sounds and even movies. You can add sound effects, such as screeching brakes or breaking glass to liven up dull presentations. You can even add your own applause, making your presentation like a TV sitcom or game show. You can also add a musical background or a narration to your presentation.

Additionally, you can insert a film clip from *The African Queen* or a picture of the space shuttle launching if you think that will help keep people awake. This chapter shows you how to add those special effects.

This chapter is short because you can't do as much with sound and video in PowerPoint as you can with, say, a professional multimedia-authoring program, such as Adobe Director or a video editor such as Adobe Premiere. Still, PowerPoint allows you to paste sound and video elements into your slide show, thus giving you the power to craft some impressive high-tech presentations. And PowerPoint 2013 allows you to perform basic edits on the videos you insert.

Getting Ready to Add Sound to a Slide

A sterile *beep* used to be the only sound you could get from your computer. Nowadays, you can make your computer talk almost as well as the computers in the *Star Trek* movies, or you can give your computer a sophomoric sense of audible distaste. At last, the computer can be as obnoxious as the user!

Investigating sound files

Computer sounds are stored in *sound files,* which come in two basic varieties:

- **Audio files:** Audio files contain digitized recordings of real sounds. These sounds can be sound effects, such as cars screeching, guns firing, or drums rolling; music; or even quotes from movies or your favorite TV shows. (Imagine Darth Vader saying to your audience, "I find your lack of faith disturbing.")

  Audio files come in two distinct varieties:

  - *Uncompressed:* This type of audio file (including the standard Windows WAV format) provides pristine, clean sound (and packs a large file size to prove it). Both Windows and PowerPoint come with a collection of WAV files that provide simple sound effects such as swooshes, blips, applause, and drum rolls.

  - *Compressed:* For longer sound clips, such as complete songs, the popular formats to use include MP3 and WMA. MP3 is a compressed format that's popular for sounds obtained from the Internet, and WMA is a newer audio format developed by Microsoft for newer versions of Windows. You can tell the format of a sound file by the filename's extension (`.mp3` or `.wma`). (There's an improved version of MP3 out called MP4, but it isn't used much yet). These files take up a lot less room, although any resident audiophile may scoff at using them. Go ahead and use them anyway — if it sounds right, go with it.

- **MIDI files:** MIDI files contain music stored in a form that the sound card's synthesizer can play. Think of it like sheet music for your digital piano player. Windows comes with several MIDI files, and you can download many more from the Internet. MIDI files have the file extension `.mid`.

To insert a sound into a PowerPoint presentation, all you have to do is paste one of these sound files into a slide. Then when you run the presentation in Slide Show View, you can have the sounds play automatically during slide transitions, or you can play them manually by clicking the Sound button.

MP3 and the Internet

MP3 files are a compressed form of wave files that allow entire songs to be squeezed into a reasonable amount of hard drive space. For example, the Steppenwolf song, "Wild Thing," weighs in at just under 2.5MB in an MP3 file. The same file in WAV format requires a whopping 26MB — more than ten times the space.

Napster, the online file exchange system that let users swap MP3 files, popularized the MP3 format. Of course, this file swapping bothered the music industry, which sued because it said users were illegally trading copyrighted music without paying for it, which of course they were, and we (oops, I mean *they*) all knew it.

These days, the most popular sources for legally obtaining MP3 files are iTunes, Amazon.com, and Xbox Music (formerly known as Zune). You can legally download music from these sources, and you can still find plenty of online sources to trade music under the table. Another popular way to obtain MP3 files is to rip them from a music CD. Windows Media player has the built-in capability to do this.

Keep in mind, however, that the legality of using copyrighted music in your PowerPoint presentations is questionable. So if you use hot MP3 files you got from the Internet or ripped from a CD, don't blame me if one day you wake up and find your house surrounded by federal agents and CNN news crews, who refer to you as a "dangerous copyright abuser" and your house as a "compound." They'll probably even interview your ninth-grade English teacher, who will tell the nation that all you could talk about when you were a troubled teen was stealing Aerosmith music from the Internet and using it in illegal PowerPoint presentations.

Fortunately, the national shortage of sound files ended years ago. PowerPoint comes with a handful of useful sound files, including drum rolls, breaking glass, gunshots, and typewriter sounds. Windows comes with some useful sounds, too. But a virtually unlimited supply of sounds is available at your disposal via the Internet. Pop into any of the popular search engines (such as www.google.com) and perform a general search, such as "WAV file collection," or a specific search, such as "Star Trek sounds."

Inserting an audio sound object

In this section, I explain how to insert a sound object onto a slide. You can configure the sound object to play automatically whenever you display the slide, or you can set it up so that it will play only when you click the sound object's icon. Note that if you want the sound to play automatically and the sound is a WAV file, it's easier to add it to the slide transition (as described in Chapter 9) than to add it as a separate object.

To insert a sound file from your hard drive onto a PowerPoint slide, follow these steps:

1. **Move to the slide to which you want to add the sound.**

2. **Open the Insert tab on the Ribbon, click the Audio button located on the right side of the tab, and then choose Audio on My PC.**

   The Insert Audio dialog box appears, as shown in Figure 15-1.

Figure 15-1: The Insert Audio dialog box.

3. **Select the audio file that you want to insert.**

   You may have to rummage about your hard drive to find the folder that contains your sound files. (In Figure 15-1, I navigated over to my Downloads folder to find some MP3 files that I recently downloaded.)

4. **Click the Insert button.**

   The audio file is inserted into the current slide, along with a toolbar of controls that let you play the sound. See Figure 15-2.

You can also insert sounds from the Internet. To do so, click the Audio button on the Insert task pane tab and then choose Online Audio. Then, you can search for the sound you want to insert.

Figure 15-2: A sound inserted onto a slide.

Here are a few other random thoughts on adding sounds to your slides:

 ✔ To play a sound while working in Normal View, double-click the sound icon. However, to play the sound during a slide show, click only once.

 ✔ Remember that you can also play audio files as a part of the slide transition. For more information, see Chapter 9.

 ✔ If you change your mind and decide that you don't want any sounds, you can easily remove them. To remove a sound, click the sound's icon (which resembles a speaker) and press Delete.

Setting Audio Options

You can control several important aspects of how an audio file is played by selecting the file to reveal the Audio Tools contextual tab on the Ribbon and then opening the Playback tab, shown in Figure 15-3. As you can see, this tab contains several controls that let you edit the way the sound file is played. The following sections explain how to use the most important of these tools.

Figure 15-3: The Audio Tools Playback tab.

Controlling when a sound is played

By default, sounds are not played until you click the sound icon that appears on the slide. If you want a sound to play automatically when the slide is displayed, change the option in the Start drop-down list (found in the Audio Options group on the Audio Tools Playback tab) from On Click to Automatically.

If you select On Click or Automatically, the sound automatically stops when you move to the next slide. To allow the sound to continue over several slides, select the Play Across Slides option from the Start drop-down list.

Looping a sound

If the sound file isn't long enough, you can loop it so that it plays over and over again. This feature is most useful when you have a subtle sound effect, such as the sound of waves crashing, that you want to continue for as long as you leave the slide visible. To loop an audio clip, just select the Loop Until Stopped check box found in the Audio Options group.

Hiding the sound icon

By default, the icon representing an audio clip is visible on the slide during your slide show. Assuming that you have set the sound to play automatically, you probably don't want the icon visible.

The Audio Options group includes a check box titled Hide While Not Playing, but it hides the icon only when the sound is not playing; the icon is visible when the sound is playing.

The easiest way to get the icon off of your slides altogether is to simply drag the icon off the edge of the slide that contains it. The sound will still be a part of the slide, so it will play automatically when the slide is displayed. But because the icon is off the edge of the slide, it won't be visible to your audience.

Fading the sound in and out

The Fade In and Fade Out controls let you gradually fade your audio clip in and out. By default, these controls are both set to 0, so the audio clip begins and ends at full volume. By changing either or both of these controls to a value such as 2 or 3 seconds, you can smoothly fade the sound in or out for a more subtle effect.

Trimming an audio clip

Clicking the Trim Audio button brings up the Trim Audio dialog box, shown in Figure 15-4. This dialog box enables you to select just a portion of the audio clip to play in your presentation by letting you choose start and end times. You can choose the start and end times by dragging the green start pointer or the red end pointer over the image of the audio file's waveform. Or, you can enter the time (in seconds) in the Start Time and End Time boxes.

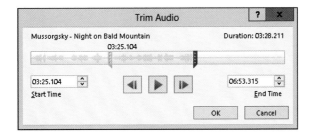

Figure 15-4: The Trim Audio dialog box.

Adding Video to Your Slides

Welcome to the MTV era of computing. If your computer has the chutzpah, you can add small video clips to your presentations and play them at will. I'm not sure why you would want to, but hey, who needs a reason?

Adding a movie motion clip to a slide is similar to adding a sound clip. A crucial difference exists, however, between motion clips and sound bites: Video is meant to be *seen* (and sometimes *heard*). An inserted motion clip should be given ample space on your slide.

If you think that sound files are big, wait till you see how big motion clips are. Ha! They consume hard drive space the way an elephant consumes veggies. The whole multimedia revolution is really a conspiracy started by hard drive manufacturers. (Be aware that you may have trouble sending a PowerPoint presentation bloated with large video files to your friends and colleagues via e-mail because many e-mail servers have limits on the size of e-mail attachments.)

The following steps show you how to add a video clip to a slide:

1. **Find a good movie and, if needed, download it or upload it to your hard drive.**

   The hardest part about using video in a PowerPoint presentation is finding a video file that's worth showing. Use Google or any other search service to find a video to insert. Then, download the video to your computer. Or, you can create your own videos using a camcorder and video-editing software.

2. **Move to the slide on which you want to insert the movie.**

   Hopefully, you left a big blank space on the slide to put the movie in. If not, rearrange the existing slide objects to make room for the movie.

3. **Open the Insert tab on the Ribbon, click Video in the Media group, and then choose Video on My PC.**

   The Insert Video dialog box, shown in Figure 15-5, appears.

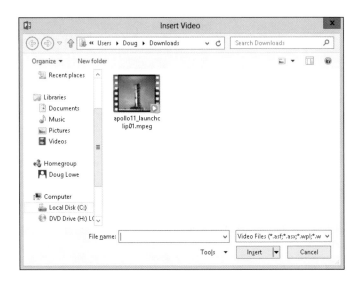

Figure 15-5: Inserting a video.

4. **Select the movie that you want to insert.**

   You may need to scroll the list to find the movie you're looking for or navigate your way to a different folder.

5. **Click the Insert button.**

   The movie is inserted on the slide, as shown in Figure 15-6.

6. **Resize the movie if you want and drag it to a new location on the slide.**

   When you resize the movie, try to do it by using one of the corner handles. If you drag one of the side handles, you distort the image.

   To play the movie while you're working on the presentation in Normal View, double-click the movie. During a slide show, a single click does the trick, unless you set the movie to play automatically. In that case, the movie runs as soon as you display the slide.

You can also insert a directly from an online source by choosing Online Video rather than Video on My PC in Step 3. Then, you can search for a video online. Note that this option inserts a link to the online video, not the video itself. That means that you must have a working network connection to play the video, and if the owner of the video removes the video, the link won't work.

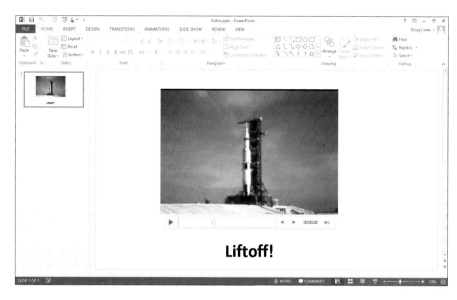

Figure 15-6: A movie inserted on a slide.

Setting Video Options

You can set various options for playing video files via the Video Tools Playback tab on the Ribbon, shown in Figure 15-7. As you can see, this tab contains several controls that let you edit the way the sound file is played. The following sections explain how to use the most important of these tools.

Figure 15-7: The Video Tools Playback tab.

Controlling when a video is played

By default, videos play when you click the Play button that appears beneath the video frame. If you want the video to start automatically when you display the slide, change the option in the Start drop-down list (found in the Video Options group on the Video Tools Edit tab) from On Click to Automatically.

Looping a video

If the video is short, you may want to repeat it over and over again until you move to the next slide. To do so, select the Loop Until Stopped check box found in the Video Options group.

Trimming a video clip

The Trim Video button summons the Trim Video dialog box, which is shown in Figure 15-8. Here, you can select the portion of the video clip you want to play in your presentation. You can choose the start and end points of the video by dragging the start pointer or the red end pointer over the image of the video's soundtrack wave, which appears immediately beneath the video frame. Or, you can enter the time (in seconds) in the Start Time and End Time boxes.

Figure 15-8: The Trim Video dialog box.

Playing the video full screen

If you want the video to take over the entire screen, select the Play Full Screen check box. Note that this option works best for high-quality videos. If the video is of lower quality, it may not look good when played in full-screen mode.

Fading the video's sound in and out

The Fade In and Fade Out controls for video clips work just as they do for audio clips (described earlier in this chapter). In other words, they affect the video's sound track, not the video image itself. You can use these controls to gradually fade the video's sound in and out.

Adding a bookmark

A *bookmark* is a marked location within the playback of a video file that can be used to trigger an animation effect. For example, a few seconds into the video of the Apollo 11 launch shown in the previous two figures, the announcer says "Liftoff!" and the rocket begins to rise. It's a simple matter to create a bookmark at that exact point in the video playback. Then, you can use that bookmark to trigger an animation that causes the word "Liftoff!" to appear beneath the video, as shown in Figure 15-9.

Figure 15-9: Using a bookmark to trigger an animation effect.

Here are the steps for creating a video bookmark and animating an object when the video playback reaches the bookmark:

1. **Add a video to the slide.**

    For this example, I added a video of the Apollo 11 launch that I downloaded from the Internet.

2. **Select the video object and then select the Video Tools Playback tab.**

    This tab was shown earlier in Figure 15-7.

3. **Click the Play button that appears beneath the video frame.**

   The video begins to play.

Add
Bookmark

4. **When the video reaches the point where you want to insert the book-mark, click the Add Bookmark button on the Playback tab (shown in the margin).**

   The bookmark is created; a small dot appears in the progress bar that appears beneath the video frame to mark the location of the bookmark.

5. **Click the Stop button beneath the video frame to stop the video.**

6. **Create an object on the slide that you will animate when the book-mark is reached during playback.**

   For this example, I created a text box with the text "Liftoff!"

7. **Click the Animations tab.**

8. **Select the object you created in Step 6 and then click the Add Animation button in the Animations tab. Select the animation effect you want.**

   For this example, I chose the Appear effect to cause the object to appear.

9. **Click the Trigger button on the Animations tab, choose On Bookmark, and then choose the bookmark you created in Step 4.**

   Doing this sets up the animation so that it is triggered automatically when the bookmark in the video is reached.

   You're done!

Here are a few additional points to ponder concerning bookmarks:

✔ You can create more than one bookmark in a single video. Each book-mark can be used as an animation trigger.

Remove
Bookmark

✔ To remove a bookmark, click the small circle that represents the book-mark in the video's slider bar. Then click the Remove Bookmark button in the Ribbon (shown in the margin).

✔ For more information about creating animations, refer to Chapter 9.

More Things to Insert on Your Slides

*T*he Insert tab on the Ribbon is chock-full of goodies you can insert into your presentations. The most important of these goodies have already been covered in other chapters: pictures clip art (Chapter 11), shapes (Chapter 12), SmartArt (Chapter 14), and movies and sounds (Chapter 15).

But you can insert a lot more, including tables, WordArt, hyperlinks, and actions. This chapter covers these items.

Inserting Tables

Tables are a great way to present lots of information in an orderly fashion. For example, if you want to create a slide that shows how many people like or hate various computer presentation programs, a table is the way to go. Or if you're considering purchasing some new computer equipment and want to list the prices for five different computer configurations from three different vendors, a table is the best way.

Creating a table in a Content placeholder

Basic tables are simple to create in PowerPoint. The easiest way to create a slide that contains a table is to use the Title and Content slide layout. Just follow these steps:

1. **Open the Home tab on the Ribbon and then click the New Slide button in the Slides group to add a slide with the Title and Content layout.**

   A new slide is created.

2. **Click the Table icon in the center of the Content placeholder.**

   The Insert Table dialog box appears, as shown in Figure 16-1.

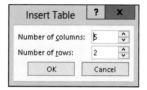

Figure 16-1: The Insert Table dialog box.

3. **Set the number of rows and columns you want for the table and then click OK.**

   The table appears, as shown in Figure 16-2.

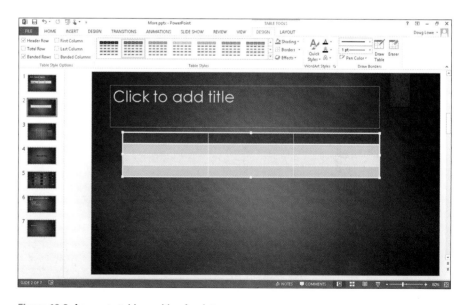

Figure 16-2: An empty table, waiting for data.

4. **Type information into the table's cells.**

   You can click any cell in the table and start typing. Or you can move from cell to cell by pressing the Tab key or the arrow keys.

5. **Play with the formatting if you want.**

   You can use Table Tools on the Ribbon, described later in this section, to control the formatting for the table.

6. **Stop and smell the roses.**

   When you're done, you're done. Admire your work.

Figure 16-3 shows an example of a finished table.

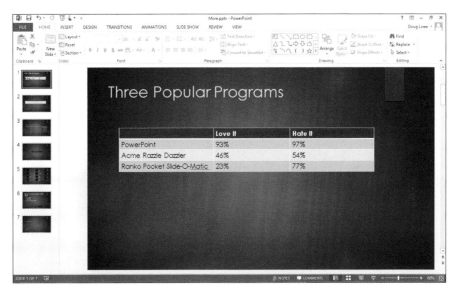

Figure 16-3: A finished table.

Inserting a table on a slide

You can use the Table button on the Insert tab to insert a table on an existing slide. When you click this button, a gridlike menu appears that enables you to select the size of the table you want to create, as shown in Figure 16-4. You can use this technique to create a table as large as ten columns and eight rows.

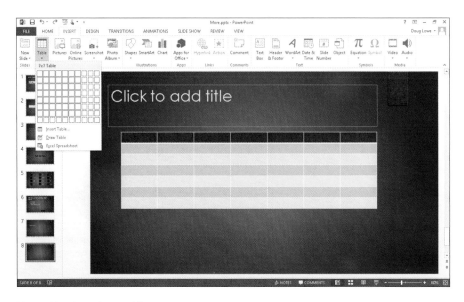

Figure 16-4: Inserting a table.

Drawing a table

A third way to create a table is to use the Draw Table command. The Draw Table command lets you draw complicated tables onscreen by using a simple set of drawing tools. This command is ideal for creating tables that are not a simple grid of rows and columns, but rather a complex conglomeration in which some cells span more than one row and others span more than one column.

Here's the procedure for creating a table by using the Draw Table tool:

1. **On the Insert tab on the Ribbon, click the Table button in the Tables group and then choose Draw Table from the menu that appears.**

   PowerPoint changes the cursor to a little pencil.

2. **Draw the overall shape of the table by dragging the mouse to create a rectangular boundary for the table.**

   When you release the mouse button, a table with a single cell is created, as shown in Figure 16-5. Notice also in this figure that Table Tools is displayed on the Ribbon.

Draw
Table

3. **Click the Draw Table button in the Table Tools Design tab (shown in the margin).**

   The mouse pointer changes into a little pencil when you click this button.

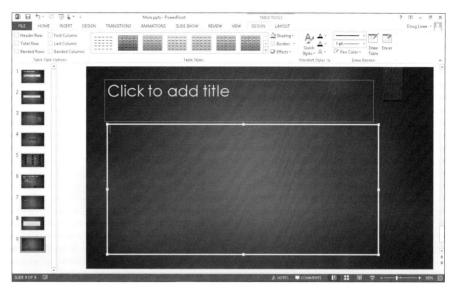

Figure 16-5: Drawing a table.

4. **Carve the table into smaller cells.**

   To do that, just drag lines across the table. For example, to split the table into two rows, point the cursor somewhere along the left edge of the table and then click and drag a line across the table to the right edge. When you release the mouse button, the table splits into two rows.

   You can continue to carve the table into smaller and smaller cells. For each slice, point the cursor at one edge of where you want the new cell to begin and click and drag to the other edge.

5. **If you want to change the line size or style drawn for a particular segment, use the Pen Style and Pen Weight drop-down controls in the Draw Borders group on the Table Tools Design tab.**

   You can change the style of a line you've already drawn by tracing over the line with a new style.

6. **If you make a mistake while drawing the table cells, click the Eraser (the one that looks like an eraser) button in the Draw Borders group and erase the mistaken line segment.**

   Or, just press Ctrl+Z or click the Undo button on the Quick Access Toolbar.

   If you want to draw additional segments after using the Erase tool, click the Draw Table button.

The most common mistake I make when drawing table cells is to accidentally create diagonal borders. If you make this common mistake, just press Ctrl+Z or click the Undo button, or use the eraser to erase the diagonal border.

7. When you're done, click outside of the table to finish drawing the table.

Figure 16-6 shows a table carved up into several cells, with various types of line styles and line weights.

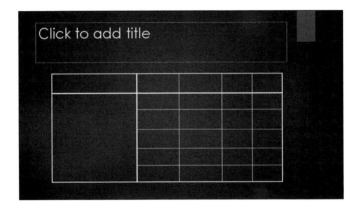

Figure 16-6: A finished table.

Applying style to a table

After you've created a table, you can set its style by using the controls under Table Tools on the Ribbon. The easiest way to format a table is by applying one of PowerPoint's predefined table styles.

Before you apply a style, however, use the check boxes that appear at the left side of the Design tab under Table Tools on the Ribbon. These check boxes determine whether PowerPoint uses special formatting for certain parts of the table:

- **Header Row:** Indicates whether the style should format the first row differently than the other rows in the table

- **Total Row:** Indicates whether the style should format the last row differently than the other rows in the table

- **Banded Rows:** Indicates whether alternating rows should be formatted differently

- **First Column:** Indicates whether the style should format the first column differently than the other column in the table

✔ **Last Column:** Indicates whether the style should format the last column differently than the other columns in the table

✔ **Banded Columns:** Indicates whether alternating columns should be formatted differently

After you've set the Quick Style options, you can apply a Table Style to the table by clicking the style you want to apply (refer to Figure 16-5). If the style doesn't appear in the Table Styles group under Table Tools on the Ribbon, click the More button to reveal the Table Styles gallery, shown in Figure 16-7. This gallery displays all the built-in styles provided with PowerPoint.

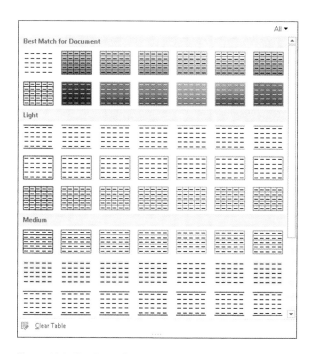

Figure 16-7: The Table Styles gallery.

In addition to using one of the preselected table styles, you can format each cell and line in your table by using the following controls under Table Tools:

✔ **Shading:** Sets the background color for the selected cells.

✔ **Borders:** Lets you control which edges of the selected cells have borders.

✔ **Effects:** Applies bevels, shadows, and reflections. (Note that you can apply bevels to individual cells, but shadows and reflections apply to the entire table.)

Working with the Layout tab

When you select a table, a special Layout tab is available, as shown in Figure 16-8. The controls on this tab let you adjust the layout of your table in various ways. Table 16-1 lists the function of each of these controls.

Figure 16-8: The Layout tab under Table Tools.

Table 16-1		The Layout Tab
Control	*Name*	*What It Does*
Select	Select	Activates the Selection cursor so you can select cells
View Gridlines	View Gridlines	Shows or hides table gridlines
Delete	Delete	Deletes a row, a column, or the entire table
Insert Above	Insert Above	Inserts a new row above the current row
Insert Below	Insert Below	Inserts a new row below the current row

Control	Name	What It Does
Insert Left	Insert Left	Inserts a new column to the left of the current column
Insert Right	Insert Right	Inserts a new column to the right of the current column
Merge Cells	Merge Cells	Merges adjacent cells to create one large cell
Split Cells	Split Cells	Splits a merged cell into separate cells
Height:	Height	Sets the row height
Width:	Width	Sets the column width
Distribute Rows	Distribute Rows	Adjusts the height of the selected rows to distribute the rows evenly
Distribute Columns	Distribute Columns	Adjusts the width of the selected columns to distribute the columns evenly
	Align Left	Left-aligns the text
	Center	Centers the text

(continued)

Table 16-1 *(continued)*

Control	Name	What It Does
	Align Right	Right-aligns the text
	Align Top	Vertically aligns the text with the top of the cell
	Align Middle	Vertically aligns the text with the middle of the cell
	Align Bottom	Vertically aligns the text with the bottom of the cell
Text Direction	Text Direction	Changes the direction of text in a cell
Cell Margins	Margins	Sets the cell margins
Height:	Height	Sets the overall height of the table
Width:	Width	Sets the overall height of the table
Lock Aspect Ratio	Lock Aspect Ratio	Fixes the ratio between height and width so that when you change the height or width individually, both values are adjusted to maintain the same ratio
Bring Forward	Bring Forward	Brings the table to the front of the slide
Send Backward	Send Backward	Sends the table to the back of the slide
Selection Pane	Selection Pane	Displays a selection task pane that lists the objects you can select on the slide
Align	Align	Aligns the table on the slide
Group	Group	Groups selected objects
Rotate	Rotate	Rotates and flips objects

Inserting WordArt

In Chapter 7, you discover how to apply WordArt formatting to any bit of text in PowerPoint 2013. WordArt also appears on the Insert tab on the Ribbon, which provides a convenient way to insert a text box with text that is already formatted with WordArt formatting.

To insert WordArt, follow these steps:

1. **Move to the slide on which you want to insert WordArt.**

2. **Click the Insert tab on the Ribbon and then click the WordArt button in the Text group.**

   A gallery of WordArt styles is displayed, as shown in Figure 16-9.

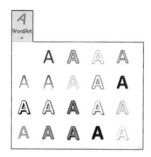

Figure 16-9: The WordArt gallery.

3. **Select the WordArt style you want to use.**

   The WordArt text box is inserted on the slide, as shown in Figure 16-10.

4. **Click the WordArt text box and then type the text you want to use.**

5. **Apply any other WordArt formatting you want.**

   For more information about WordArt formatting, refer to Chapter 7.

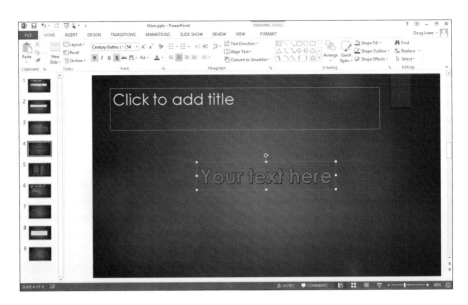

Figure 16-10: A WordArt text box.

Using Hyperlinks

In PowerPoint, a *hyperlink* is simply a bit of text or a graphic image that you can click when viewing a slide to summon another slide, another presentation, or perhaps some other type of document, such as a Word document or an Excel spreadsheet. The hyperlink may also lead to a page on the World Wide Web.

For example, suppose that you have a slide that contains a chart of sales trends. You can place a hyperlink on the slide that, if clicked during a slide show, summons another slide presenting the same data in the form of a table. That slide can in turn contain a hyperlink that, when clicked, summons an Excel spreadsheet that contains the detailed data on which the chart is based.

Another common use for hyperlinks is to create a table of contents for your presentation. You can create a slide — usually the first or second slide in the presentation — that contains links to other slides in the presentation. The table of contents slide may include a link to every slide in the presentation, but more likely, it contains links to selected slides. For example, if a presentation contains several sections of slides, the table of contents slide may contain links to the first slide in each section.

Hyperlinks are not limited to slides in the current presentation. Hyperlinks can lead to other presentations. When you use this kind of hyperlink, a person viewing the slide show clicks the hyperlink, and PowerPoint automatically loads the indicated presentation. The hyperlink can lead to the first slide in the presentation, or it can lead to a specific slide within the presentation.

A common use for this type of hyperlink is to create a menu of presentations that can be viewed. For example, suppose that you have created the following four presentations:

- The Detrimental Effects of Pool
- Case Studies in Communities Destroyed by Pool Halls
- Marching Bands through the Ages
- Understanding the Think System

You can easily create a slide that lists all four presentations and contains hyperlinks to them. The person viewing the slide show simply clicks a hyperlink, and off he or she goes to the appropriate presentation.

Here are a few additional thoughts to ponder concerning hyperlinks:

- **Hyperlinks aren't limited to PowerPoint presentations.** In PowerPoint, you can create a hyperlink that leads to other types of Microsoft Office documents, such as Word documents or Excel spreadsheets. When the person viewing the slide show clicks one of these hyperlinks, PowerPoint automatically runs Word or Excel to open the document or spreadsheet.

- **A hyperlink can also lead to a page on the World Wide Web.** When the user clicks the hyperlink, PowerPoint runs Internet Explorer to connect to the Internet and displays the web page.

- **Hyperlinks work only when the presentation is shown in Slide Show View.** You can click a hyperlink all you want while in Outline View or Slide Sorter View, and the only thing that happens is that your finger gets tired. Links are active when viewing the slide show. In Normal View, you can activate a link by right-clicking it and choosing Open Hyperlink.

Creating a hyperlink to another slide

Adding a hyperlink to a presentation is easy. Just follow these steps:

1. **Select the text or graphic object that you want to make into a hyperlink.**

   The most common type of hyperlink is based on a word or two of text in a slide's body text area.

2. **Choose Insert⟶Links⟶Hyperlink.**

   Alternatively, click the Insert Hyperlink button found on the standard toolbar or use the keyboard shortcut Ctrl+K. One way or the other, the Insert Hyperlink dialog box, shown in Figure 16-11, appears.

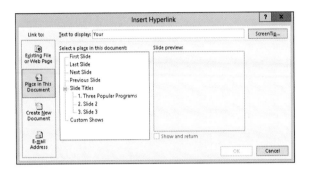

Figure 16-11: The Insert Hyperlink dialog box.

The dialog box has four icons on the left side, as follows:

- *Existing File or Web Page:* You can link to another file in another application, or to a web page on the Internet.
- *Place in This Document:* You can link one part of your PowerPoint presentation to another part.
- *Create New Document:* You can, however, choose now or another time to edit the new document by clicking the appropriate button.
- *E-mail Address:* Use this to link to an e-mail address. This feature is useful in an intranet or Internet setting because this link allows the reader to write an e-mail to the e-mail address that you link to.

3. **Click the Place in This Document icon on the left side of the dialog box.**

   A list of the slides in the current presentation appears in the dialog box.

4. **Click the slide that you want the hyperlink to lead to and then click OK.**

   The Insert Hyperlink dialog box vanishes, and the hyperlink is created.

If you selected text in Step 1, the text changes color and is underlined. If you selected a graphical object, the picture isn't highlighted in any way to indicate that it is a hyperlink. However, the cursor always changes to a pointing hand whenever it passes over a hyperlink in Slide Show View or Reading View, thus providing a visual clue that the user has found a hyperlink.

Creating a hyperlink to another presentation or to a website

Creating a hyperlink that opens another presentation is much like the procedure described in the preceding section, "Creating a hyperlink to another slide," but with a couple important differences:

1. **Select the text or graphical object that you want to make into a hyperlink.**

2. **Click the Hyperlink button in the Links group on the Insert tab.**

   The Insert Hyperlink dialog box appears (refer to Figure 16-11).

3. **Click the Existing File or Web Page icon in the list of icons on the left side of the dialog box.**

   You can also link to a specific slide within another presentation by clicking the Bookmark button in the Insert Hyperlink dialog box. This brings up another dialog box listing the slides in the selected presentation. Choose the slide you want to link to; then click OK to return to the Insert Hyperlink dialog box.

4. **Click Current Folder.**

5. **Select the file that you want to link to.**

   You might have to rummage about your hard drive to find the presentation.

   The presentation that you link to doesn't have to be in the same folder or even on the same drive as the current presentation. In fact, you can link to a presentation that resides on a network file server.

6. **Click OK.**

When you follow a link to another presentation, PowerPoint automatically opens the other presentation. This means that you now have both presentations open. When you're finished viewing the second presentation, close it to return to the original presentation.

If you want to create a hyperlink to an existing web page, just type the address of the web page in your outline or on your slide and a hyperlink automatically appears. You can select any page of a website as long as you know the URL for that specific page.

To remove a hyperlink, right-click the hyperlink that you want to zap and then choose Remove Hyperlink from the menu that appears. To change a hyperlink, right-click it and choose Edit Hyperlink.

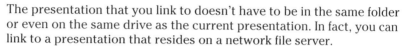

Adding Action Buttons

An *action button* is a special type of AutoShape that places a button on the slide. When the user clicks the button during a slide show, PowerPoint takes whatever action you've designated for the button. A well-planned arrangement of action buttons scattered throughout a presentation can make it easy for someone to view the presentation in any order he or she wants.

The following sections describe how action buttons work and show you how to add them to your presentations.

Assigning button actions

When you create an action button, you assign both a shape for the button (you have 12 shapes to choose from; the shapes are described a bit later in this section) and an action to be taken when the user clicks the button or merely points the cursor at it. The action for a button can be any of the following:

- ✔ **Activate a hyperlink:** This is the most common button action. It causes a different slide in the current presentation, a different presentation altogether, a non-PowerPoint document, or even an Internet web page to appear.

- ✔ **Run a program:** For example, you can set up a button that runs Microsoft Word or Excel.

- ✔ **Run a macro:** PowerPoint lets you create *macros,* which are programs written in a powerful programming language called Visual Basic for Applications.

- ✔ **Play a sound:** This is just one way to add sound to a PowerPoint presentation. For more ways, refer to Chapter 15.

Choosing button shapes

PowerPoint provides a selection of built-in shapes for action buttons. Table 16-2 lists the action button shapes that you can place in your presentation and indicates what type of action is associated with each type.

Table 16-2		Action Buttons
Button Image	**Name**	**What the Button Does**
◀	Back or Previous	Displays the preceding slide in the presentation
▶	Forward or Next	Displays the next slide in the presentation
◀▏	Beginning	Displays the first slide in the presentation
▶▏	End	Displays the last slide in the presentation

Button Image	**Name**	**What the Button Does**
	Home	Displays the first slide in the presentation
	Information	No default action for this button type
	Return	Displays the most recently viewed slide
	Movie	No default action for this button type
	Document	No default action for this button type
	Sound	No default action for this button type
	Help	No default action for this button type
	Custom	No default action for this button type

Creating a button

To add a button to a slide, follow these steps:

1. **Move to the slide on which you want to place a button.**

2. **Open the Insert tab on the Ribbon, click the Shapes button in the Illustrations group, and select one of the Action Button shapes found at the bottom of the gallery that appears.**

3. **Draw the button on the slide.**

Start by pointing to the spot where you want the upper-left corner of the button to appear. Then click and drag to where you want the lower-right corner of the button to appear.

When you release the mouse button, the Action Settings dialog box appears, as shown in Figure 16-12.

Figure 16-12: The Action Settings dialog box.

4. **If you want, change the action settings for the action button.**

   In most cases, the default setting for the action button that you chose is appropriate for what you want the button to do. For example, the action setting for a Forward or Next button is Hyperlink to Next Slide. If you want the slide to hyperlink to some other location, change the Hyperlink To setting.

5. **Click OK.**

   The Action Settings dialog box vanishes, and the button is created.

Here are some additional thoughts concerning action buttons:

- **Change the look of a button:** You can format action buttons like any other shape object. Therefore, you can use Drawing Tools on the Ribbon to apply fill colors, line styles, or shape effects such as bevels and 3-D rotations. For more information, refer to Chapter 12.

- **Move a button:** To move a button, just click it to select it. Then use the mouse to drag the button to a new location.

✔ **Change the action setting for a button:** You can change the action setting for a button by right-clicking the button and choosing the Action Settings command.

Creating a navigation toolbar

Grouping action buttons into a navigation toolbar makes a slide show easy to navigate. You can add a set of navigation buttons to the bottom of your Slide Master. Figure 16-13 shows a slide with navigation buttons in the lower-right corner. These buttons make getting around the show a snap. For this example, I use Beginning, Backward (Previous), Forward (Next), and Ending buttons, but you can include any buttons you want.

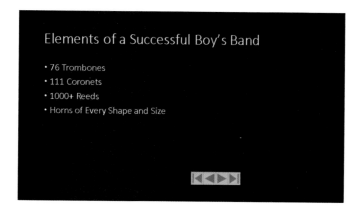

Figure 16-13: A slide with navigation buttons.

To create a navigation toolbar that appears on every slide, follow these steps:

1. **Switch to Slide Master View.**

   From the View tab on the Ribbon, click the Slide Master button in the Presentation Views group. Or if you like shortcuts, hold down the Shift key and click the Normal View button in the lower-left corner of the PowerPoint window.

2. **Create the action buttons that you want to include.**

   Follow the procedure described in the preceding section, "Creating a button," to create each button. Make sure that all the buttons are the same size and line them up to create a tight cluster of buttons.

You can easily duplicate a button by holding down the Ctrl key while you drag the button to a new location. This technique makes it easy to create several similar buttons, such as navigation buttons.

3. **Return to Normal View.**

Click the Normal View button or click the Normal button in the Presentation Views group on the View tab.

The buttons that you created appear on every slide in your presentation.

Inserting Equations

Steven Hawking has said that his editor told him that every mathematical equation he included in his classic book *A Brief History of Time* would cut the book's sales in half. So he included just one: the classic $e=mc^2$. See how easy that equation was to type? The only trick was remembering how to format the little 2 as a superscript.

My editor promised me that every equation I included in this book would double its sales, but I didn't believe her, not even for a nanosecond. Just in case, Figure 16-14 shows some examples of the equations you can create by using PowerPoint's handy-dandy Equation feature. You wouldn't even consider using ordinary text to try to create these equations, but they took me only a few minutes to create with the Equation tool. Aren't they cool? Tell all your friends about the cool equations you saw in this book so that they'll all rush out and buy copies for themselves.

You don't have to know anything about math to use PowerPoint. I don't have a clue what most of the equations in Figure 16-14 do, but they sure look great, don't they?

Don't forget to tell your friends how great the equations in Figure 16-14 are. Those alone are worth the price of the book.

$$A = \pi r^2$$

$$(x + a)^n = \sum_{k=0}^{n} \binom{n}{k} x^k a^{n-k}$$

$$(1 + x)^n = 1 + \frac{nx}{1!} + \frac{n(n-1)x^2}{2!} + \cdots$$

$$f(x) = a_0 + \sum_{n=1}^{\infty} \left(a_n \cos \frac{n\pi x}{L} + b_n \sin \frac{n\pi x}{L} \right)$$

$$a^2 + b^2 = c^2$$

$$x = \frac{-b \pm \sqrt{b^2 - 4ac}}{2a}$$

$$e^x = 1 + \frac{x}{1!} + \frac{x^2}{2!} + \frac{x^3}{3!} + \cdots , \qquad -\infty < x < \infty$$

$$\sin \alpha \pm \sin \beta = 2 \sin \frac{1}{2}(\alpha \pm \beta) \cos \frac{1}{2}(\alpha \mp \beta)$$

$$\cos \alpha + \cos \beta = 2 \cos \frac{1}{2}(\alpha + \beta) \cos \frac{1}{2}(\alpha - \beta)$$

Figure 16-14: These equations will probably not affect the sales of this book one way or another.

To add an equation to a slide, follow these steps:

1. **Click the Insert tab of the Ribbon and then click the Equation button to reveal the gallery of equations, as shown in Figure 16-15.**

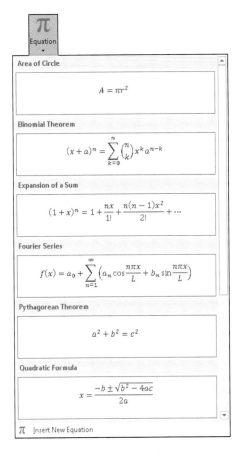

Figure 16-15: Inserting an equation.

2. **If one of the preformatted equations in the gallery meets your needs, select it. Otherwise, select Insert New Equation found at the bottom of the gallery.**

The rest of this procedure assumes that you've chosen to insert a new equation. A placeholder for the equation appears in the slide, and the Equation Tools Design tab appears on the Ribbon, as shown in Figure 16-16.

3. **Start typing your equation.**

PowerPoint watches any text you type in an equation and does its level best to figure out how the text should be formatted. If you type the letter **x**, for example, PowerPoint assumes that you intend for it to be a variable, so the x is displayed in italics. If you type **cos**, PowerPoint assumes that you mean the cosine function, so the text is not italicized. If you use the mathematical operators +, −, *, and /, PowerPoint will automatically format them using the equivalent equation symbols.

Don't worry about how the equation is formatted. When you press Enter, PowerPoint formats the equation automatically. For example, suppose you enter the following:

a = (b + 2c) / 2b

When you press Enter, the equation is formatted as follows:

$$a = \frac{b+2c}{2b}$$

4. **To add a symbol that's not on the keyboard, use one of the buttons in the Symbols section of the Equation Tools Design tab.**

The Symbols section contains a gallery of mathematical symbols most of which only Robert Oppenheimer could understand. To use this gallery, first click the More button in the bottom-right corner of the Symbols section. Then choose the symbol category from the drop-down menu that appears at the top of the gallery. For example, Figure 16-17 shows the Operators gallery. Additional galleries contain basic math symbols, Greek letters, negated relations, and other obscure symbols.

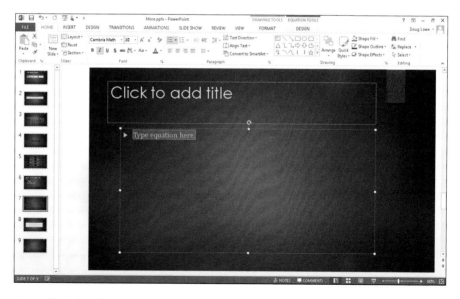

Figure 16-16: Creating a new equation.

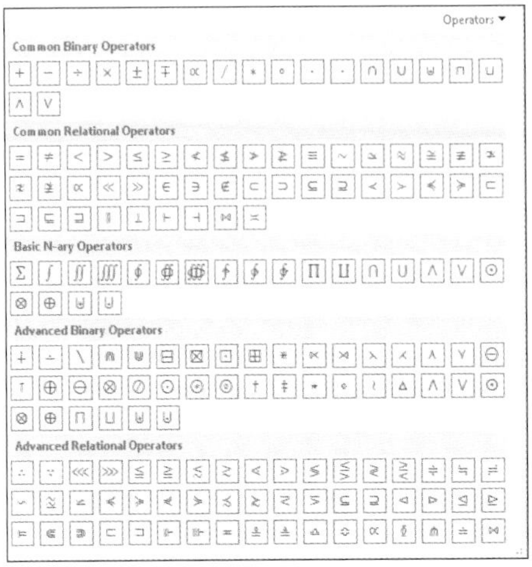

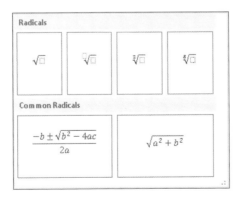

Figure 16-17: The Operators symbol gallery.

5. **To create symbols stacked upon each other in various ways, use the controls in the Structures section of the Equation Tools Design tab.**

   Each button in the Structures section reveals a gallery of structures that you can use to create equations with stacked symbols. Most structures include a symbol and one or more slots, in which you type text or insert other symbols or other structures. For example, Figure 16-18 shows the gallery of templates that are displayed when you click the Radical button. These structures let you insert a square-root sign along with slots in front of and inside the sign.

Radicals

$$\sqrt{\square} \qquad \sqrt[2]{\square} \qquad \sqrt[3]{\square} \qquad \sqrt[8]{\square}$$

Common Radicals

$$\frac{-b \pm \sqrt{b^2 - 4ac}}{2a} \qquad \sqrt{a^2 + b^2}$$

Figure 16-18: The Radical structures gallery.

6. **When you're done, click outside of the equation to return to the slide.**

Confused? I don't blame you. After you latch on to the idea behind structures, you can slap together even the most complex equations in no time. But the learning curve here is steep. Stick with it.

Here are a few additional points to keep in mind when editing equations:

✏ Spend some time exploring the symbols and structures available on the Equation Tools Design tab. There's enough stuff here to create a presentation on how to build your own atomic bomb. (None of the equations in Figure 16-14 have anything to do with atomic bombs. Honest.)

✏ Don't use the spacebar to separate elements in an equation — let PowerPoint worry about how much space to leave between the variables and the plus signs. The only time you should use the spacebar is when you're typing two or more words of text and you need the space to separate the words.

✏ The Enter key has an interesting behavior in an equation: It adds a new equation slot, immediately beneath the current slot. This technique is sometimes a good way to create stacked items.

✏ The denominator is the bottom part of a fraction, not an Arnold Schwarzenegger movie.

Part IV
Working with Others

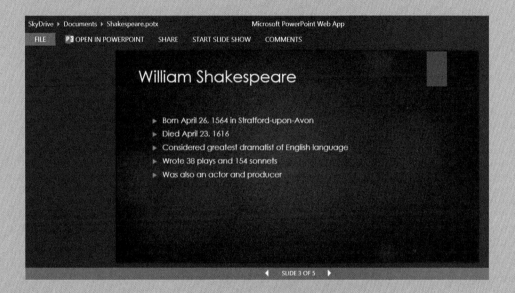

In this part . . .

- Find out about the several simple PowerPoint tools that let you distribute your presentation to others and allow others to add comments to the presentation so you can get their feedback.

- Understand how to reuse slides, including how to set up and use a slide library.

- Discover how to use a variety of PowerPoint features that let you save your presentations in formats other than the standard PowerPoint file format.

- Learn how to add comments to a slide when working collaboratively with others on a presentation at `www.dummies.com/extras/powerpoint2013`.

# 17

Collaborating in the Cloud

*"W*orks well with others" is more than standard fare for rookie resumes. It's also one of the PowerPoint mantras. Many presentations are designed not by and for a single presenter, but by a team of presenters. Fortunately, PowerPoint includes several simple tools that let you distribute your presentation to others and allow others to add comments to the presentation so you can get their feedback.

This chapter shows you how to use those features.

Sharing a Presentation in the Cloud

Recently, the term *cloud computing* has become one of the most popular of all computer buzzwords. Cloud computing refers to the idea of not being limited to local computer resources (such as disc storage or CPU cycles), but instead taking advantage of the nearly limitless resources that are available to you via *the cloud* (aka the Internet).

Microsoft has integrated cloud computing into PowerPoint 2013 by providing its own dedicated cloud storage resource, called *SkyDrive,* and designating it as one of the primary places you can store your PowerPoint presentations. When you install Office 2013, you are given the opportunity to create a free SkyDrive account that offers up to 7GB of free cloud storage, with the capability to purchase additional storage.

In addition to storing PowerPoint presentations on SkyDrive, you can also share your presentations with other SkyDrive users so that you can collaboratively view and edit your work. Before you can share a presentation with another user, you must first save the presentation to your SkyDrive account. To do so, just follow these steps:

1. **Choose File➪Save As.**

   The Save As page appears, which offers several locations to which the presentation can be saved as shown in Figure 17-1. The default location is your SkyDrive account.

Figure 17-1: Saving a presentation.

2. **Click the Browse button.**

   The Save As dialog box appears, as shown in Figure 17-2. As you can see, this dialog box automatically navigates to your SkyDrive account's Documents folder.

3. **Navigate to another SkyDrive folder or create a new SkyDrive folder.**

   You can navigate SkyDrive as if it were a local hard drive. And you can create a new folder by clicking the New Folder button.

4. **Change the filename and then click Save.**

   The presentation is saved to your SkyDrive.

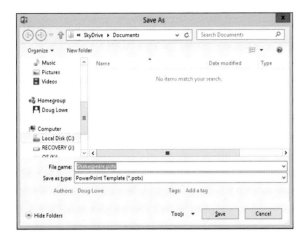

Figure 17-2: Browsing to your SkyDrive Documents folder.

Sharing a Presentation with Other Users

You can easily share a presentation with a friend or colleague by sending an invitation via e-mail. The invitation e-mail will include a link that will open the presentation in a web-based version of PowerPoint called the PowerPoint Web App. From the PowerPoint Web App, the user can view the presentation. If the user has PowerPoint installed on his or her computer, the user can also open the presentation in PowerPoint, edit the presentation, add comments (as described later in this chapter), and save the edited presentation in the original SkyDrive location.

Here are the steps to send an invitation:

1. **Save your presentation to SkyDrive.**

2. **Choose File⇨Share and then click Invite People.**

    The Invite People page appears, as shown in Figure 17-3. On this page, you can craft an e-mail message that will be sent to the people with whom you'd like to share the presentation.

3. **Type one or more e-mail addresses in the Type Names or E-mail Addresses text box.**

    If you have more than one e-mail address, just separate the addresses with commas or semicolons.

    You can click the Address Book icon to the right of the text box to bring up your address book. Then, you can select names from your address book rather than type the e-mail addresses manually.

Figure 17-3: Sending an invitation.

4. **Choose the sharing permission you want to grant.**

   The two options are Can Edit and Can View. Use the drop-down list to the right of the Address Book icon to select the permission.

5. **If you wish, type a message in the Include a Personal Message with the Invitation text box.**

   The message is included in the e-mail that is sent to the recipients.

6. **If you want to add extra security, select the Require User to Sign-In Before Accessing Document option.**

   If you select this option, users will have to log in to SkyDrive before they can access your presentation.

7. **Click Share.**

   A confirmation message appears, indicating that the e-mails have been sent.

Figure 17-4 shows a typical invitation e-mail.

To open a shared presentation in PowerPoint Web App, simply click the link in the invitation. Figure 17-5 shows a presentation opened in Web App. You can view the entire presentation in Web App, or you can open the presentation in PowerPoint by clicking the Open in PowerPoint button. (Note that to open the presentation in PowerPoint, you must have a copy of PowerPoint installed on your computer).

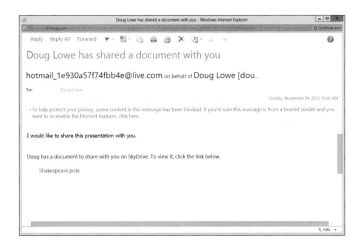

Figure 17-4: An invitation to a shared PowerPoint presentation.

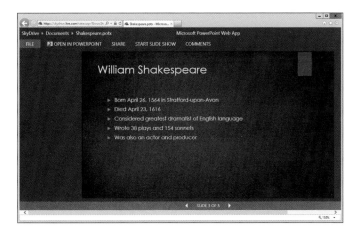

Figure 17-5: A shared presentation open in the PowerPoint Web App.

If you want to manually send your own e-mail with a link that allows users to view or edit your presentation, you can choose File➪Share➪Get a Link. This displays a page that allows you to create a View Link or an Edit Link, which you can then copy and paste as needed.

Sharing a Presentation on Social Networks

Another way to share a presentation is via a social network such as Facebook or Twitter. To do that, choose File➪Share➪Post to Social Networks. This displays the page shown in Figure 17-6, which lists the social networks that you have associated with your SkyDrive account. Select the permission option (Can View or Can Edit), add a personal message if you wish, and then click Post.

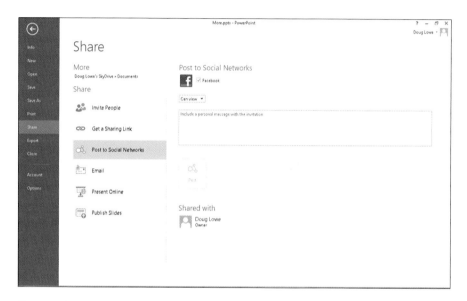

Figure 17-6: Sharing a presentation via social media.

Figure 17-7 shows how a PowerPoint presentation appears when posted on Facebook. Your friends can click the link to view or edit the presentation in the PowerPoint Web App.

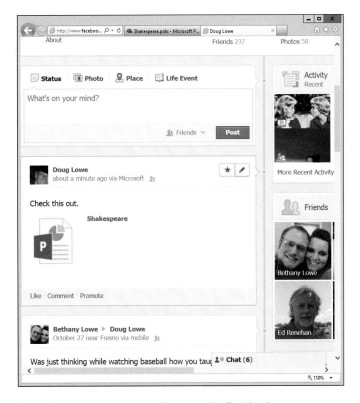

Figure 17-7: A shared presentation posted to Facebook.

Sending Slides for Review Via E-mail

Another way to share a presentation with colleagues is to simply e-mail them a copy of the presentation. PowerPoint includes a built-in feature for doing that. Here are the steps:

1. **Open the presentation that you want to send out for review.**

   If the presentation is already open, choose File⮕Save to save any changes you made since you opened it.

2. **Choose File⮕Share⮕Email.**

   PowerPoint displays the page shown in Figure 17-8, which offers five options for sending the file. The five options are

   - *Send as Attachment:* This is the most commonly used option. It simply creates an e-mail message with the presentation file inserted as an attachment.

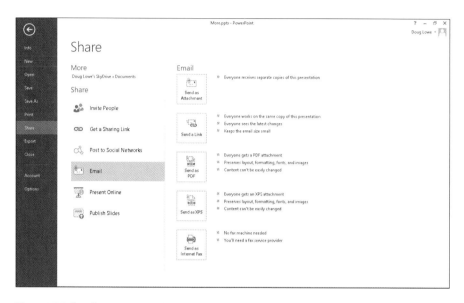

Figure 17-8: Sending a presentation via e-mail.

- *Send a link:* This option works best if you've saved the presentation to SkyDrive. It then creates an e-mail that contains a link that the recipient can click to open the presentation.

- *Send as PDF:* This option creates a PDF version of the presentation, and then creates an e-mail that contains the PDF version as an attachment.

- *Send as XPS:* This option creates an XPS version of the presentation (XPS is Microsoft's attempt at competing with PDF) and then creates an e-mail that contains the XPS version as an attachment.

- *Send as Internet Fax:* If you have an account with an Internet fax service, you can use this option to send a fax of your presentation. (This option would be more useful in today's world if it could also send your presentation back in time, so that, for example, the recipient would receive the fax in 1983 — when faxing was popular.)

3. Click the option you want to use to send the e-mail.

Outlook fires up and creates an e-mail message with the correct attachment or link, depending on which option you choose.

4. In the To field, add an e-mail address for each person to whom you want to send a review copy.

You can type the e-mail addresses directly into the To field, or you can click the To button to open the Address Book. You can then use the Address Book to select your reviewers.

If you want to send the presentation to more than one person, separate the e-mail addresses with semicolons.

5. **If you want, change the Subject field or message body.**

   By default, PowerPoint uses the filename as the message's subject and leaves the message body blank. You probably want to say something a little more cordial.

6. **Set any other e-mail options you want for the message.**

   Depending on the program you use for your e-mail, you have a bevy of options to set for e-mail messages, such as high or low priority, signatures, stationery, read receipts, plain or HTML formatting, and more.

7. **Click the Send button.**

   Your message is whisked away and will be delivered as soon as possible.

Using Comments

So far in this chapter, I've showed you several ways to share a presentation with others so that two or more people can collaborate on a document. But after the presentation has been shared, what exactly can you do to work collaboratively? In this section, I show you one of the best ways to collaborate — by adding comments to a presentation.

A comment is a lot like a sticky note. The beauty of comments is that you can turn them on and off. Therefore, you can view the comments while you're editing your presentation, and you can turn them off when it's time for the show.

To add a comment to a presentation, follow these steps:

1. **Call up the slide to which you want to add a comment.**

2. **Click where you want the comment to appear.**

   You can click anywhere in the slide.

3. **Open the Review tab on the Ribbon and then click the New Comment button.**

   A comment bubble appears on the slide, and the Comments task pane opens to the right of the slide.

4. **Type whatever you want in the Comment pane.**

   Offer some constructive criticism. Suggest an alternative approach. Or just comment on the weather. Figure 17-9 shows a completed comment.

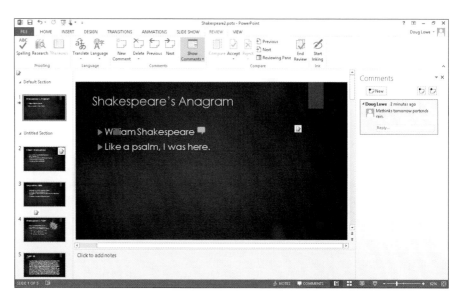

Figure 17-9: Creating a comment.

5. If you want, move the comment bubble.

You can move the comment closer to the slide item on which you're commenting by dragging the comment tag around the slide.

Here are some additional thoughts concerning working with comments:

- To view a comment, click the comment bubble.

- To change a comment, click the comment in the Comments pane and then edit the text in the comment until you're satisfied.

- You can move a comment by dragging it. Note that comments are not attached to any particular slide object or text. Therefore, if you move a comment near the text or object that the comment applies to and then edit the slide so that the text or object moves, the comment will *not* move along with the text or object. You have to manually move the comment if you want it to stay near the text or object it applies to.

- To delete a comment, click the comment to select it and then press Delete.

- To delete all the comments on a particular slide, click the down arrow beneath the Delete button on the Review tab. Then choose Delete All Markup on the Current Slide.

- To delete all the comments in a presentation, click the down arrow beneath the Delete button and choose Delete All Markup in This Presentation.

✓ You can quickly scan through all the comments in a PowerPoint presentation by using the Previous and Next buttons on the Review tab on the Ribbon.

✓ You can use the Show Comments button on the Review tab to show or hide comments from a presentation.

Comparing Presentations

The Compare feature lets you compare the differences between two versions of a presentation and accept or reject the differences. This feature is useful if you've sent a copy of the presentation to a reviewer and you want to selectively incorporate the reviewer's changes.

Using the Compare feature is easy. Here are the steps:

1. **Open the original version of the presentation.**

2. **On the Review tab of the Ribbon, click the Compare button.**

   A dialog box appears that lets you open the revised version of the presentation.

3. **Navigate to the revised version of the presentation, select it, and click Open.**

   This action opens the revised version of the presentation and merges the two presentations together, keeping track of the differences between the original presentation and the revised version.

   The differences between the original and the revised versions are highlighted, as shown in Figure 17-10. As you can see, the revisions are shown as check boxes, which allow you to select the individual changes you want to accept or reject. You can also select the All Changes . . . check box to accept or reject all the changes for a given object.

4. **Use the check boxes to select the changes you want to accept or reject; then click either Accept or Reject on the Review tab of the Ribbon.**

   If you click Accept, the selected changes are incorporated into the drawing. If you click Reject, the original version of the selected changes is restored.

5. **Click the Next button found in the Compare section of the Review tab to move to the next set of edits.**

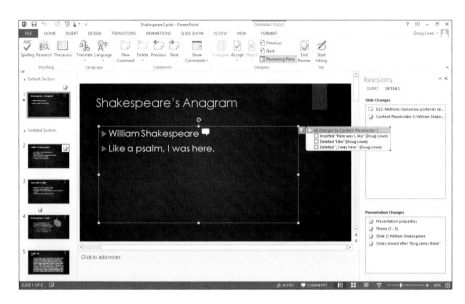

Figure 17-10: PowerPoint shows the differences between the original and revised versions of a presentation.

6. **Repeat Steps 4 and 5 until you have accepted or rejected all the edits to the presentation.**

7. **Click the End Review button (in the Compare group of the Review tab of the Ribbon) when you're finished.**

This step hides any remaining edits that you haven't yet accepted or rejected.

8. **Save the presentation.**

18

Using a Slide Library and Other Ways to Reuse Slides

In This Chapter

▶ Stealing slides from another presentation

▶ Saving slides in a slide library

▶ Stealing slides from a slide library

*W*hat do you do when you're plodding along in PowerPoint and realize that the slides you're trying to create probably already exist in some other presentation somewhere? You do what I do: You borrow the slides from the other presentation. This chapter shows you how to do that.

Note that in the old days, the only way to steal slides from another presentation was to get on your horse and chase down the other presentation (that is, find the presentation on your hard drive), jump on board (open the presentation), and steal the slides at gunpoint (copy the slides you want to steal and paste them into the new presentation).

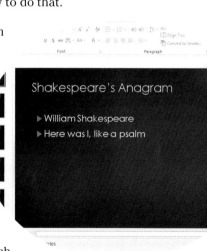

You can still steal slides that way — in fact, Microsoft has created a special command that makes it easy to steal slides directly from another presentation. But if you steal slides often and want to become a career criminal, the real way to do it is to set up a *slide library,* which is a central repository for slides. The slide library lives on a server, so anyone can access it, and it's managed by SharePoint, so it has a bunch of nice SharePoint-like features.

Stealing Slides from Another Presentation

Stealing slides from another presentation isn't a serious crime. In fact, Microsoft provides a special command on the Insert tab on the Ribbon to let you do it. Here are the steps:

1. **Open the presentation you want to copy slides into (*not* the one you want to steal the slides from).**

2. **Click the Home tab on the Ribbon and then click the New Slide button and choose Reuse Slides. (Reuse Slides appears at the bottom of the New Slide menu.)**

   This step displays a Reuse Slides task pane, which appears on the right side of the screen, as shown in Figure 18-1.

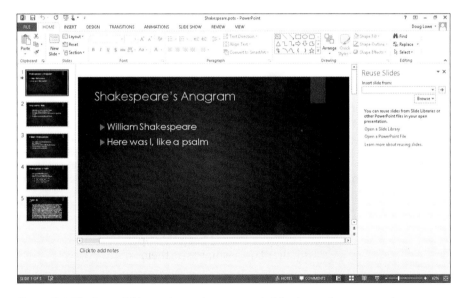

Figure 18-1: The Reuse Slides task pane lets you steal slides from other presentations.

3. **Click the Open a PowerPoint File link in the Reuse Slides task pane.**

   This summons a Browse dialog box.

4. **Locate the presentation you want to steal slides from and then click Open.**

   The slides from the presentation you selected are displayed in the Reuse Slides task pane, as shown in Figure 18-2.

Figure 18-2: Steal these slides!

You're now privy to one of the coolest effects in PowerPoint: When you point at one of the slides in the Reuse Slides task pane, the slide magnifies to twice its original size so you can better see the contents of the slide.

5. **(Optional) Select the Keep Source Formatting check box if you want the slides to retain their original formatting.**

   Normally, you should keep this option deselected. With the option deselected, the slide assumes the theme of the presentation it is inserted into.

6. **Click the slides you want to steal.**

   Each slide you click is added to the presentation.

7. **When you're done, click the X at the top right of the Reuse Slides task pane to dismiss it.**

That's about all there is to stealing slides from other presentations.

Saving Slides in a Slide Library

If you're lucky enough to work at a company that uses SharePoint, you have several additional PowerPoint features at your disposal. One of the most useful is the capability to create and use *slide libraries,* which are special types of document folders that store individual slides, not whole documents. When you've saved slides in a slide library, you can easily insert them into a presentation. And as an added bonus, you can have PowerPoint check to see whether the slides have changed and automatically update them with the changes. Pretty cool, eh?

To save one or more slides to a slide library, you must first create the slide library. That's a task better left to a SharePoint system administrator, so you can skip that step here. Instead, assume that the slide library has already been created for you, and you've been provided with the URL (that is, the web address) of the slide library and any login credentials you might need to access it.

Here are the steps for adding slides to a slide library:

1. **Open the presentation that contains the slides you want to add to the library.**

2. **Choose File⇨Share⇨Publish Slides; then click the Publish Slides button.**

   This step brings up a dialog box that allows you to select the slides you want to share.

3. **Select the slides you want to add to the library.**

   To select an individual slide, select the check box next to the slide thumbnail. To select all the slides in the presentation, click the Select All button.

4. **Enter the URL of the slide library in the Publish To text box.**

   Or if you prefer, you can click the Browse button to browse to the library.

5. **Click the Publish button.**

   The slides are copied to the slide library.

6. **(Optional) Play a game of Solitaire.**

   Depending on the speed of your local network and how many slides you selected, PowerPoint might take a while to publish the slides (probably not long enough for a game of Solitaire, but your boss doesn't have to know that).

   You're done!

The slides have now been added to the library.

Stealing Slides from a Slide Library

To incorporate a slide from a SharePoint slide library into a presentation, just follow these steps:

1. **Open the presentation you want to copy slides into (*not* the one you want to steal the slides from).**

2. **Click the Insert tab on the Ribbon and then click the Add Slide button and choose Reuse Slides.**

   This step displays a Reuse Slides task pane (refer to Figure 18-1).

3. **Click the Open a Slide Library link in the Reuse Slides task pane.**

   This step summons a Browse dialog box.

4. **Locate the Slide Library you want to steal slides from and then click Open.**

   The slides from the presentation you selected are displayed in the Reuse Slides task pane, in the same way that slides from a PowerPoint file are shown. Refer to Figure 18-2.

5. **(Optional) To keep the original formatting for the slides, select the Keep Source Formatting check box.**

   Normally, you should keep this option deselected.

6. **Click the slides you want to steal.**

   Each slide you click is added to the presentation.

7. **When you're done, click the X at the top right of the Reuse Slides task pane to dismiss it.**

19

Exporting Your Presentation to Other Formats

In This Chapter

▷ Exporting to PDF

▷ Exporting to a video

▷ Exporting to a Word document

*T*his chapter shows you how to use a variety of PowerPoint features that let you save your presentations in formats other than the standard PowerPoint file format. You can save you presentation as a PDF file which can then be viewed using Adobe's Acrobat software. Or, you can create a video that can be viewed over the web, using a media player, or even on a DVD that can be played on a standard DVD player. You can also create a self-contained presentation that can be saved to a CD or flash drive and viewed with a free PowerPoint viewer. And finally, you can convert a pre-sentation to a Word document that you can give to your attendees as handouts.

All these features are available from the File⇨Export page.

Creating a PDF File

PDF, which stands for *Portable Document Format,* is a popular format for interchanging files. You can easily con-vert a PowerPoint presentation to PDF format by following these steps:

1. **Choose File⇨Export⇨Create PDF/XPS Document.**

2. **Click the Create PDF/XPS button.**

    This brings up the dialog box shown in Figure 19-1.

Figure 19-1: Creating a PDF document.

3. **Navigate to the location where you want to save the file, and change the filename if you wish.**

   The default is to save the file in the same folder as the PowerPoint presentation, using the same name but with the extension PDF.

4. **Select the appropriate optimization setting.**

   The two choices are to optimize for standard use or to minimize the file size. The quality will be slightly reduced if you opt to minimize the file size.

5. **Click Publish.**

   The presentation is converted to a PDF file.

Crafting a Video

PowerPoint is great for preparing presentations to give in person. But what about giving presentations when you can't be there? With digital video cameras practically being given away in cereal boxes these days, just about anyone can record a video of himself giving a presentation. Wouldn't it be great if you could easily combine the slides from a PowerPoint presentation with a video of you presenting it? Then anyone can watch the presentation later, when you can't be there.

Good news! Beginning with PowerPoint 2013, you can! In fact, creating a video version of your presentation is a snap. First, you set up the timing you want for each slide and for each animation within each slide. You can even add a voice narration to each slide. After the timings and narration are all set up, you just click a few times with the mouse, and your presentation is converted to video.

Adding timings and narration

PowerPoint includes a nifty feature that lets you record the timings for each slide and for each animation element (such as bullet points appearing). At the same time, you can record your own voice to use as a narration for the presentation.

To record the timings, you essentially rehearse the presentation as if you were giving it to an audience. PowerPoint keeps track of the time between each mouse click or other action and records those timings along with the presentation.

As for the narration, you simply speak your narration into a microphone, and PowerPoint attaches your recorded voice to each slide. Then, when you play back the presentation, the slides are automatically synchronized with the narrations you recorded.

Note that you can also record PowerPoint's built-in laser pointer. Then, when you play back the show or create a video, the pointer will dance across the screen automatically! For more information about using the laser pointer, refer to Chapter 6.

You need a microphone plugged into your computer to record narrations. I recommend you get the kind that's built into a headset rather than a hand-held microphone. The headset microphone will provide more consistent voice quality, plus it will leave your hands free to work your keyboard and mouse while you record the timings, narration, and laser pointer.

To record timings and narration, first plug a microphone into your computer's microphone input jack. Then, open the presentation and follow these steps:

1. **Open the Slide Show tab, choose Record Slide Show and then choose Start Recording from Beginning.**

   The Record Slide Show dialog box, shown in Figure 19-2, appears. This dialog box simply asks whether you want to record slide timings or narration.

Figure 19-2: Specify what elements you want to record.

2. **To record slide timings, select the Slide and Animation Timings check box. To record narrations and the laser pointer, select the Narrations and Laser Pointer check box.**

    You'll almost always want to select the Slide and Animation Timings check box. Select the Narrations and Laser Pointer check box only if you want to add your voice narration, the laser pointer, or both.

    If you don't want to record a narration but you would still like the laser pointer to appear in your final video, select the Narrations and Laser Pointer check box. Then, in Step 4, just skip the part about speaking into the microphone.

3. **Click OK to begin recording the slide show.**

    The first slide of your presentation is displayed, and a small toolbar titled Record Slide Show is displayed, as shown in Figure 19-3.

Figure 19-3: The Record Slide Show toolbar.

4. **Speak your narration into the microphone. Press Enter or click the mouse button each time you want to advance to a new slide or call up a new animation element (such as a bullet point).**

5. **If you want to use the laser pointer on a slide, hold down the Ctrl key and then click and hold the mouse button and use the mouse to control the laser pointer.**

    When you release the mouse button, the laser pointer disappears. (For more information about working the laser pointer, see Chapter 6.)

6. **If you need to pause the recording at any time, click the Pause button that appears in the Record Slide Show toolbar.**

    The recording is suspended, and a dialog box appears with a button that lets you resume the recording. When you're ready to continue, click this button.

7. When you're finished recording, press Esc.

PowerPoint ends the recording and switches to Slide Sorter View, which displays the timings associated with each slide, as shown in Figure 19-4.

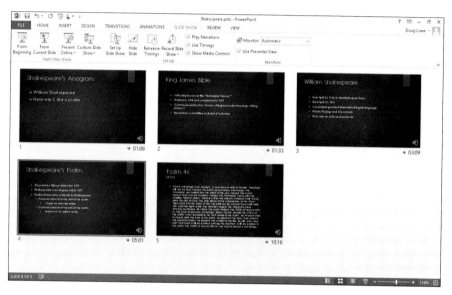

Figure 19-4: PowerPoint displays the slide show in Slide Sorter View so you can see the timings.

8. If you messed up on any slide, select that slide, click Record Slide Show, and then choose Start Recording from Current Slide. Then re-record the timings and narration for that slide. Press Esc to stop recording.

You can re-record more than one slide in this way; just press Enter or click the mouse to advance through all the slides you want to re-record. Press Esc to stop recording.

9. Press F5 or click the Slide Show button on the right side of the status bar to begin the slide show so you can see whether your narration works.

The slide show begins. The narration plays through your computer's speakers, and the slides advance automatically along with the narration. The laser pointer should also appear if you used it during the recording.

Here are some additional things to keep in mind about narrations:

- ✔ As you record the narration, leave a little gap between each slide. PowerPoint records the narration for each slide as a separate sound file and then attaches the sound to the slide. Unfortunately, you get cut off if you talk right through the slide transitions.

- ✔ The narration cancels out any other sounds you placed on the slides.

- ✔ To delete a narration, click the Record Slide Show button, click Clear, and then click either Clear Narrations on Current Slide (to delete narration from just one slide) or Clear Narration on All Slides (to delete all narration).

Creating a video

Creating a video from your presentation couldn't be much easier. Here's the procedure:

1. **(Optional) Record the slide timings and any narration you want to use.**

   For the procedure to record timings and narration, refer to the preceding section. If you skip this step, each slide will be displayed for a fixed duration in the resulting video.

2. **Choose File⇨Export⇨Create a Video.**

   The Create a Video Backstage View screen is displayed, as shown in Figure 19-5.

3. **Select the video quality.**

   The first drop-down list on the Create a Video page lets you choose whether your video is targeted at computer displays, the Internet, or portable devices.

4. **Select whether to use recorded timings and narrations.**

   If you choose not to use recorded timings, you can set the duration to display each slide. (The default is 5 seconds.)

5. **Click Create Video.**

   A Save As dialog box appears.

6. **Select the folder where you want to save the file and enter the filename you want to use.**

   By default, the video file will be saved in the same folder as the presentation and will have the same name, but with the extension .wmv.

Figure 19-5: Creating a video.

7. **Click Save.**

    The video is created.

    Depending on the size of the presentation and the quality you selected, the video may take a long time to create. A progress bar appears in the status bar to indicate the video's progress. You can continue doing other work in PowerPoint while the video is being created, but your computer will probably respond sluggishly until the video is finished.

8. **When the progress bar completes, the video is finished!**

You can view the video in Windows Media Player by navigating to it in Windows Explorer and double-clicking the video's .wmv file.

Packaging Your Presentation on a CD

Often, you may need to share a PowerPoint presentation with someone who doesn't own a copy of PowerPoint. Fortunately, PowerPoint includes a Package for CD command that creates a CD with the presentation and a special program called the *PowerPoint Viewer* that can display the presentation on a computer that doesn't have PowerPoint installed.

Unfortunately, the PowerPoint Viewer program that's placed on the CD isn't able to display all the features of PowerPoint 2013 presentations with the same quality that PowerPoint 2013 displays them. As a result, your presentation may look slightly different when you view it with the PowerPoint Viewer.

To create a CD with your presentation, follow these steps:

1. **Open the presentation in PowerPoint and then choose File⇨Export⇨Package Presentation for CD. Then click the Package for CD button.**

   The Package for CD dialog box appears, as shown in Figure 19-6.

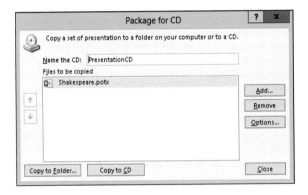

Figure 19-6: The Package for CD dialog box.

2. **Click the Options button.**

   This step summons the Options dialog box, shown in Figure 19-7.

Figure 19-7: The Options dialog box.

3. **Look over the options and change any that aren't set the way you want.**

   The following list describes each of the options that are available:

   - *Linked Files:* Select this option to include any linked files, such as videos or large audio files.

   - *Embedded TrueType Fonts:* Select this option to ensure that the fonts you use in your presentation will be available when you show the presentation on another computer.

   - *Password to Open Each Presentation:* Enter a password if the presentation contains top-secret information, such as the true whereabouts of Jimmy Hoffa.

   - *Password to Modify Each Presentation:* Enter a password if you want to prevent unauthorized people from changing the presentation.

   - *Inspect Presentations for Inappropriate or Private Information:* Sorry, this option doesn't check your presentation for off-color jokes or naughty pictures. Instead, it checks for any personal information that might be embedded in your presentation.

4. **Click OK to return to the Package for CD dialog box.**

5. **If you want to add other presentations to the CD, click Add Files, select the files that you want to add, and then click Add.**

   You can put as many files as will fit on the CD. You can add other PowerPoint presentations or any other files you'd like to add to the CD, such as Word documents or text files.

6. **Click Copy to CD.**

   If you haven't already inserted a blank CD into the drive, you're prompted to insert one now. Go ahead and insert a blank CD when prompted.

   PowerPoint copies the files to the CD. This might take a few minutes, so now is a good time to catch a few *z*'s. When the CD is finished, the drive spits it out and asks whether you want to make another copy.

7. **Remove the CD and then click Yes if you want to make another copy. Otherwise, click No and then click Close.**

   You're done!

The CD is set up so that the presentation should start running all by itself when you insert it into a computer. If it doesn't, open a My Computer window and then open the CD drive and double-click `pptview.exe`. A list of presentations on the CD appears. Double-click the one that you want to run, and off you go.

Creating Word Handouts

The final Export topic for this chapter is using the Create Handouts command to create a Word document that you can then print and distribute to your audience. Using this feature is simple; just follow these steps:

1. **Choose File⇨Export⇨Create Handouts, then click the Create Handouts button.**

   This brings up the dialog box shown in Figure 19-8.

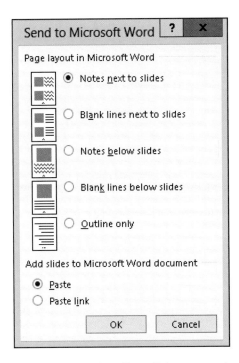

Figure 19-8: Exporting a PowerPoint presentation to Word.

2. **Choose the formatting option you want to use.**

   You have several options for the page layout:

   - Slides on the left and notes on the right
   - Slides on the left and blank lines on the right
   - Slides at the top of the page and notes below the slides
   - Slides at the top of the page and blank lines below the slides
   - Just the outline

3. Click OK.

PowerPoint grinds and whirs for a bit, then regurgitates the presentation in the form of a Word document, as shown in Figure 19-9.

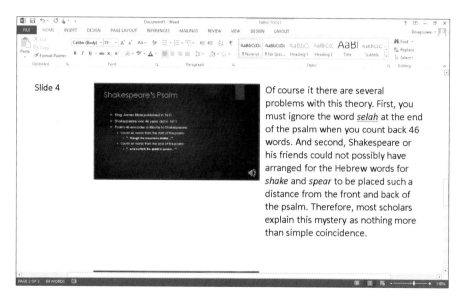

Figure 19-9: A PowerPoint presentation converted to Word.

4. Edit the document as you see fit, then save it.

You're done!

Note that if you don't plan on editing the document in Word, there's no real advantage to exporting the presentation to a Word document. Instead, you can simply print the slides and notes by using PowerPoint's Print command.

Part V

Enjoy an additional PowerPoint 2013 Part of Tens chapter online at www.dummies.com/extras/powerpoint2013.

In this part . . .

- ✔ Get familiar ten PowerPoint commandments — obey these commandments and it shall go well with you, with your computer, and even with your projector.

- ✔ Find out a few tips and pointers that will help you produce readable slides.

- ✔ Explore some things you can do to prevent the audience from falling asleep during the presentation.

- ✔ Enjoy an additional PowerPoint 2013 Part of Tens chapter online at www.dummies.com/extras/powerpoint2013.

Ten PowerPoint Commandments

And the hapless Windows user said, "But who am I to make this presentation? For I am not eloquent, but I am slow of speech and of tongue, and my colors clasheth, and my charts runneth over." And Microsoft answered, "Fear not, for unto you this day is given a program, which shall be called PowerPoint, and it shall make for you slides, which shall bring forth titles and bullets and, yea, even diagrams."

— Presentations 1:1

nd so it came to pass that these ten PowerPoint commandments were passed down from generation to generation. Obey these commandments and it shall go well with you, with your computer, and yea even with your projector.

1. Thou Shalt Frequently Savest Thy Work

Every two or three minutes, press Ctrl+S. It takes only a second to save your file, and you never know when you'll be the victim of a rotating power outage (even if you don't live in California).

11. Thou Shalt Storeth Each Presentation in Its Proper Folder

Whenever you save a file, double-check the folder that you're saving it to. It's all too easy to save a presentation in the wrong folder and then spend hours searching for the file later. You'll wind up blaming the computer for losing your files.

III. Thou Shalt Not Abuseth Thy Program's Formatting Features

Yes, PowerPoint lets you set every word in a different font, use 92 different colors on a single slide, and fill every last pixel of empty space with clip art. If you want your slides to look like ransom notes, go ahead. Otherwise, keep things simple.

IV. Thou Shalt Not Stealeth Copyrighted Materials

Given a few minutes with Google or any other search engine, you can probably find just the right picture or snippet of clip art for any presentation need that might arise. But keep in mind that many of those pictures, clip art drawings, and media files are copyrighted. Don't use them if you don't have permission.

V. Thou Shalt Abideth by Thine Color Scheme, Auto-Layout, and Template

Microsoft hired a crew of out-of-work artists to pick the colors for the color schemes, arrange things with the slide layouts, and create beautifully crafted templates. Humor them. They like it when you use their stuff. Don't feel chained to the prepackaged designs, but don't stray far from them unless you have a good artistic eye.

VI. Thou Shalt Not Abuse Thine Audience with an Endless Array of Cute Animations or Funny Sounds

PowerPoint animations are cute and sometimes quite useful. But if you do a goofy animation on every slide, pretty soon your audience will just think you're strange.

VII. Keep Thy Computer Gurus Happy

If you have a friend or co-worker who knows more about computers than you do, keep that person happy. Throw him or her an occasional Twinkie or a bag of Cheetos. Treat computer nerds as if they're human beings. After all, you want them to be your friends.

VIII. Thou Shalt Backeth Up Thy Files Day by Day

Yes, every day. One of these days, you'll come to work only to discover a pile of rubble where your desk used to be. A federal agent will pick up what's left of your computer's keyboard and laugh. But if you back up every day, you won't lose more than a day's work.

IX. Thou Shalt Fear No Evil, for Ctrl+Z Is Always with Thee

March ahead with boldness. Not sure what a button does? Click it! Click it twice if it makes you feel powerful! The worst that it can do is mess up your presentation. If that happens, you can press Ctrl+Z to set things back the way they should be.

If you really mess things up, just close the presentation without saving. Then open the previously saved version. After all, you did obey the first commandment, didn't you?

X. Thou Shalt Not Panic

You're the only one who knows you're nervous. You'll do just fine. Imagine the audience naked if that will help. (Unless, of course, you're making a presentation to a nudist club and they actually are naked, in which case try to imagine them with their clothes on.)

21

Ten Tips for Creating Readable Slides

. . . .

*T*his chapter gives you a few random tips and pointers that will help you produce readable slides.

Try Reading the Slide from the Back of the Room

The number-one rule of creating readable slides is that everyone in the room must be able to read them. If you're not certain, there's one sure way to find out: Try it. Fire up the projector, call up the slide, walk to the back of the room, and see whether you can read it. If you can't, you need to make an adjustment.

Remember that everyone's eyesight might not be as good as yours. If you have perfect vision, squint a little when you get to the back of the room to see how the slide might appear to someone whose vision isn't perfect.

If a projector isn't handy, make sure you can read your slides from 10 or 15 feet away from your computer's monitor.

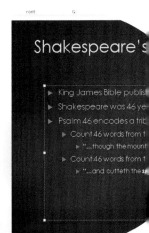

Avoid Small Text

If you can't read a slide from the back of the room, it's probably because the text is too small. The rule to live by is that 24-point type is the smallest you should use for text that you want people to read. A 12-point type might be perfectly readable in a Word document, but it's way too small for PowerPoint.

No More Than Five Bullets, Please

Have you ever noticed how David Letterman uses two slides to display his Top Ten lists? Dave's producers know that ten items is way too many for one screen. Five is just right. You might be able to slip in six now and again, but if you're up to seven or eight, try breaking the slide into two slides.

Avoid Excessive Verbiage Lending to Excessively Lengthy Text That Is Not Only Redundant but Also Repetitive and Reiterative

See what I mean? Maybe the heading should have been "Be Brief."

Use Consistent Wording

One sign of an amateur presentation is wording in bullet lists that isn't grammatically consistent. Consider this list:

- Profits will be improved
- Expanding markets
- It will reduce the amount of overseas competition
- Production increase

Each list item uses a different grammatical construction. The same points made with consistent wording have a more natural flow and make a more compelling case:

- Improved profits
- Expanded markets
- Reduced overseas competition
- Increased production

Avoid Unsightly Color Combinations

The professionally chosen color schemes that come with PowerPoint are designed to create slides that are easy to read. If you venture away from them, be careful about choosing colors that are hard to read.

Watch the Line Endings

Sometimes, PowerPoint breaks a line at an awkward spot, which can make slides hard to read. For example, a bullet point might be one word too long to fit on a single line. When that happens, you might want to break the line elsewhere so the second line has more than one word. (Press Shift+Enter to create a line break that doesn't start a new paragraph.)

Alternatively, you might want to drag the right margin of the text placeholder to increase the margin width so that the line doesn't have to be broken at all.

Web addresses (URLs) are notoriously hard to squeeze onto a single line. If your presentation includes long URLs, pay special attention to how they fit.

Keep the Background Simple

Don't splash a bunch of distracting clip art on the background unless it's essential. The purpose of the background is to provide a well-defined visual space for the slide's content. All too often, presenters put up slides that have text displayed on top of pictures of the mountains or city skylines, which makes the text almost impossible to read.

Use Only Two Levels of Bullets

Sure, it's tempting to develop your subpoints into sub-subpoints and sub-sub-subpoints, but no one will be able to follow your logic. Don't make your slides more confusing than they need to be. If you need to make sub-sub-subpoints, you probably need a few more slides.

Avoid Bullets Altogether If You Can

Bullets have become cliché. If possible, eliminate them altogether from your presentation. A single, well-chosen photograph is often a far better way to communicate a key point than a list of bullet points.

Keep Charts and Diagrams Simple

PowerPoint can create elaborate graphs that even the best statisticians will marvel at. However, the most effective graphs are simple pie charts with three or four slices and simple column charts with three or four columns. Likewise, pyramid, Venn, and other types of diagrams lose their impact when you add more than four or five elements.

If you remember only one rule when creating your presentations, remember this one: *Keep it simple, clean, and concise.*

22

Ten Ways to Keep Your Audience Awake

Nothing frightens a public speaker more than the prospect of the audience falling asleep during the speech. Here are some things you can do to prevent that from happening. (Yawn.)

Don't Forget Your Purpose

Too many presenters ramble on and on with no clear sense of purpose. The temptation is to throw in every clever quotation and every interesting tidbit you can muster that is even remotely related to the topic of your presentation. The reason that this temptation is so strong is that you most likely haven't identified what you hope to accomplish with your presentation. In other words, you haven't pinned down your *purpose.*

Don't confuse a presentation's title with its purpose. Suppose that you're asked to give a presentation to a prospective client on the advantages of your company's new, improved, deluxe model ChronSimplastic Infindibulator. Your purpose in this presentation is not to convey information about the new Infindibulator, but to persuade your client to buy one of the $65 million beasties. The title of your presentation might be *Infindibulators for the 21st Century,* but the purpose is "Convince these saps to buy one, or maybe two."

Don't Become a Slave to Your Slides

PowerPoint makes such beautiful slides that the temptation is to let them be the show. That's a big mistake. *You* are the show — not the slides. The slides are merely visual aids, designed to make your presentation more effective, not to steal the show.

Your slides should supplement your talk, not repeat it. If you find yourself just reading your slides, you need to rethink what you put on the slides. The slides should summarize key points, not become the script for your speech.

Don't Overwhelm Your Audience with Unnecessary Detail

On November 19, 1863, a crowd of 15,000 gathered in Gettysburg to hear Edward Everett, one of the greatest orators of the time. Mr. Everett spoke for two hours about the events that had transpired during the famous battle. When he finished, Abraham Lincoln rose to deliver a brief two-minute postscript that has become the most famous speech in American history.

If PowerPoint had been around in 1863, Everett probably would have spoken for four hours. PowerPoint practically begs you to talk too much. When you start typing bullets, you can't stop. Pretty soon, you have 40 slides for a 20-minute presentation. That's about 35 more than you probably need. Try to shoot for one slide for every two to five minutes of your presentation.

Don't Neglect Your Opening

As they say, you get only one opportunity to make a first impression. Don't waste it by telling a joke that has nothing to do with the topic, apologizing for your lack of preparation or nervousness, or listing your credentials. Don't pussyfoot around; get right to the point.

The best openings are those that capture the audience's attention with a provocative statement, a rhetorical question, or a compelling story. A joke is okay, but only if it sets the stage for the subject of your presentation.

Be Relevant

The objective of any presentation is to lead your audience to say, "Me, too!" Unfortunately, many presentations leave the audience thinking, "So what?"

The key to being relevant is giving your audience members what they need, and not what you think is interesting or important. The most persuasive presentations are those that present solutions to real problems rather than opinions about hypothetical problems.

Don't Forget the Altar Call

What would a Billy Graham crusade be without the altar call? A wasted opportunity.

The best presentations are the ones that entice your audience to action. That might mean buying your product, changing their lifestyles, or just being interested enough to do more research into your topic.

But the opportunity will be wasted if you don't invite your audience to respond in some way. If you're selling something (and we're all selling something!), make it clear how your audience can buy. Tell them the toll-free number. Give them a handout with links of websites they can go to for more information. Ask everyone to sing *Just As I Am*. Do whatever it takes.

Practice, Practice, Practice

Back to good ol' Abe: Somehow a rumor got started that Abraham Lincoln hastily wrote the Gettysburg Address on the train, just before pulling into Gettysburg. In truth, Lincoln agonized for weeks over every word.

Practice, practice, practice. Work through the rough spots. Polish the opening and the closing and all the awkward transitions in between. Practice in front of a mirror. Videotape yourself. Time yourself.

Relax!

Don't worry! Be happy! Even the most gifted public speakers are scared silly every time they step up to the podium. Whether you're speaking to one person or 10,000, relax. In 20 minutes, it will all be over.

No matter how nervous you are, no one knows it except you. That is, unless you tell them. The number-one rule of panic avoidance is to never apologize for your fears. Behind the podium, your knees might be knocking hard enough to bruise yourself, but no one else will notice. After you swab down your armpits and wipe the drool off your chin, people will say, "Weren't you nervous? You seemed so relaxed!"

Expect the Unexpected

Plan on things going wrong, because they will. The projector may not focus, the microphone may go dead, you may drop your notes on the way to the podium. Who knows what else may happen?

Take things in stride, but be prepared for problems you can anticipate. Carry an extra set of notes in your pocket. Bring your own microphone if you have one. Have a backup projector ready if possible.

Don't Be Boring

An audience can overlook almost anything, but one thing they'll never forgive you for is boring them. Above all, do not bore your audience.

This guideline doesn't mean you have to tell jokes, jump up and down, or talk fast. Jokes, excessive jumping, and rapid speech can be unimaginably boring. If you obey the other instructions in this chapter — if you have a clear-cut purpose and stick to it, avoid unnecessary detail, and address real needs — you'll never be boring. Just be yourself and have fun. If you have fun, so will your audience.

Index

• *K* •

pple & Mac

ad 2 For Dummies,
d Edition
78-1-118-17679-5

hone 4S For Dummies,
h Edition
78-1-118-03671-6

od touch For Dummies,
d Edition
78-1-118-12960-9

ac OS X Lion
or Dummies
78-1-118-02205-4

logging & Social Media

tyVille For Dummies
78-1-118-08337-6

acebook For Dummies,
h Edition
78-1-118-09562-1

om Blogging
or Dummies
78-1-118-03843-7

witter For Dummies,
nd Edition
78-0-470-76879-2

ordPress For Dummies,
h Edition
78-1-118-07342-1

usiness

ash Flow For Dummies
78-1-118-01850-7

vesting For Dummies,
h Edition
78-0-470-90545-6

Job Searching with Social Media For Dummies
978-0-470-93072-4

QuickBooks 2012
For Dummies
978-1-118-09120-3

Resumes For Dummies,
6th Edition
978-0-470-87361-8

Starting an Etsy Business
For Dummies
978-0-470-93067-0

Cooking & Entertaining

Cooking Basics
For Dummies, 4th Edition
978-0-470-91388-8

Wine For Dummies,
4th Edition
978-0-470-04579-4

Diet & Nutrition

Kettlebells For Dummies
978-0-470-59929-7

Nutrition For Dummies,
5th Edition
978-0-470-93231-5

Restaurant Calorie Counter
For Dummies,
2nd Edition
978-0-470-64405-8

Digital Photography

Digital SLR Cameras &
Photography For Dummies,
4th Edition
978-1-118-14489-3

Digital SLR Settings & Shortcuts
For Dummies
978-0-470-91763-3

Photoshop Elements 10
For Dummies
978-1-118-10742-3

Gardening

Gardening Basics
For Dummies
978-0-470-03749-2

Vegetable Gardening
For Dummies,
2nd Edition
978-0-470-49870-5

Green/Sustainable

Raising Chickens
For Dummies
978-0-470-46544-8

Green Cleaning
For Dummies
978-0-470-39106-8

Health

Diabetes For Dummies,
3rd Edition
978-0-470-27086-8

Food Allergies
For Dummies
978-0-470-09584-3

Living Gluten-Free
For Dummies,
2nd Edition
978-0-470-58589-4

Hobbies

Beekeeping
For Dummies,
2nd Edition
978-0-470-43065-1

Chess For Dummies,
3rd Edition
978-1-118-01695-4

Drawing For Dummies,
2nd Edition
978-0-470-61842-4

eBay For Dummies,
7th Edition
978-1-118-09806-6

Knitting For Dummies,
2nd Edition
978-0-470-28747-7

Language & Foreign Language

English Grammar
For Dummies,
2nd Edition
978-0-470-54664-2

French For Dummies,
2nd Edition
978-1-118-00464-7

German For Dummies,
2nd Edition
978-0-470-90101-4

Spanish Essentials
For Dummies
978-0-470-63751-7

Spanish For Dummies,
2nd Edition
978-0-470-87855-2

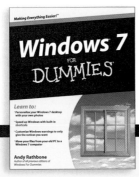

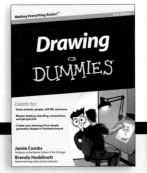

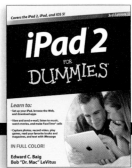

Math & Science

Algebra I For Dummies,
2nd Edition
978-0-470-55964-2

Biology For Dummies,
2nd Edition
978-0-470-59875-7

Chemistry For Dummies,
2nd Edition
978-1-1180-0730-3

Geometry For Dummies,
2nd Edition
978-0-470-08946-0

Pre-Algebra Essentials
For Dummies
978-0-470-61838-7

Microsoft Office

Excel 2010 For Dummies
978-0-470-48953-6

Office 2010 All-in-One
For Dummies
978-0-470-49748-7

Office 2011 for Mac
For Dummies
978-0-470-87869-9

Word 2010
For Dummies
978-0-470-48772-3

Music

Guitar For Dummies,
2nd Edition
978-0-7645-9904-0

Clarinet For Dummies
978-0-470-58477-4

iPod & iTunes
For Dummies,
9th Edition
978-1-118-13060-5

Pets

Cats For Dummies,
2nd Edition
978-0-7645-5275-5

Dogs All-in One
For Dummies
978-0470-52978-2

Saltwater Aquariums
For Dummies
978-0-470-06805-2

Religion & Inspiration

The Bible For Dummies
978-0-7645-5296-0

Catholicism For Dummies,
2nd Edition
978-1-118-07778-8

Spirituality For Dummies,
2nd Edition
978-0-470-19142-2

Self-Help & Relationships

Happiness For Dummies
978-0-470-28171-0

Overcoming Anxiety
For Dummies,
2nd Edition
978-0-470-57441-6

Seniors

Crosswords For Seniors
For Dummies
978-0-470-49157-7

iPad 2 For Seniors
For Dummies, 3rd Edition
978-1-118-17678-8

Laptops & Tablets
For Seniors For Dummies,
2nd Edition
978-1-118-09596-6

Smartphones & Tablets

BlackBerry For Dummies,
5th Edition
978-1-118-10035-6

Droid X2 For Dummies
978-1-118-14864-8

HTC ThunderBolt
For Dummies
978-1-118-07601-9

MOTOROLA XOOM
For Dummies
978-1-118-08835-7

Sports

Basketball For Dummies,
3rd Edition
978-1-118-07374-2

Football For Dummies,
2nd Edition
978-1-118-01261-1

Golf For Dummies,
4th Edition
978-0-470-88279-5

Test Prep

ACT For Dummies,
5th Edition
978-1-118-01259-8

ASVAB For Dummies,
3rd Edition
978-0-470-63760-9

The GRE Test For
Dummies, 7th Edition
978-0-470-00919-2

Police Officer Exam
For Dummies
978-0-470-88724-0

Series 7 Exam
For Dummies
978-0-470-09932-2

Web Development

HTML, CSS, & XHTML
For Dummies, 7th Edition
978-0-470-91659-9

Drupal For Dummies,
2nd Edition
978-1-118-08348-2

Windows 7

Windows 7
For Dummies
978-0-470-49743-2

Windows 7
For Dummies,
Book + DVD Bundle
978-0-470-52398-8

Windows 7 All-in-One
For Dummies
978-0-470-48763-1

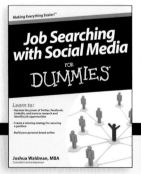

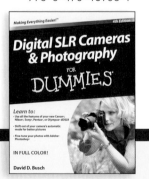

Available wherever books are sold. For more information or to order direct: U.S. customers visit www.dummies.com or call 1-877-762-2974.
U.K. customers visit www.wileyeurope.com or call (0) 1243 843291. Canadian customers visit www.wiley.ca or call 1-800-567-4797.

Connect with us online at www.facebook.com/fordummies or @fordummies